PHILOSOPHICAL ASPECTS OF CULTURE

Philosophical Aspects of Culture

BERTRAM MORRIS

"For moral philosophy is nothing else but the science of what is good, and evil, in the conversation, and society of mankind."

THOMAS HOBBES, *Leviathan*
Part I, ch. 15.

THE ANTIOCH PRESS · 1961

Published by The Antioch Press
Yellow Springs, Ohio

Copyright 1961
by Bertram Morris

Library of Congress Catalog Card
Number 60-15086

Printed in the United States of America

To Judy and Susie,
both of whom have had a hand in this.

CONTENTS

PREFACE

THE PROBLEM OF HOW TO BE A HUMAN BEING IS difficult at any time. Today it is agonizingly difficult. Power-mad persons go to almost any extreme to achieve their ends. Little persons with well-meaning instincts are caught in the struggle. More sensitive persons turn their backs to the power world and cynically refuse to be a part of it. A few try to make sense of the world without benefit of dogma or stale orthodoxies. This study is an attempt to interpret what lies behind these various attitudes, to fix on the major aspects of the modern conflicts, and to suggest the kinds of methods which give promise of transforming them into issues less degrading and less estranged from the human spirit.

If the point of view I have adopted in this study needs a name, it can be called functionalism. This functionalism is utilitarian in the sense that it means to respect the requirements of man's so-called material existence. It does not shun questions of health, housing, social security—and in general, standards of living—on the ground that they satisfy only low-level living and that they destroy the heroic stature which makes one a man. The functional theory regards this criticism as a piece of snobbery which needs to be understood not as above the human context but as a part of it, so limited as to have no independent validity.

Again, this functionalism is humanitarian in the sense that it means to respect the human impulses which lead men to invent, to love, to laugh, to question, and to think. It shuns no impulses; it requires no tabus; and it demands no orthodoxies. But it does insist upon the need for rigorous criticism of, as well as sensitive appreciation for, whatever man does that has import beyond his irresponsible subjectivities.

In developing this kind of functionalism, I have emphasized the institutional embodiments, for this has seemed to me the only feasible way of understanding the perplexities of our own society as well as those of other societies. My reasons for proceeding in this way are two: first, institutions appear to be the only reasonable units of analysis, and secondly, a knowledge of their interrelations seems to be the only way one can understand the concreteness of moral life. This is to say that in practice one needs to read concreteness as a manifestation of culture, since it alone is broad enough to permit human actions to become intelligible.

If this intelligibility is to succeed, it becomes imperative, I believe, that a distinction between the authentic and the false be respected. Certainly the most difficult question I have tried to face in this work is how to clarify the meaning of this distinction. I realize the clarification is only partially successful. Should the reader be convinced, however, that the distinction is of first importance and should he himself be encouraged to clarify it further, I am satisfied that he will come to recognize the major philosophical aspects of culture and that my efforts have been to some purpose.

It is not fitting for me to suggest what novelty there may be in any ideas expressed in this volume. I know where my major borrowings have been and most of these I have tried to acknowledge in my Notes.

Parts of Chapter 8 have appeared in article form in *The Colorado Quarterly* and parts of Chapter 10 in *The Antioch Review*. I am indebted to the editors of both publications for their help and for their permission to include the material in this volume.

Finally, I wish also to acknowledge stimulation and help I have received over the years from students and especially from colleagues both in philosophy and in other departments at the University of Colorado. I name only one to whom I feel most indebted, Professor J. W. Cohen. The Council on Research and Creative Work has from time to time collectively given me tangible support, especially in the faculty fellowship it made possible for me in the Fall of 1958. Individually, I have got moral support from the members. I thank them. Also, philosophers, neighbors, and librarians at Swarthmore College I thank for their indulgence and help during my fellowship stay there. At Antioch I wish to thank George Geiger and my captivating editor, Paul H. Rohmann. Other acknowledgments are more personal and I prefer to make them in private.

BERTRAM MORRIS
Boulder, Colorado

INTRODUCTION

My purpose in this study is to look beyond the descriptive aspects of culture to what may be called its metaphysical and ethical aspects. It seems reasonable to distinguish at the outset metaphysical from ethical questions, even though in the final analysis the two may merge into one. The metaphysical are those which pertain to the sense in which we may regard culture as real—whether it is an expression of reality, or whether it is a sham, a deception, an illusion, to cover up realities man cannot quite bring himself to acknowledge. The ethical questions, which are certainly related to the metaphysical, pertain to the wholeness, the completeness, the perfection of cultures, and secondarily to their capacity to evoke stirrings in men which lead to the promotion of civil life. Some elaboration of the questions may prove helpful as an introduction to what is to follow.

It is doubtful whether metaphysical questions can ever quite be eliminated from philosophical debate. Especially in matters relating to culture, it is doubtful whether they can reasonably be eliminated. Culture is by its very nature a trans-individual affair —or so it seems—and therefore the extra-private character of it becomes of prime concern. It would seem to be so because we want to know how things are interrelated, whether some are epiphenomenal expressions of others or whether there are independent existences, and if so, which are independent, and consequently which are dependent, and the like. Again, we want to know whether culture engenders the vitalities of human existence, and if it relates men to the world or if it only alienates them from it. To provide the reader with further clues, it may be well to specify more particularly what is involved in some of these questions.

In describing various cultures as whole cultures, the ethnologist usually tells us about the patterns which seem to characterize the life of a people, as if the reality lay in the pattern itself. We need not be hypercritical of his descriptions, even if they are idealized versions which only approximately fit the facts. Nevertheless, there is a residue of perplexities pertaining to the human psyche and its relation to culture defined as a configuration of actions, beliefs, attitudes, and the customs, institutions, and artifacts which are their results. Besides knowing about these configurations, we want to know what kinds of realities there are in the relations between them and individual persons. Is the life of the individual a reflection in his consciousness of the pattern which characterizes the life of his people? Is his a life dominated by the cultural pattern? Is his seemingly individual conduct a function of an order of which he is barely aware and over which he has little or no control? Or is he an independent and free agent who is responsible for the creation of cultural patterns and, moreover, an agent who is indefinitely capable of further altering them as his wisdom may dictate?

Again, there are important questions in connection with the relation of culture and nature. Is culture a spiritual kind of entity, more akin to the life of the mind than it is to the physical environment, which may be regarded as only the theater of the life of a people? We want to know whether the physical world is at best a means of sustaining the animal in man, even if it permits cultural life to evolve its own free expressions in religion, the arts, and philosophy, independent of the origins which provide for man's biological needs. Or on the contrary, may it be that the world of nature itself becomes humanized in culture in a way that makes it possible for man to become at home in the world? An insistent aspect of this question turns upon what science and technology have done to convert the question into a new form. A world of sprites and spirits domiciled in nature and presiding over aspects of it, such as the Greek gods and spirits did—has not this basic humanism been defeated once and for all by an impersonal science which discloses a world indifferent to the humanized world of the emotions and sentiments? Has not science with its panoply of protons, electrons, neutrons, deuterons, and the like, destroyed the opportunities of making the world over to conform to the heart's desires? By virtue of the gross impersonalities of the natural world, is man not compelled to find solace in an inner world impervious to the indignities of the world of matter and space?

The defeat of the human spirit may originate, of course, in any number of different quarters. Besides technology, which may be said by some to be the determinant of cultural life, there may be a variety of explanations said to constitute the "real" determinants—such as the imposition of the will of one people upon another, whether this is regarded as having its source in the providence of God, in manifest destiny, in the white man's burden, in the superiority of the Aryan race, in the inexorable laws of economic progress, or what-not. Theory does not permit us to play fast and loose with actual causal factors which may be at work as determinants of human culture. But it is also true that no dogmatic assertion that "x" is the determinant of cultural patterns makes "x" the determinant. Although the singling out of some one determinant of culture is indulged in by some metaphysicians, the legitimacy of this kind of explanation becomes more doubtful as we move on from the metaphysical to the ethical questions.

The locus of the ethics of culture appears to be civil life itself. If this is actually so, then the ethical predicate applies to the whole length and breadth of culture. Indeed, there appears to be good reason to question the correctness of any attempt to limit the ethical or moral quality of a culture to some part of it, less than the whole. Possibly it is like the proverbial egg, which is either all good or all bad, and any pronouncement on a part only is incompetent. I do not mean to conclude that there is no sense in using moral predicates distributively to refer to particular acts, beliefs, dispositions, intents, motives, and the like. But one may suggest that the moral predicate as applied to culture must apply to its whole range, if it is not to suffer possible total defeat in the disenchantment which arises from the advance from partial to more complete knowledge.

Even institutions taken singly, although they can lend themselves to functional analysis, cannot be properly evaluated apart from their basic interrelations with the totality of institutions that comprise a cultural pattern. On this score, the church or the state or the family or the arts—no single institution can be regarded as unqualifiedly good, however effectively it performs a function, unless its function furthers the life of a people. Piety, freedom, power, security, sentiment—these and other virtues have to be validated in a complex which gives them meaning, or else they become shibboleths of a people weary of thought and given to an orthodoxy which only debilitates. Even though there may be private gratifications sufficient to tide men over the unmeaning of impersonal monotonies and frustrations, they surely are not sufficient compensation to render a culture satisfactory, or even legitimate.

Cultures are thoroughgoingly social in character. Even aberrations become from this point of view paradoxically social—that is, in the attitudes which are taken towards social deviants and the ways in which they are treated in accordance with formal discipline or informal opinion. Because culture is so thoroughly social in character, it is capable of displaying civic virtue. The serious question we consequently need to contend with is whether it is not by reason of this fact that the supreme essence of morality is to be found in cultural relations and cultural relations alone. On such an assumption we would certainly need to doubt the validity of, if not completely reject, those time-honored theories which make of truth-telling or promise-fulfilling and such-like acts the prototype of moral conduct. If wholeness of persons in a whole culture is the locus of morality, then we would interpret moral injunctions such as the above in the light of their meaningful connections, if any, within a cultural configuration.

In opposition to the stringent ethic of moral injunctions, there is a current version which appears to be more culturally oriented. In its semi-popular form it may very well represent a revolutionary change in the approved ideal of the American character—a change from the inner-directed to the outer-directed man, or as it has become known in a derivative rendering, the change from the "Protestant ethic" to the "social ethic." We need not quarrel with these accounts of what is happening in present-day American life. They appear to be sufficiently well documented to make a convincing case for the beginning of a radically new pattern of morality in our scientific-industrial world. The new pattern calls for interpretation rather than for either indignation or friendly acceptance. Indeed, the authors who describe these new patterns are not advocating their adoption. Instead of regarding them as satisfactory goals of contemporary culture, they strongly suggest that they fall short of the requirements of an authentic culture.

By and large, the new "social ethic" is social in the most uncritical of ways. It emphasizes "belongingness" and "togetherness" in terms of the most adolescent of standards. The individual's attachment to a group is primarily sentimental in that it admits of no serious consideration of function and his selection of associates is based mostly on considerations of prestige. Moreover, since prestige is determined not by what he regards as valuable and since he cannot quite rely on the judgments of other persons, because others are in turn relying on his, the vicious circle is likely to be broken by those who hide behind the scene and who manipulate "public opinion" in subtle ways.

Two interesting conclusions may be drawn from the "social ethic." First, this ethic is not just an expression of an inherent goodness in human nature. On the contrary, it is a product of a culture (at least in its middle-class range) which honors an ease and comfort of life, as well as status and belongingness appropriate to a new-found opulence to which the majority can aspire. The second is that this ethic cries out for an authentication, which is denied it by virtue of its refusal to be critical of its gratifications. Its standards of taste are accordingly more responsive to fad than they are to genuine cultural demands. And this brings us back to what is without doubt the crucial ethical problem.

If social relations are not to be merely a function of some alien—and therefore mechanical—force, they must be a response to the authentic needs of a society. And the result will have to be the enjoyment of meaningful relations—not the banalities and monotonies of a round of existence stimulated, not even by animal spirits, but only by cooked-up gladness. The philosophical quest, it seems, must be for that principle of authenticity by which, in Edward Sapir's happy distinction, we can distinguish the genuine from the spurious. The existence of patterns or configurations of culture is not enough to aid much in the answer to the ethical question unless we can move from them to the normative function of culture. In fact, the major problem lies precisely in the appropriate sense in which culture is capable of supplying a norm for our actions, beliefs, dispositions and their objective expression in the artifacts and institutions which are indispensable to their expression. The appeal to something more than sentiment or power or gratification, but which includes sentiment and power and gratification and is at the same time capable of legitimating them—this is what seems to be called for in order to arrive at some satisfactory conception of a genuine culture. The task is indeed formidable.

Mainly, the task is formidable because it presupposes a knowledge of the actual working of institutions that probably no one can possess. Yet without making a stab at what appears to be the basic principles of their workings, only formal—and probably in the last analysis only arid—discussion can result. To avoid aridity, we need to seek out the interconnections between principles and institutions which we may hope will lead to a better understanding of each. To deal with the questions analytically, some division is necessary. It appears to me that the least arbitrary division for such purposes is into institutions of power and institutions of expression, together with the principles appropriate to each. In so dividing things, I expect only to bring the ethical problem of culture into focus, not to solve it. This expectation conforms with the axiom that the nature of culture is such that no single individuals can either create or destroy it. By its very nature, it is a matter of joint and public efforts, not of idiosyncratic and private ones. Better then that we turn directly to a consideration of it.

PART ONE

On Culture

"I do not call one greater and one
  smaller,
That which fills its period and
  place is equal to any."

Walt Whitman,
Song of Myself

Chapter 1

FROM CULTURAL PATTERNS TO CULTURAL NORMS

IT IS FASHIONABLE TODAY TO REGARD HUMAN LIFE as being indissolubly linked with the peculiar culture in which it flourishes. There is no greater commonplace than that which asserts that man is a dependent creature, incapable of maintaining himself, not just apart from nature and its fruits, but also apart from those who nourish him, teach him, and upon whom his social life depends. Man's mutuality with man has long been recognized in political thought by its engendering such a concept as "the general welfare," without which a concept of political life is inconceivable. Culture connotes an advancement beyond the barbarities of crude biological existence, and in the modern mode it further connotes a singularity of life which marks off one people from another and which supplies a kind of integrity of human relationships sustained by traditions unique to a people.

The fact of the existence of cultures has been obscured from the beginnings of occidental thought for a variety of reasons. It was obscured to the classical Greeks by virtue of their narcissistic bias to regard all who were not Greeks as barbarians. It was obscured to later religious thinkers, typified by St. Augustine, by their universalizing the antagonistic precepts of the way of the flesh and the way of the spirit, precepts which made inconsequental or incoherent the particularities of social life. And in modern political thought it has been obscured in quite opposite directions, partly by the dominance of nationalism and chauvinism, and partly by the dominance of individualism and subjectivism. Inevitably imperialistic in its bias, the former has been accompanied by the invidious distinction between superior and inferior peoples. Secularly monastic in its outlook and impervious to the authentic sources of a person's support, the latter has looked to the individual will as the spring of all significant human activity.

Paradoxically, a variety of institutional structures has conspired to conceal from occidental man the role of culture in his own life as well as in that of other peoples. The city-state, the church, the nation, commerce, and property have served in various ways to blind him from almost limitless divergence of cultures, each with its own viable customs, artifacts, and ideals, not to speak of the endless aberrations found in individual actions.

The modern emphasis on culture at least has the virtue of attempting to do justice to the richness and variegated patterns of social life, as well as of giving us pause in formulating alleged necessities of social existence from the limited outlooks of our own parochial points of view. Once we recognize the range of customs that pertains to the business of life and the range of attitudes that is expressed in men's judgments about the worthiness of various kinds of activities, we are in a position to gain a sense of the endless complexities of the facts of social existence together with the values they are thought to contain. Birth, puberty, marriage, death, along with the sustaining activities of art, religion, craftsmanship, exchange of goods, and use of power, come to be seen in their illimitable expressions, subject only to the genius of a people in making them significant in their lives.

By recognizing the wide variations of social life, the study of man almost inevitably leads to an attitude of tolerance of, if not respect for, the ingenuity of human beings in achieving viable forms of social existence. The fertility of social invention not unjustly leaves the student of culture with a sense of awe, and his contagious enthusiasm finds expression in his urging others to a compassionate appreciation of alternative cultural forms. Contemporary anthropologists reject as incompetent any merely antiquarian interest for penetrating to the substance of cultural life. On the contrary, they insist upon the need for an intimate knowledge of the various structures which give to culture an integrity and character of its own.

The contemporary fashion is thus to see in peoples as divergent as those of Dahomey or Ponape, of Dobu or the Crow Indians, of the Chukchee or the Haitians, an integrity and uniqueness of culture which clearly differentiates one people from

4

another. It is this which puts a stamp of individuality upon a people and which, some say, renders ineffectual the collecting and cataloguing of folkways in disregard of their particularized embodiment in actual cultural life.[1] The process of patterning, as Ruth Benedict speaks of it, is what is regarded as being crucial to the very conception of culture. Presently, I shall want to analyze this with some care, but at the outset it suffices to note that anthropologists appears to be entirely in accord that it is the organization or patterning of customs and institutions that constitutes a culture as a unique kind of entity. Through variegated patterns of culture, different peoples have discovered ways of living with themselves and of coping with nature adequately enough to support their ways of life. How this is done is obviously very complex, and the various transformations it brings about in man himself are especially noteworthy.

What appears most remarkable is that the process of enculturation is one which changes the very stuff of man from a limited biological organism into a social or human being. Although it is true the metamorphosis has never actually been observed, we can nevertheless observe in the cultural processes qualities that we cannot attribute simply to the expression of animal drives and their biological expression. Even in so-called primitive societies, the utilization of knowledge, the accommodation of person to person and of group to group, the communication of meanings, the ways of enjoying vicarious experiences, the development of imaginative and creative life—these very special phenomena cannot be expressed through literal, biological concepts. And whatever correlations there may be between the biological and the social, they are not such that cultural facts are intelligible by a reading of the physiological processes which sustain them. Our assumption, to be further explicated in the sequel, is that to understand the peculiar nature of man is to understand the cultural activities of which he is capable. As we have already observed then, this is to understand him as able to enter into the variegated patterns, such as those which anthropologists have made familiar to us by their recognition of the range of cultures, and not just limited to that which is familiar to us in our own native life. This assertion is, of course, no more than platitude today.

5

What is somewhat less platitudinous is the observation that culture is a condition both of a person's security as well as of his liberation. The case is easily enough made today to show that security is a function of social organization, that the preservation of man is accomplished by factors varying all the way from sexual reproduction to role-differentiation and assignment, to communication and shared articulated sets of goals, to the regulation of affective expression and the control of disruptive forms of behavior.[2] Although the theorists of the social contract were not always clear about the ends of civil society, nor always agreed upon them, the unmistakable truth is that the state of nature is, if not impossible, so fraught with danger, insecurities, and inconveniences as to make life scarcely human at all. It was, at least in their language, "uncivil." Political discussion in the modern mode recognizes that security is a function of social organization, and popular criticism seldom avoids the cliché of contrasting security with liberty, as if the two were totally incompatible. No doubt, the complexities of modern life have made it increasingly difficult for contemporary man to achieve a sense of individuality in the face of the complicated technology of the world in which he lives.

Despite the truth which popular criticism contains, culture has a liberating influence as well as a conserving one. To liberate activity is to give expression to power, and this is to channel activities to consummations, rather than to dissipate them into formless outpourings. No doubt, liberation requires the fashioning of activities in accordance with patterns, and we may assume, until we can explore the theory, that the patterning which is provided by culture is a condition of significant freedom of action. This theory is, of course, not new; on the contrary, it belongs to much of the idealistic tradition of Western thought. In modern political thought, Rousseau and Hegel have been especially prominent in their attempts to reconcile freedom with the exigencies of social life. When the problem is cast in terms of culture, the challenging question is how to reconcile the drives and necessities peculiar to particular individuals with the power and authority inherent in the institutions of a culture.

Although culture provides the conditions of liberation of

6

activities, clearly, unless we employ culture as a question-begging term, it can also be harsh and stifling. It is axiomatic that in any society that is to continue, restraining power must be exercised for its preservation. When the restraints that are exercised are incommensurate with the consummatory activities made possible by them, then a culture may be properly said to be authoritarian and the liberations so engendered, spurious. Culture is always restraining, but the nice question is whether restraint constitutes a condition of productive discipline, or of discipline for the purpose of effecting inequitable distribution of goods and prestige, or of discipline just for the sake of discipline.

A major fault in adopting a point of view which insists that all cultures are of equal worth and that all are good is that inequities and stupidities may thus be condoned. Those in positions of power may maintain themselves through preferential treatment and rewards disproportionate to any service they perform for their society. Shamans are often able to employ their rank to perpetuate superstitions that enchain, rather than liberate, a people. A priestcraft may not always be useful to a culture, and the assertion that it always justifies itself is somewhat more than debatable.[3] Even when superstition and magic do play a useful role within a culture, anthropologists are often quick to point out that, like the oracles of ancient Greece, those who wield superstitious and magical powers are careful to provide an "out" if their powers are not effective in a given instance. Moreover, those who follow the prescriptions and proscriptions of magic rely upon settled and effective craftsmanship where ends are controlled by known and tested means rather than upon supernatural forces over which the individual has no sure control.[4] The fact that magic is not permitted to contravene technology is evidence of the respect that even primitive man shows for natural knowledge, to the extent to which he is capable of developing techniques for knowing and controlling his world.

The preliminary conclusion to be drawn from the above discussion is that there are manifest virtues in regarding the life of man as culture-bound and that there are serious doubts concerning the legitimacy of regarding cultures as being beyond the pale of criticism and evaluation. The paradoxical character of this conclusion suggests the need for inquiring more deeply into the nature of culture. To this end, the interrelated questions we may profitably consider are, first, what is it in the conception of culture that commends itself as possessing postive worth; second, are there supra-cultural factors that render cultures measurable upon an objective, evaluative scale, and, if so, what is the nature of these factors? I wish to consider these questions in order.

The above discussion has already suggested an aspect of culture that requires a more searching analysis—namely, the patterning process by which a society is formed into a culture. Cultures are, of course, complex entities. They are capable, consequently, of being viewed from many different perspectives, no doubt all of which are useful for some purpose or other. Kroeber and Kluckhohn have collected hundreds of definitions of "culture."[5] I have no desire to add to the number, nor does it seem necessary, inasmuch as my chief purpose is to spell out those implications of culture which look primarily to its intrinsic value in the life of a people and therefore which attribute to that life a kind of integrity of its own.

For this reason, the process of gathering, enumerating, and classifying folkways gives little promise of throwing light upon the nature of the values intrinsic to a people's mode of life. The use of a painstaking, empirical method for obtaining the data of cultural life is without question indispensable to the objectives of anthropological science; but these data are nevertheless only raw material out of which the anthropologist must somehow fashion his concept of the kind of culture that belongs to a people, and by which he must test the adequacy of the concept he has fashioned. There is no doubt that the task of accumulating the data is enormous, but the more relevant task for our purpose is that of ascertaining a pattern inherent in them, by virtue of which a people may be said to have a culture.

Besides calling attention to factors which are constituents of cultures, anthropologists are likely to warn that the summation of these factors does not itself constitute a culture. The acts, the ideas, the language, the attitudes, the artifacts of a people constitute a culture only as they are integrated according to a more

8

or less consistent pattern. Ruth Benedict gives clear expression to this when she writes:

> A culture, like an individual, is a more or less consistent pattern of thought and action. Within each culture there come into being characteristic purposes not necessarily shared by other types of society. In obedience to these purposes, each people further and further consolidates its experience, and in proportion to the urgency of these drives the heterogeneous items of behavior take more and more congruous shape. Taken up by a well-integrated culture, the most ill-assorted acts become characteristic of its peculiar goals, often by the most unlikely meta-morphoses. The form that these acts take we can understand only by understanding first the emotional and intellectual mainspring of that society.[6]

The context in which this passage appears clearly suggests the need for a nice balance between the discoverable empirical elements which go into the structure of a culture and the form which it assumes by virtue of the various relationships that obtain among the elements.

There is, of course, a two-fold danger in looking to patterns as if they constituted the essence of culture. First, they are at best only imperfectly embodied in the actual comings and goings of a people; hence, a romanticized version of actions is taken for the actual actions where no articulatable pattern is discoverable. The danger is not entirely allayed by use of the adjectival phrase "more or less consistent" as qualifying the noun "pattern." One might wish here to fall back upon the sociologist's notion of an "ideal type." As a matter of fact, the use of some such notion is almost inevitable if the term "culture" is to be employed both as a theoretical concept and as one which is intended to have denotative significance. The difficulty in employing the term in this double sense is really no more than an exaggerated one of applying any concept to empirical entities. The exaggeration arises from the doubt whether there exists a thoroughly clear rule as to how the term "pattern" is to be applied empirically, and consequently from whether the anthropologists are able to arrive at a sufficient degree of agreement for regarding their investigations as scientific.

The questions raised by these doubts do not allow of facile answers, and I do not propose to attempt any such. Nevertheless, there are clues towards answers that look promising and that seem to accord with the procedures anthropologists actually employ in their investigations. I do not intend to discuss the reliability of anthropological techniques, the use of informers, and the like. This requires first-hand knowledge by those who have actually practiced in the field. Yet it is abundantly clear that a skilled practitioner will distinguish between actions and attitudes that are typical in the life of a people and those that are aberrant, however difficult the distinction is to make. Homicide, for example, may have many different forms, and whether it is indulged in out of malice, social or religious necessity, or out of any number of other causes, will call for widely divergent descriptions of its meaning in cultural life. The facts themselves are of an elementary sort, even though the methods of ascertaining them are anything but elementary.

In its most simple form we may say that the patterning of a culture is a function of the institutions of a society, since an institution may be conceived of as a society's ingrained practices or customs. By its very nature of being customary, an institution possesses a degree of persistence. Moreover, by virtue of its persistence, it expresses itself as a character of that society, and consequently may ordinarily be regarded as characteristic of it. A people's customary technologies, their forms of education or worship, their characteristic dress, their treatment of property, of criminals, of their leaders, their kinds of play or amusement, warfare and burial—all of these are institutions, as well as all other formalized practices shared by all or most of the people, or even some of them, when the practices express a function recognized by all or most, even though not shared by them, as for example in those functions served by specialized craftsmen or constituted authorities.[7] In addition, there are peripheral institutions, especially proliferated in our own complex industrial society, in which groups spring up for almost any interest imaginable, even the most asocial, such as fishing, playing chess, or driving automobiles.[8] Ordinarily, however, institutions would appear to be more fundamental to the life of a society and to express more basic attitudes towards the problems of man.

As in all definitory and classificatory schemes pertaining to empirical things, there is in respect to institutions too a difficulty of setting exact boundaries. On the one side, the concept may shade off into individual habits that may be more personal than social. And on the other, it may be so extended in scope that it entails the idea of institutions within institutions. Should, for example, the office of mayor within the institution of local government, or the role of fatherhood within the wider institution of the family, or the institution of animal sacrifice within that of religion be regarded as constituting separate institutions? No dogmatic answers are very helpful, and proposed legislation for answering them is dogmatic. Usage provides some guides, even if not without confusion. Perhaps the best guide is one which looks to a statement of the function or purpose of repeated, persistent, and pervasive activities expressed in and through material artifacts.

This suggestion at least has the advantage of pointing to the complex nature of institutions. They express social purposes, biological and psychological motivations infuse life into them, and artifacts stand as mute testimony to the pains a people are willing to take in order to give their purposes embodiment of some permanence. The total process involved engenders the minimum of what we expect to find in the interpretation of human actions. It involves a motivating source of action; it involves cognitive processes with ends as well as with mediating judgments; it involves the actual action itself; and, finally, it involves the results of this action both upon the actor and upon his environment—in short, the affects and the effects.[9] There is little doubt that institutions involve all these factors as well as the more complicating ones of communication and co-operative enterprise, without which there could be no institutions of a society.

The purposes expressed in institutions are as varied as life itself. They run the gamut from the celebration of birth to the consolation of death and all the intermediate sustaining activities, including many of man's frivolities. Some of the purposes are naturally similar, because some of the circumstances of human life are common to life wherever it is lived. Professor Kluckhohn succinctly asserts this in these terms:

Every society's patterns for living must provide approved and sanctioned ways for dealing with such universal circumstances as the existence of two sexes; the helplessness of infants; the need for satisfaction of the elementary requirements such as food, warmth, sex; the presence of individuals of different ages and of differing physical and other capacities.[10]

Although some peoples do borrow institutions from others, the general rule seems to be that in each culture an institution has its own peculiar timbre, and this is likely to be the case even with borrowed institutions. When, for example, a new religion permeates a culture, its nature is likely to be a fusion of the new with the old. The greatest similarities would seem to be those which depend upon basic technologies, especially where variations are likely to be less rather than more productive of the intended ends.

The purpose of an institution, being an ideal or norm to be expressed in action and consequently to give it direction, can ordinarily be realized only more or less perfectly. Simple purposes may be expressed rather completely by simple folk, complicated ones by geniuses. But those that require continuing activities by numbers of persons are likely to fall far short of their mark. Whatever the degree of realization, clear-cut, well-defined purposes are essential to intelligent action, since only as they are capable of being articulated is it possible to implement them into action, to ascertain correctness or incorrectness of action, and accordingly to modify action. Finally, a clarity of apprehension and statement is a condition of the evaluation of purposes. Although discussion of the nature of the evaluative process is better postponed, we may observe here that clarity of purpose is a condition of the vitality of a culture. Otherwise, a society is given over to drift and flux of circumstance.

However clearly the ends of social life may be stated, they can have no vitality without the urgencies supplied by human beings. The conception of a human being can never prove adequate if it ignores man's biological base. We do well to recur to the great tradition which constantly reminds us that man belongs to the genus animal. Accordingly, we are reminded of the ubiquitous facts of metabolism and reproduction, together with the activities in human life which sustain them. However much these activities are overlaid with the sophistications of culture, we can easily discover the carnal which lies beneath them, even in what appear to be the most transcendental of man's activities.

Were there no biological grounding, it would be inconceivable that there should be a "go" of culture. But inasmuch as the variety of cultures belies the assumption of simple drives which manifest themselves in repeated patterns throughout all cultures, there appears no alternative but to recognize that these drives undergo transformations in the actions of enculturated persons. Malinowski italicizes this transformation when he writes, "Although culture is primarily born out of the satisfaction of biological needs, its very nature makes man into something essentially different from a mere animal organism. Man satisfies none of his needs as mere animal."[11] The fact of the transformation of animal drives into patterned customs is scarcely debatable, even though our knowledge of the processes by which it occurs is not reliable. Instead of venturing into this field of analysis, however, prudence suggests the wisdom of leaving it to the psychologists and social scientists to analyze these processes with the ingenuity at their command.

Nevertheless, we may modestly observe that an aid to the discrimination of the processes, and, we may add, further evidence for their existence, is found in the artifacts created by them. A host of material things results from the institutional activities of men, ranging all the way from houses, schools, churches, shrines, to tools, works of art, seals, limitless insignia, banners, and dressware, from plain to exotic. Through these artifacts (sometimes popularly thought of as institutions themselves) purposes are expressed and actions, by conducting their urgencies to states of quiescence, come to fulfilment. Social purposes endure in the works of man, and these works are embodied more or less permanently in material culture, which is indispensable to the life of any society. If there is confusion between houses and homes, churches and religion, art and creation, armies and warfare, and the like, these confusions are only the inevitable outcome of identifying actions with the materials through which they come to be expressed.

We should not, of course, confuse "the emotional and intellectual mainsprings of a society" (Benedict) with its artifacts,

13

but surely we cannot understand these "mainsprings" without understanding what they issue into. The confusion at this point is attended by the danger of reducing social to psychological phenomena, with the consequence that the peculiar character of the social is lost in reductive psychological analysis. The only sure protection against this unwarranted reduction is to regard institutional patterns as the basic data of social life and to fit the psychological (and biological) factors into the schemata of institutions and the interstitial relations that exist between them. Actually, in this way we come to a better knowledge of the authentic attitudes and beliefs of a people, for we can see them as operative factors concretely expressed in institutional structures. In short, the best test we have of the ideals of a people is the observation of the continuance of their institutions over a span of time, for institutions stand as the crucial testimony of how a people think and act and how they feel towards one another and towards their world.

By way of conclusion we may say then that an institution is a unit of culture, of some duration, which expresses a more or less vital function, and which, taken together with other units, constitutes that which is distinctive of a society. Insofar as functions are discriminable, whether complex or simple, institutions may be said to constitute the fundamental units of a culture.[12] In regarding them as the basic units of society, we look to units which on the one hand are functions (and therefore identifiable) and on the other preserve the essential character of being social, and consequently are not reduced to elements of a different order. The next question in order is to inquire into the interrelations of these units in their more complex whole, which is culture. In this further inquiry we shall be addressing ourselves specifically to the question previously raised: what is it in a culture that commends itself as possessing positive worth?

If, as has been repeatedly suggested, the essence of a culture consists in a distinctiveness of social life, and if, as has been asserted, the basic units of social life are its institutions, we properly look for the distinctiveness in the interrelationships of its institutions. Our immediate task is, first, to see how these may be adequately construed and then to offer some suggestions for ascertaining how the distinctive qualities may actually be found in the life of a people. In doing this, we are in essence moving from a descriptive and explanatory conception of culture to a normative one. I shall therefore attempt to make the steps quite explicit.

Our analysis, following the lead of newer movements in anthropology, has first of all rejected as a faulty preconception of culture that which consists in a mere collection of unrelated items in the lives of people, and which consequently is constituted as an agglomeration or, at best, a classification of social beliefs and practices. It also has rejected the study of individual behavior separated from social context, for the sufficient reason that the clues are destroyed as to whether such behavior is sanctioned or is aberrant and merely tolerated. Unless we know the social rewards and punishments that are visited upon individuals' behavior, we cannot know what is typical and what is not typical within that society.

It is only through the typical that we can come to know what is distinctive of a society and, consequently, what its culture is. But the problem of knowing what the culture of a society is, is much more complicated than that of knowing the typical actions which are constituted as separate institutional structures: it is, in Ruth Benedict's terms, the discovery of a "pattern" or, better, a "configuration" which is characteristic of a whole society. In other words, it is that of knowing how the various institutions themselves fit together. An expression which Sapir and others often use to denote this is what they call the "genius" of a society. This is an appropriate term for marking the passage from a descriptive to a normative point of view.

In his redefinition of culture, Sapir briefly characterizes it as "civilization insofar as it embodies the national genius."[13] Although he explicitly borrows from the technical ethnological conception of culture that which is said "to embody any socially inherited element in the life of man, material and spiritual" as well as from the idea of culture as "individual refinement[s] . . . that have the sanction of a class of long standing," he is forced to reject certain trivia contained in each in order to arrive at a definition useful in an evaluative sense.[14]

The genius of a culture is necessarily reflected in its daily activities, but unless some principle of selection is employed, we cannot distinguish between those activities that are prosaic and trivial and those that in a special way express the distinctive attitudes of a people. Some institutions are freighted with meaning that requires the support of others in order that they may run their course. Accordingly, there will inevitably be in the minds of the people an order of significance as to what they can and what they cannot achieve in their lives. The directive powers of this order in some cases reinforce activities, in some cases prohibit them, and in still others just tolerate or remain indifferent to them. What this amounts to in the social behavior is a selective system of activities—a system of purposive behavior that is restricted by a more or less rigorous priority of ends. Thus when conflicts arise, actions regarded as of inferior worth must make way for those regarded as superior.

To ascertain the concrete meaning of any such purposive system is to explore the relative order of its institutions and to discover the peculiar character of its institution or institutions which impose limitations upon those which are made subordinate. Thus a society which, for example, is given over to warfare will be one in which family life and educational institutions will especially inculcate the manly virtues, respect for leadership, and the like. It will emphasize sports and encourage meeting the challenges of danger. It will spurn most indulgences and emphasize frugality. In short, it will create a Spartan pattern that has traditionally and rightly been called *militarism*. And although the militaristic attitude has been repeated throughout history, its specific embodiments will always be founded in the military technologies peculiar to the civilization of any given epoch.

Militarism, of course, is only one of the many ideals of a society. Actually, we are familiar with a large number of them, many of which have become familiar to us in the language of "isms" and "cracys," such as industrialism, materialism, spiritualism, aestheticism, urbanism, professionalism, bureaucracy, theocracy, plutocracy, democracy, etc. All of these terms have in common the magnifying of some one aspect of life and making it into a dominating trait. As is the case with most genius, they achieve the enhancement of some qualities by minimizing or rejecting others. Like a work of art, so a culture too realizes unique qualities by contrasts and subordinations, not to speak of the exclusions which intensify these particular ones by the elimination of others. Thus, pacificism gives way in the face of militarism, handicrafts in the face of industrialism, paternalism in the face of progressivism, and so on.

In the Western world, critics from the time of Thales and Xenophanes to those of Augustine and Acquinas, Erasmus and Hobbes, Voltaire and Paine, Marx and von Mises, to take a few names at random, have called attention to the overemphases on some of our cultural activities and the need for redirecting them in quite other ways. Whether it is religion or commerce or sports or what-not that is emphasized, activities that conflict with those central to a society will be suffocated. The priorities characteristic of society have been commonly regarded as the "dominant institutions" of it.[15] In a well illustrated discussion bearing upon this topic, Professor Herskovits has employed the happy expression "cultural focus" to emphasize the directive powers contained in some principal activity or activities of a society. He defines cultural focus as "the tendency of every culture to exhibit greater complexity, greater variation in the institutions of some of its aspects than in others."[16] As instances in point, he refers us to activities such as those of the dairy operations among the Toda, including the sanctifying and ritualistic procedures as well as the techniques of milking, churning, and the like. The buffalo dairy is thus "the particular institution that orients and gives meaning to life."[17] In contrast, among the Ponape, he asserts, it is the cultivation of the yam that marks its cultural focus, including its economic system as well as its system of prestige in social relationships.

We may regard the cultural focus of a society, then, as that institution or set of institutions that marks the genius of a people, that gives their activities a direction and meaning, and that provides them with a system of priorities. Prestige, a degree of order and security, the reasonable expectations of persons, the services they are compelled to perform and the rewards they are entitled to—these together with what sustain them are included in a

17

society that possesses a cultural focus. The power and authority included in the system provide increased liberation of action for just those interests that constitute the focus of a society. In turn, they stifle those activities and interests at odds with the focal ones. Hence, the areas of social necessities, prohibitions, and permissivenesses are defined by cultural focus.

In turn, the existence or non-existence of a cultural focus can be determined by inquiry to discover just what in a society is necessary, prohibited, or permitted. Once we ascertain what a society demands of its members or enjoins them from doing through its various sanctions, we possess the clue to its focal activities. The kind of punishments and rewards it employs as sanctions will be peculiar to itself, but insofar as they are effective in directing conduct, they will show what a people believe in and the pains they are willing to take to infuse their beliefs into their actions.

The focal institutions embody within a culture its supreme powers. Accordingly, the major energies of a people will be expended principally upon its buffalos or its yams or its shrines, and the like, as its focus is a buffalo-culture or a yam-culture, or a theocracy. How the authority is wielded within a culture is itself a matter to be understood in terms appropriate to that culture. No doubt, the educational scheme in any culture will incorporate within it a respect for those qualities and a preparation for those activities that are encouraged by the focal institutions. The extent to which, in addition to the education of the youth, special authorities need to be constituted for the perpetuation and enhancement of focal activities—these are matters to be learned in their particularities by empirical study, rather than by a priori assumption. Sometimes, it would seem to require some kind of special police force (probably never completely lacking), sometimes the power of public opinion (probably also never completely lacking), or various degrees of combinations of the two, ranging all the way from full-fledged authoritarianism to democracy based upon voluntary consent and guided by agreement at least on fundamentals, if not particulars.

A viable culture must develop a whole range of institutions to satisfy the requirements of a more or less self-sustaining society.

Besides providing for the material goods which support a people, and at least the rudiments of government whereby they resist disruptive encroachments, they must also devise means for the care and nurture of the young, for effecting some kind of community of feeling, and for celebrating it both in social relations and in artifacts; and in addition they will have to develop techniques for sharing some kind of intellectual outlook and which appropriately make room for vastly different talents through which persons can share in that outlook. These various functions are commonly recognized in the institutions which we catalog as the economic, political, legal, educational, technological, artistic, religious, and the like.[18] Although some one of these may be the primary focus of what is focal to a society, we should nevertheless expect the whole range of institutions to be appropriately colored by the focal, even though the shadings will necessarily vary in accordance with the various subordinations which are dictated by its system of priorities.

Two opposite but weighty objections may be urged against this conception of cultural focus. On the one hand, one may insist that the focal, by virtue of its disproportionate exaggeration of some qualities to the elimination of others, is precisely what accounts for the *absence* of culture within a society. The objection not unjustly assumes that a cultured society is precisely one which encourages legitimate activities, not one which prohibits them. On the other hand, one may insist that no society is so highly organized that it has a single cultural focus. Societies, as we know them, the objection continues, always involve varieties of conflicting interests, dissents, and precarious balances so that powers are always in flux, and what order there is, is always changing accordingly as some interests are capable of maintaining themselves either over against others or simply because they are separate and at least temporarily not in conflict. Consequently, since there exist no cultural foci, our own oversimplification and falsification must be responsible for our asserting that they do. Both of these objections are impressive and call for the replies that may be possible on the merits of the case.

No doubt, it is true that when some one interest focussed in some one institution is a people's primary concern, that interest not only overshadows all others but it also tends to suffocate other legitimate interests. This is commonly and properly spoken of as a dehumanizing process, just because it chokes off other human aspirations, the expression of which would make for a more complete and satisfactory life. Whether it is religion or industry or warfare that is the all-compelling pursuit of a society, life does become poverty stricken to the extent that the recurrent promptings of other human impulses are frustrated and therefore incapable of being satisfied through the creation of modes of life satisfactory to these promptings. The members of a society, so far from being content with being denied those further possible satisfactions, would be certain to voice their objections and to insist upon effecting the appropriate changes to make them actual. What is involved in their procedures is nothing more nor less than moral criticism which, in envisaging new alternatives for the expression of human aspirations, agitates for their realization.

Social criticism at its best has the function of helping men to overcome the inadequacies of their society. As significant, it is imaginative, and therefore not just captious; and as imaginative, it discloses the conditions of its own realization, and therefore is not just fanciful. Significant social criticism consequently aims at the rise of more vital persons, fitted for occupying new positions, encouraged to perform new services, and, singly and collectively, stimulated to a heightened appreciation of functions engendered in the transformed society. What the new functions are and how they mark an advance in social life has been eloquently described by George Mead. Explaining this through a kind of dialectical movement, he interprets for example the movement of ancient Rome from a militaristic to an administrative society in the following terms:

> There is the sense of pride of the Roman in his administrative capacity as well as in his martial power, in his capacity to subjugate all the people around the Mediterranean world and to administer them. The first attitude was that of subjugation, and then came the administrative attitude which was more of the type to which I have already referred as those of functional superiority. It was that which Virgil expressed in his demand that the Roman should realize that in his ruling he was possessed with the capacity for administration. This capacity made the

Roman Empire entirely different from the earlier empires, which carried nothing but brute strength behind them. The passage in that case is from a sense of political superiority and prestige expressed in a power to crush, over into a power to direct a social understanding in which there is a larger co-operative activity. The political expression starts off with a bare self-assertion, coupled with a military attitude, which leads to the wiping-out of the other, but which leads on, or may lead on, to the development of a higher community, where dominance takes the form of administration. Conceivably, there may appear a larger international community than the empire, organized in terms of function rather than force.[19]

The focal character, as for example in the case of militarism, may be so limited that it cannot satisfy legitimate human cravings. Consequently, in order that it may continue to exist, a society may be forced to transform itself in such ways as to effect new kinds of human relationships, through which men may come to a new sense of dignity.

The characteristics of classical Greek society have proved especially attractive to students of culture precisely because it was able to overcome the limitations inherent in previous cultures. In its Apollonian phase, at least, it was capable of incorporating a range of activities which denied neither the spiritual nor the material, neither the aesthetic nor the political, neither the communal nor the individual. It found the essence of human qualities to lie in a balance that satisfied the requirements of reason and justice. Reason provided a rationale, an intelligibility, that could give to life intrinsic satisfaction and meaning. And justice signified not merely legal equality but that balance which constituted virtue entire; in short, all a man could with elegance do in his waking and sane life. This was a life that eschewed asceticism, commandments, and mechanical formulas of action. On the contrary, its "Nothing to excess" made possible the flourishing of a Sophocles, an Ictinous, a Pericles, a Phidias, an Ephialtes, a Democritus, and a Protagoras, to name only a few of the greats. I do not mean to suggest that Athenian culture should be taken as our ideal today. On the contrary, it is particularly embarrassing, to put it in Nietzschean terms, to reconcile the Apollonian with the Dionysiac elements of human life. Despite this embarrassment, however, the recognition of the Apollonian qualities forces upon us the need for coming to terms with the humanistic qualities that the Athenians, especially, made focal in at least one period of their lives.[20] Whatever our considered appraisals of the Athenians may be, certainly we should not ignore the ideals they prized so highly, even if we dare not emulate at this date the particular institution which was their particular vehicle for achieving these ideals—the city-state. We need to take these matters into further account in a reconsideration of the nature of culture.

Before doing so, however, there is point in recurring to the second objection raised against the idea of cultural focus—namely, that which regards it as an oversimplified abstraction, which distorts the real nature of social life as it is found in actual societies. The contention is that a society is not so well knit as to exhibit within it a single cultural focus; on the contrary, it is held, actual societies more truly exist as a kind of battleground in which varieties of particular interests for the most part contend with one another for a supremacy that no one of them is capable of achieving. To this objection, too, must be conceded some truth.

Historians have made us sufficiently aware of the oversimplifications by which we have characterized our own past. We have attributed consistencies to epochs which the facts will not bear out. We characterize, for example, the Middle Ages as if men's only real concern were the salvation of their souls, as if this world were but a vale of tears, and as if the mundane could properly be regarded only as a testing ground for eternal life or damnation. We attribute an orderly hierarchy to the organization of the Church, and we attribute a similar organization to the manor house as constituting its secular counterpart in the feudal system. For some purposes, this description, adequately filled out in its details, may have worth; but there is no doubt that it is inadequate as a description of fact. When we come to recognize the many facets of medieval life that were anti-feudal and even democratic, including especially the freeholders, when we come to see how disorganized from a hierarchical point of view many of the spiritual and secular social systems actually were, when we come to recognize the interest in scientific descriptions of nature for its own sake, or the extent to which capitalistic enterprise was a part of medieval times—when we recognize these as well as other so-called anomalies of medieval life, we come to appreciate what in the apt words of G. G. Coulton may be called "the medieval panorama."

The complexities and inconsistencies of social life in medieval times appear likewise to have their counterparts in other so-called epochs of the occidental world, as well as in the oriental world and in primitive societies. Does the great history of China, for example, allow itself to be adequately described in terms of ancestor worship and reverence for learning? Or can we satisfactorily describe the Ute Indians in terms of noble savagery? Surely, descriptions of the sort indicated here will be found to be not very adequate.

Despite such considerations, the objection is somewhat wide of the mark, since it pertains to the degree of adequacy of historical description, rather than to what, in principle, is signified by cultural focus. No historical description is more than an approximation to truth, and consequently its adequacy is always open to challenge. The correction of historical description surely may cause us to discard what we may have alleged to be the particular focus of a given society. We may nevertheless justly seek for—and discover—another focus that more appropriately characterizes the nature of that society. This procedure can be justified even in the face of exceptions that distort the focus attributed to that society, inasmuch as a focus is intended to disclose an emphasis in the life of a people and asserts consequently the existence of a character that is *by and large* true.

Further encouragement for the adoption of the ideal of cultural focus comes from a large number of social scientists who regard societies as structures in which the various institutions are well knit. So much is this the case that it is a commonplace among them that alterations in one basic institution are bound to produce alterations in other basic institutions. In fact, the principal argument used especially by economists for not interfering, for example, with the economy of a society is that such changes reverberate throughout politics, the law, the schools, the churches, the press, the family, and consequently affect virtually the total life of the individual. Political scientists and sociologists in large numbers seem to add the weight of their testimony to this, and much of the burden of anthropological investigation supplements the thesis in the case of non-literate peoples.

We need not be led through dogmatism, however, to assume that there is one and only one cultural focus within a society. On a priori grounds there may be two or three or even more foci. But if there is more than one focus, we have every right to expect that the two or more foci exist in harmony and mutually affect and reinforce one another, the exception, of course, being the case of internal strife in a society where change appears iminent; that is, when a society is in, or is about to enter upon, a period of radical transformation. Addressing himself to the question of whether there is a dominant character in every culture, Franz Boas, referring to Ruth Benedict, writes:

> As the author points out, not every culture is characterized by a dominant character, but it seems probable that the more intimate our knowledge of the cultural drives that actuate the behavior of the individual, the more we shall find that certain controls of emotion, certain ideals of conduct, prevail that account for what seem to us as abnormal attitudes when viewed from the standpoint of our civilization. The relativity of what is considered social or asocial, normal or abnormal, is seen in a new light.[21]

The "new light" does not cause us to impugn the existence of a cultural character (the "controls of emotion" or the "ideals of conduct") but on the contrary provides the very illumination by which we can apprehend what is "social or asocial, normal or abnormal."

To put it differently, we may suggest that the real question is whether a culture that has no character, or order of subordinations and superordinations of institutional activities, is properly called a culture at all. If a society is divided against itself, it is two, not one, with separate interests, separate loyalties, and the minimum of communication between the two, precisely because there appears to exist no common ground through which there can be genuine intercourse and the possibility of arriving at common agreements and mutually respected functions. If this is true of a society split in two, it is all the more true when there exists a larger number of factions. Factionalism makes the continuance of social life precarious and makes, as long as it lasts, impossible anything that might reasonably be called culture. (Its extreme form is, of course, the mythical war of all against all—the state of nature, which is the complete denial of the social.) Hence, although a condition which we call factionalism obviously may prevail, it is a condition contrary to the existence of culture.

The solution of the question of whether a culture always involves a dominant character that is its cultural focus is more than verbal. Our discussion does call for a verbal distinction, nevertheless, between that kind of society which is marked by internal strife, factional dispute, and discord, on the one hand; and that which is marked by balance, harmonious agreements, and concord, on the other. The distinction is one of kind. If, however, we wish to call them both a form of culture, we need to recognize the distinction in some other form, say, that of Sapir's in his distinction between the spurious and the genuine. Actually, this formulation has the distinct advantage of calling attention to the normative element in the definition of culture. Sapir makes this clear in the following passage:

> The genuine culture is not of necessity either high or low; it is merely inherently harmonious, balanced, self-satisfactory. It is the expression of a richly varied and yet somehow unified and consistent attitude toward life which sees the significance of any one element of civilization in its relation to all others. It is, ideally speaking, a culture in which nothing is spiritually meaningless, in which no important part of the general functioning brings with it a sense of frustration, of misdirected or unsympathetic effort.[22]

I suggest that this definition commends itself to us inasmuch as it attempts to cope with both the vitalities of social life and the individualities of human existence.

A genuine culture possesses vitality, first of all, insofar as it has an integrity and therefore a kind of self-sufficiency. Unlike a single institution, it is a totality capable of sustaining a way of life over a period of generations. Although an institution may reflect a kind of life, it clearly cannot sustain it. Only as all the social necessities are cared for can a way of life persist as a complex, functioning thing. Accordingly, the institutions must possess a degree of harmony that will support the continuity of movement from one kind of action to another. In education, for example, the processes must be such that the young can take their places in adult life and in turn either become parents or devise institutions for the care and education of the next generation. Educational vitalities will necessarily incorporate what is immediately significant to the child as well as what is significant in the life of the culture. The animating ideals will be precisely those which animate adult life, whatever the practices may be which give them substance.

As in education, so in the other institutions of a genuine culture, there is no energy wasted in irreconcilable opposites. Ideals and practices are consequently in harmony or else persons dissipate their vitalities in fruitless hypocrisies. Torn in contrary directions, they are, so far, incapacitated from achieving ends of any magnitude. Apropos of this topic, Sapir further writes of the genuine culture that:

> . . . if it builds itself magnificent houses of worship, it is because of the necessity it feels to symbolize in beautiful stone a religious impulse that is deep and vital; if it is ready to discard institutionalized religion, it is prepared also to dispense with the homes of institutionalized religion. It does not look sheepish when a direct appeal is made to its religious consciousness, then make amends by furtively donating a few dollars toward the maintenance of an African mission.[23]

To generalize further, we may characterize a genuine culture as one which spurns all ritualistic practices that neither better fit a people for the business of its life nor celebrate their fruitful and satisfying pursuits. Otherwise they are merely distracted from those pursuits that bear meaning.

There is danger, of course, in suggesting that a genuine culture is one so perfectly integrated that to admit of any extraneous or new elements in it is to admit only of what is contaminating. The suggestion can, of course, lead only to a caricature of what any actual culture is and, consequently, so far depart from any reality as to make the concept useless for practical purposes. New elements are, no doubt, constantly injected into the life of a people, and any conception of culture, normative or otherwise, that fails to take this factor into account cannot but be grossly unsatisfactory. To correct, consequently, what would otherwise be an unseemly romantic idea of culture, we need to recognize that the injection of new elements in the life of a people, however it comes about, constitutes discontinuities, and that a major problem of any people is to transform discontinuities into continuities—to incorporate the new into the old, and thus to engender in them new potencies. This kind of achievement involves the ingenuities of man to learn and to invent new ways of doing things.

The dynamics of cultural change make it increasingly clear that natural knowledge and technologies built upon that knowledge are indispensable to the tapping of cultural vitalities. The invention of the wheel, of levers and pulleys, the domestication of animals, the smelting of ore and molding of metals, to suggest only some elements that have gone into cultural dynamics, rest upon natural knowledge and implicate techniques for the advancement of cultural ends. How these were utilized in particular societies and the virtual revolutions they created have constituted the subject matter for extended treatises. I wish here only to italicize the principle that there are no social vitalities that do not either directly or indirectly involve both knowledge and technologies passed on in the traditions of cultural life. There appear to be no exceptions to this principle. One might possibly conceive of some that are not social—namely, those immediate and largely uncontrollable, biological responses of individuals— but if they become social, they become transformed into patterns subject to criticism and capable of being incorporated in significant social technologies. Again, an exception may be thought to reside in those celebrations or rituals or forms of belief pertaining to matters beyond the world of nature and beyond the controls over it man may devise by reason of his knowledge of causal connections. In response to this allegation, I would suggest that celebrations, rituals, religions, which are disconnected from nature lose vitality to the extent that they are disconnected. In other words, they are constituted as forms of asceticism, and although individuals may be ascetics, a whole culture cannot. So far from being ascetic, primitive religions (and possibly more often than not, advanced religions too) appear to be intimately interwoven with the worship of nature and consciously reflect man's sympathetic responses to the cyclical processes found in nature. When this connection is broken, a separate priestcraft with its own interests comes into being and, instead of contributing to the urgencies of a culture, it is more likely to dissipate

27

them by playing upon a people's fears and exploiting their tensions. We shall have to reckon with the theory that technological advance is the mark of the heights to which a culture may soar. There is an obvious sense in which a people who, for example, can develop a horse collar and thus utilize the energies of horses without half-choking them to death possess more vitality than a people who can utilize but a fraction of the power horses can provide. Examples of this kind of advance can, of course, be extended indefinitely. The question at issue, however, is not that of comparing the worth of culture with culture, but rather that of discovering the identity of a genuine culture.

The marks of a genuine culture include the activities of social life found to be more or less self-contained, functional, mutually supporting, and grounded upon natural knowledge, as well as possessing a dimension of totality in which there is play given to a wide range of human conduct. Moreover, vitalities are sustained only when consummatory activities are reconciled with the instrumental, and both engage a range of talents and a range of satisfactions consonant with the range of variations found in human life. Although inevitably some talents must be discouraged and some satisfactions denied, nevertheless, unless the vast majority of persons can exercise themselves rather completely and enjoy themselves rather fully, a society would probably not be said to have a culture, and certainly not a genuine one.

This observation brings us back to our insistence that in addition to the social vitalities a genuine culture liberates the individualities of human existence. The two are, of course, opposite faces of one and the same thing. Although it has been fashionable to believe that individuality can be achieved only when the social necessities are reduced to a minimum, this is more the result of economic dogma than a conclusion justified by a serious study of society. Individualities, just as individuals, may, of course, be crushed by a society—that is, by major forces within a society. What is equally true is that individualities, just as individuals, may be sustained by a society—that is, again, by major forces within it. In any society there will be capacities for acting, for making, for thinking, for enjoying. But how they exist and how they come to be expressed will be a matter, not just of the capacities themselves, but also of the kind of culture in which those who possess them live, and which gives direction to them. The idioms of their thoughts and actions can be sustained only as there are common symbols and forms of communication peculiar to that culture. In other words, although culture is a context of creative thought and action, obviously it is individuals who feel a sense of frustration or of liberation, and it is through their expressions that a culture is realized as either spurious or geuine. In this connection, Sapir observes, "The major activities of the individual must directly satisfy his own creative and emotional impulses, must always be something more than a means to an end."[24] If the activities of the individual normally suffer from "no sense of spiritual frustration," it is because of the fact that individuality is a correlate of the social processes and that a genuine culture is one which is essentially liberative and capable of sustaining individuality.

On the other hand, a spurious culture is a malfunctioning culture. It is full of hypocrisy, lowered sensitivities, frustrations, and general debilitation. It is a mixture of inchoate and incompatible ideals, incapable of sustaining for long any direction in activities. It encourages ideals it cannot support. Its appeals consequently are to social loyalties, but its springs of action are narrowly expedient and opportunistic. Its powers derive from the inculcation of fears; its enthusiasms are avoidances; its emotions, sentimentalities; and its artistic creations decorative exaggerations of the obvious, the horrors of emotional derangements, or abstractions devoid of any responsible connection with pulsating life. Finally, its spiritual orientation is one of gaudy ritual, obtrusively separating the sabbatical from the quotidian.

In the actualities of social life, there is no completely genuine culture, just as there is no absolutely spurious culture. The former represents an ideal of community life that could not be very closely approximated, and the latter represents an absence of social concern to such an extent as to signify something like the universal warfare of all with all. It is fair to assume, however, that there is a continuity between the spurious and the genuine such that the higher degrees of the one shade into the lower degrees of the other, and that only by an arbitrary decision could we separate one from the other. The chief virtue of the two conceptions lies in the recognition of principles by which it is possible to pass from a descriptive to a normative treatment of culture, and to accomplish this without creating a hiatus so great as to prevent our norms from having any recognizable connection with ways in which social life is actually carried on. Both the spurious and the genuine may consequently be regarded as extrapolations from modes of life that can be observed in literate as well as in primitive cultures. By reason of the intimate connection between the descriptive and the normative, we derive the double advantage of enriching what would otherwise be hopeless abstractions in value theory and of giving point to anthropological descriptions which would otherwise remain simply as antiquarian lore or even romantic primitivism.

I suggest our discussion reveals that by conceiving cultures as falling upon a scale from the spurious to the genuine, we come upon principles which give us leverage for understanding them according to what may be regarded as their moral worth, and that we can do this precisely because we become aware of principles which are definitely cultural principles, rather than imports from the outside. Discussion of the principles themselves leads us to the very heart of value theory. Such discussion, however, we might better postpone until we can see more clearly what the principles can signify in action; that is, how they may be construed for purposes of evaluating cultures themselves.

The evaluation of cultures is especially complicated by virtue of the fact that there is an important sense in which they are incomparable. A genuine culture satisfies the most rigorous of standards of achieving human ends. It encourages the fullest liberation of the human spirit individually and collectively; its prohibitions are only those in the absence of which frustration would be increased rather than decreased; its technologies are subordinated to indispensable services and functional craftsmanship, rather than to individual gain and titillating art; and its institutions and their tangible manifestations are harmoniously designed to produce both the necessities of, and elegance in, human life. For reasons such as these, a genuine culture possesses positive worth. Moreover, like the worth often attributed to persons, its worth is unique and intrinsic. In Sapir's terms, a genuine culture implicates a "somehow unified and consistent attitude toward life." The "unified and consistent attitude" we have seen fit to call a "cultural focus." A cultural focus is the mark of the individuality of a genuine culture, just as personality is the mark of the individuality of a person, and both are in much the same sense precious and incomparable. Despite this alleged uniqueness, we can nevertheless turn profitably to the further questions we earlier raised—namely, are there supra-cultural factors of a society which are measurable upon an objective, evaluative scale, and, if so, what is their nature?

Chapter 2

CRITICISM AND CULTURE

NOTHING IS MORE REASONABLE THAN TO ASSUME that cultures, like individuals, have shortcomings and that they are capable of being criticized and of being improved. Any assumption to the contrary appears to appeal to a fatalism that is belied by the facts of intelligent conduct, both individual and collective. To believe that human betterment can come about through criticism is not to believe that all things can be changed, or even that anything can be changed without serious, concerted, intelligent effort. Assuming that change is possible, consequent upon criticism, I wish to inquire first into what is the nature of grounded and legitimate criticism and secondly how it can be effective in altering the quality of social life. These two parts of the question are obviously closely related.

One form of criticism is that which sympathetically elucidates the nature of something by rigorously carrying out its implications and thus by marking it off from everything else in the world. Accordingly, whatever has an end can be defined by the processes that disclose what that end is, and it will be defined proximately or absolutely as the end is proximate or absolute. The processes that define the end are the means to it, and as contributory to the definition of it, they are of necessity relevant, everything else being irrelevant or non-contributory. Since a culture has an end, it is definable, however complexly, by those elements which, taken together, are contributory to, and consequently taken in their entirety are definitory of, that culture. Ordinarily, we think of cultures as proximate ends and of works of art as absolute ends, but either may be thought of the other way around.

The elements by which a culture is best defined, as we previously insisted, are the institutions which contribute to its definition, and these institutions will be relevant as they contribute or fail to contribute to the end. When they are relevant, they are constituted in such a way as to sharpen the focus of a society. In this they are analogous to the instrumental parts of a symphony, such that whether they carry the melody or the ground bass or the figured tenor, they mutually contribute to the definition of the composition. Although each part engenders tensions, their resolution is to be found in the parts as they complement one another and not in the parts taken separately. Likewise, the institutions of a culture—that is, of a genuine culture—have only a quasi-autonomy, since they must all be contributory to a common end. Effective criticism will be that which intensifies life by the continuous redefinition of its cultural focus through a total range of institutions capable of eliciting all available human energies and expressing them in that life.

This form of criticism is immanent in the processes of culture and consequently may be called immanent criticism. By means of it a genuine culture is validated. The organization of energies for utilizing natural resources, the definition of common ends, and the employment of concerted effort for maintaining them, regularized provision for caring for the young, the weak, and the old, ingrained ways of sustaining communication and the arts and of effecting social solidarity—all of these, together with whatever other institutions can contribute to the intensification of human living, will constantly undergo that criticism by which men will judge whether their capacities are directed or misdirected, used or misused, consummated or dissipated. Immanent criticism involves the reciprocal process, on the one hand, of determining whether institutions of a culture contribute to its primary end, that is, the sharpening of the cultural focus; and, on the other hand, of defining that end through the parts played by the institutions. The process, being circular, requires further explanation.

The end of a culture is just the functioning of its institutions, and it includes all the social actions of the component persons in a society. There is no culture apart from the actions and creations of actual persons. Consequently, the end which a culture is, is that totality of actions and creations which a people conjointly realize. Yet there is no culture unless their conjoint achievements together make a configuration. The end cannot be an ideal separate and apart from the actual lives which a people lead.

Nor can it be realized in the life of a person or of some persons short of the vast majority.[1] Those who would find culture in an unrealized ideal are incapable of defining the ideal, just because as a culture it can exist only in a certain kind of a people and is precisely defined only in and through that life.

The matter is quite parallel to that of a painter who would define his painting by asserting the idea of it without actually painting it. A painting, of course, is a painting, just that, nothing more and nothing less. Cezanne's *The Gamblers* can never be known or appreciated by someone's telling us how Cezanne would have painted the picture, or what the end is apart from the painting itself. Plato would, of course, mislead us by suggesting that there is a Form of a thing which is its ideal, which is knowable, and which gives it reality. But Plato never knew Cezanne's gamblers, nor is it likely that he could have known them, nor even could Plato's God have known them, unless he knew how to paint like Cezanne; and that, as Plato insisted, would be beneath his dignity, and would even destroy the purity of his nature, because it would require him to be a deceiver and an inferior creature.[2]

An appeal to a *Weltgeist* to account for the common spirit which is present and appropriately manifested in the institutions of a culture is an enticing, even if dangerous, assumption. It is enticing just because a spirit which is manfested in a range so extensive as religion and dress, economics and sport, politics and art, manners and technology, would seem to be something of a miracle. This kind of miracle—the achievement of a unity of outlook, a coherence of life running through a whole society—surely could not be the result of casual tinkering nor of the haphazard transformations of animal and individual psychological drives, such as is the result of unplanned biological and psychological conditioning processes. Rejecting this kind of explanation as unsatisfactory, those who look to the deeper meaning of the unity of spirit found as a pervasive characteristic of culture are likely to seek for some metaphysical principle which will account for it. In this view, a sufficient ground of the unity is to be sought for in some providential plan that reveals a transcendental intelligence at work far beyond the capacities of finite minds.

Yet, as with all miracles, there is something left out of account, and in this case it is the multitudinous instances in which the spirit fails man, and societies are rent by a plurality of heterogeneous forces. The miracles should explain the exceptions as well as the rule, and the kind of thing in question appears to have many more instances of exceptions than of those that follow the rule. We have seen grounds for believing that genuine cultures are rare, and then perhaps only passing phases in human life. An appeal to a transcendental intelligence then needs to be made again to account for the occasions where there is an absence as well as a presence of unity in social phenomena. It follows that the ground for our knowledge of all social phenomena, not just the unusual ones, is transferred to transcendental realms. Although this is helpful for inculcating a very proper sense of what has been called "natural piety" towards the things in this world, any further understanding of the factors involved would lead us to those factors themselves.

The evidence seems to point to the fact that a culture is created by a strenuous, even an agonizing, process of criticism, that it involves many false starts and still-born results, and that through the trying elimination of the false and the easy acceptance of the satisfactory men achieve a degree of success. Again we may say that a culture, like a work of art, is a series of tentative attempts to achieve an end, never clearly defined, nor even definable, until it has been achieved. And then definition is otiose or a matter for history. Thus, the relevance of various attempts is incapable of being precisely ascertained until a culture is well realized, just as the relevance of the brush strokes can be ascertained only in the completed design of the painting. The difficulties in understanding how the designers of a culture carry on their work are certainly immense, but we can point to some clues toward an understanding of the process.

Anyone who participates in the re-forming of a culture is a person sensitive to his cultural past as well as to the exigencies of the present. As a creature of the past, he possesses momentum for action. Habit, tradition, the institutions of his society, as well as his present needs move him to expressions satisfactory to his needs and appropriate to the conditions of social life. Sensitive to the

35

world in which he lives and from which he draws his substance, he can exploit only the techniques he knows; and even his innovations are extensions made possible by past accumulations of cultural life. In other words, significant innovation—inventions, modifications of life, creativities—is always an advance from a cultural base, and is significant to the degree to which the base is in turn appropriately altered to make the innovation a permanent part of an enhanced life. To alter the base is, therefore, to alter the very institutions of the life of a people. The natural resistance to innovations is enormous, for they throw out of phase accumulated habits in conflict with them.

The difficulty of introducing innovations is thus seen to consist in the fact that the natural resistance to them comes from the cultural base which itself must become altered if they are to be successful. The resistance resides in the whole weight of cultural life (or as it is often called, 'cultural lag') which must be moved in order to lodge the innovation. He who would move this mass must find a fulcrum for moving a whole society. His appeal must be therefore not just to the advantages that accrue directly from the innovation itself but also either to the positive advantages that accrue indirectly to other cultural activities or to their comparatively trivial disadvantages.

It is no wonder that the single individual ordinarily has little direct influence on cultural change and only rarely a powrful indirect influence. The genius, the hero, can affect his culture in important ways only as circumstances conspire with his particular talents to bring about any far-reaching results. Technological change would appear to be the most easily introduced, for example, as in the introduction of the horse collar, the advantages being obvious and the disadvantages minimal or concealed. On the other hand, resistance to what is less demonstrably advantageous, especially when it touches the sanctities of life, is virtually absolute. In fact, if it were to come about at all, it would seem to be either through the corrosive effects of concealed disadvantages concomitant with technological change or through those conditions that produce a crisis in a society, or both. The displacement of bronze by iron, of hand-copied manuscripts by the printing press, of steam power by hydro-electric power, and the like, have corroded such institutions as state monopoly, feudalism, and private capitalism. Crises can, of course, come about through an endless number of causes, but they will always be of such a nature as to threaten the destruction of a whole way of life, whether this comes about through depletion of natural resources, warfare, divided loyalties, criminal negligence, usurpation, emancipation, or the business cycle. Revolutions occur when there is a conjunction of social crisis and technological advance, such as to provide the fulcrum for altering virtually every aspect of society. Disaffections which precede revolutions are necessary for loosening cultural bonds. Because of the dislocations they produce, it is easy to understand why so few of them are bloodless.

We can see better now why a culture always appears as "a somehow unified and consistent attitude toward life." In the first place, if it weren't rather well unified and fairly consistent, it would not be a culture— that is, a genuine culture—at all. But less taxonomically speaking, a culture is a fairly stable kind of being. To exist at all it necessitates developed institutions—that is, *traditional* ways of doing things, ways that persist through time. To be sure, a tradition has momentum, but as an institution it cannot support itself unless it is buttressed by other institutions. Hence, when support is taken from it, it must change in ways appropriate to altered circumstance. Royalty cannot exist without thrones, thrones cannot exist without taxes, taxes without work, work without workers, food, some modicum of love and care and hope and well-being. Any alteration in any of these affects a whole chain of institutions.

Social movements vibrate throughout a whole culture, no matter where the fulcrum for initiating change may be found. Artistic creation, for instance, is a response of the artist to his world, and whether the poet sings of princes or of the open road, whether the painter paints portraits of his patrons or characters in third-class carriages, his is an artistic response to the world in which he lives. And even the escapist in art provides willy-nilly a commentary on his world, whether his dreams are the sentimental idylls of the woods or the frenzied nightmares of the psyche. The artist is always critic of his world, and for this reason no culture can be without him. But if art (and we should, of course, add philosophy) is man's critical response to his world, that art, always new, always critical, feeds upon the world in which it lives and is always relevant to it. It cannot but give a man a vision of himself. And what is true of the consciously articulate pursuits of art and philosophy is also true in their own way of the other cultural institutions.

Industry, business, government, the family, manners, religion, sports must cohere in any genuine culture. When, for example, business or government or sports usurp power over the young, family and religious life feel the effects almost at once. The most dramatic instance of the immediate impact of change on institutions is that of present-day warfare. It is commonplace that warfare today is "total war," which leaves virtually no aspect of life untouched whether it be sex and marriage, ways of telling time, transportation, amusements, or neighborhood organization. Again, speaking of a special case in our particular world of opulence today, Professor Galbraith calls attention not merely to the "input-output tables" in which expansion in one part of the economy demands an expansion in another part, as for example production of automobiles and production of steel, but also, more interestingly, to the need for public services to keep abreast of the sector of economic life called "private economy," as for example the need for parking places, public regulation, building of roads, and what-not, if automobiles are to be used. He shows unmistakably the need for preserving what he calls "the social balance."[3] Although the balance to which he calls attention is especially relevant to a complex industrial society with a mixed economy, it is nevertheless another dramatic instance of the interdependences characteristic of all cultural phenomena. I press for the recognition of these interdependencies, not with any dogmatic intent, but simply that we may turn back once more to the meaning of immanent criticism, observing the relationship of particular institutions to that of a culture itself.

The drive for the criticism of an institution comes only in part from that institution. Mostly, it comes from the clash of institutions. And that is why immanent criticism is not a mysterious kind of activity. Roads may be criticized by the kind of automobiles we have, or automobiles by the kinds of roads, or, more concretely, both may be criticized and geared to each other in terms of speed, safety, reasonable expenditures, enjoyments, truck traffic, and the like. Similarly, institutions may be criticized, altered, and even created. Such criticism is always contextual, and the nerve of it is found primarily in the oppositions and clashes in the interstices of institutional life. Administrative law, for instance, came into being to fill gaps falling between various parts of legal machinery. The need for regulatory bodies to meet the difficulties of management-labor disputes, of interstate commerce, of aeronautical traffic, stock and bond sales, control and development of public power, and the like, has led to the emergence of whole new sets of legal institutions that could not properly be provided for according to the traditional three-fold division of government. Each of the kinds of activities above mentioned has required constant adjustment to the problems of man in twentieth century industrial society. This, of course, is nothing new in history of law. In Roman times, too, when the law was not adequate, some fiction would be invented, such as that for certain legal purposes a non-Roman would nevertheless be regarded as a Roman citizen.[4]

The clue to the understanding of the reciprocal relations between means and end in immanent criticism is to be found in the unifying forces of social life. We are now in a position to assert that although such forces are not inevitable, they are always incipient in a society and there is good reason for them to prevail. The simple logic is that a divided society is an unstable society, just as a divided person is an unstable person. This society is especially unstable because it contains antagonistic institutions which constantly tug at the same persons in opposite directions. It is consequently even less stable than that which contains antagonistic classes, which though opposed, nevertheless possess a degree of internal harmony. The drives of the former are more insistent than the latter, and call for attention. Thus, if the organization of business makes demands on family life, such as happens when the home is frequently moved from one place to another, either the organization of business or of the family or of both must yield, and the chances are it will be both.

The direction of the change will be determined by the

resultant vectors of life-forces. The stronger the force, the less it will yield, and the more the character of a culture will be determined by that force. But this is exactly what we mean by the cultural focus—that set of interests which qualifiies most of a people's activities and which provides them with a set of priorities. The focus, being the dominant interest in a culture, will be embodied in its sustaining activities, will be sung by its poets, will be revered by its priests, and justified by its philosophers. It will persist in the platitudes of the people, often even when through the necessities of circumstance it has actually shifted to new qualities of life.

The law of inertia applies to a cultural focus, even as it applies to moving bodies. The choices a person is free to make in any society are limited. There is always an area in which he is free to do as he likes—that is, the private area. But the private is circumscribed by the social and the public—both the informal and the formal restrictions placed upon his actions whether through his early training from which he cannot depart, the organization of society which makes certain choices only nominally free, or that which officially enjoins forms of conduct. The cultural focus consequently limits the activities of persons and qualifies the objectives they may pursue. The language in which they are couched is the myths or ideologies of a people, except in a spurious culture in which the myths are no longer operative beliefs.

Immanent criticism is effective just because it is concerned with the operative forces actually present in a society, not with its mythologies. Its objective is satisfactorily to overcome the concrete evils of a society, rather than to impose upon it an abstract good derived from extraneous sources. Its motivation is to relieve tensions or to satisfy those cravings that have been starved by maladjustments in institutional life. Impoverishment of life takes multitudinous social forms unpredictable in advance of intimate knowledge of institutions in context. Effective criticism involves intimate knowledge and concerted action which evolves new forms of social life more responsive to human requirements.

The focus of a genuine culture is primarily a resultant and only secondarily (and with somewhat dubious value) a cause. A people do not set up a yam-culture or a Christian culture or a humanistic culture. Cultures are not set up; they grow or evolve —out of the social processes themselves. When they come to have a kind of unity, an integrity, a self-contained meaningfulness, and are without recurring, needless frustration, they may be said to be genuine. They are the results of critical examination and an acceptability implicating tacit consent. Their unity is an achievement gained through unifying processes, and not a pre-figured unity. The central activities, the more important ones, are focal and constitute the focus.

Activities can be carried on effectively only as specific virtues are capable of being singled out and practiced. They become the "mystique" of a culture. Piety, thrift, frugality, physical exercise, truth-saying, honor, amiability, and so on, have in various ways become the mystiques of various cultures. In fact, they are so intimately connected with a particular kind of culture that they often become confused with it, and are taken for it. Actions, therefore, instead of being evaluated in terms of ends, are evaluated by the mystiques which are indispensable to the cultural focus. Good and bad are thus converted into right and wrong, and rules or laws are the surrogates for the critical consideration of conduct.

Mystiques are inevitable in any society. Rules of action are necessary for carrying on the business of life. Situations repeat themselves; patterned actions simplify living and give a sureness to it that is lost in the fumbling quality of critical thought. Even complex situations can be met deftly by those who have acquired a proper mystique. Rules of piety, regularity in business procedures, indoctrination into the cultivation of yams—these are the daily activities that sustain a cultural focus, a way of life. Mystique is the translation of the genius of a people into distinctive cultural traits. It affords them power for building into society the contours which lead action on to specified outcomes. The artifacts of a society, the churches, the banks, the plowshares—these are the tools that cannot easily be used but for the ends of religion, business, or agriculture, even though they may not always be sufficiently exploited to preserve human vitalities.

It is a well know fact that through no fault of their own, virtues often become vices. Changed circumstances or an extension of rules of practice from their appropriate fields to inappropriate ones turn them from helpful guides to stultifying, or even vicious, impediments to human ends. Mystiques often do just this. As substitutes for thought they are employed to insure conformity of practice. Although conformity of itself is neither good nor bad, that which has mystique as its sole justification is necessarily unintelligent, if not unintelligible. And to the extent that it imposes practices that must be unquestioningly followed, it can only be for the ends of a priestcraft who is perpetuating a cult, not of one who is interested in enhancing a culture. A mystique that silences criticism of either the ends of an institution or of the ways in which it is conducted is, through force or ignorance, silencing the very criticism which is indispensable to the creation and maintenance of a genuine culture. Virtue can be its own reward as it is both instrumental and consummatory; otherwise, it is power wielded by those who stand to gain over those who stand to lose, or even worse, it is tragic illusion forcing the destruction of both the wielders of power and also of the powerless.

Immanent criticism, we may conclude, is stillborn if it seeks to evaluate either ends, irrespective of the concrete means by which the ends can come into being, or means dissociated from the ends. The first is sentimentality or wishful dreaming; the second, opportunism or technological madness. The circularity that realistically counts in immanent criticism is that which moves through the chain of interconnected institutions in order to effect changes through which individuals can share in justice the stimulations and rewards that are the fruits of a genuine culture. For some limited purposes, the ends may be abstracted and used to illuminate, celebrate, and even further extend the bounties of life. But unless there is opportunity for serious criticism of ends—of the cultural foci—there will result a slowing, rather than a quickening, of the cultural body.

A further element is needed to explain why immanent criticism in a genuine culture is a continuous, never-ending process. Criticism has as its proper end the effecting of enhanced continuities in social life. Consequently, it is called for only as discontinuities obtrude upon life and create discord where harmony before prevailed. If life were an Arcadian paradise, if all were continuities, criticism would be an impertinence. The sentimentalities of Arcadia, however, prove to be as far removed from reality as dust from the Arctic. The obtrusions upon life are more or less insistent. They are the irritabilities, if not the crises, that require attention and at least some degree of alleviation. Discontinuities do not have to be manufactured. They constantly arise.

There would seem to be three natural sources of discontuities. They may arise from individuals themselves who are endowed with natures that are not satisfied by the substance available to them in their culture. They may arise from the introduction of new materials or inventions or processes injected into a culture. Or they may arise from the impingement of one culture upon another. Although any combinations of these three factors may co-operate to intensify the discontinuities, discussion is facilitated by considering each as if it could exist separately.

Ordinary personalities can be satisfied by ordinary conditions, extraordinary cannot. Where to draw a line between the ordinary and the extraordinary is not at all clear. Some differences are only of degree, as a Gargantuan appetite is not different in kind from a lesser one. It only requires more of the same in order to be satisfied. Big men eat more than little men; weak men need more rest than strong men—and so of any of the appetites known to man. Any viable culture provides for these kinds of individual differences. The tastes which satisfy appetites of this kind are nevertheless similar and easily constitute an ingredient in a particular culture. By and large, the Eskimo will be satisfied with blubber, the Chinese with rice, the Todas with dairy products, etc. Although cravings could develop for exotic things, they are not likely to become serious concerns or make for serious discontinuities. Criticisms arising from them will therefore not be regarded as serious.

Serious criticism arises from cravings of a more far-reaching nature. The serious critic will aim to destroy the pomposities, the conceits of a culture or, at the other extreme, to rise above the commonplaces and stupidities. Whether in the form of travesties and burlesques, parables or tragedies, moral suasion or religious teaching, he will hope to reveal the inadequacies of the life of a people together with its potentialities for a renewed spirit. The writer, the philosopher, the moralist, the preacher, has often conceived his historic task as one which calls on man to acknowledge and to live up to his human and spiritual capacities. The call may be in vain, and the capacity for reformation stunted; but as long as forums, theaters, stoa, and churches exist, they are capable of having a new spirit infused in them and of more or less permanently affecting the lives of a people. A Sophocles, an Aristophanes, a Protagoras, a Jesus, a Mohammed, a Calvin, a Leonardo, a Jefferson, a Whitman, have, in varying measures, done just this.

Spiritual and moral appeals are not likely to quicken the pulse of cultural life unless they are supported by external circumstance. The disenchantments they presuppose, the call to life they sound, are facilitated by the substitution for worn and squeaky institutions, which bear greater weight than they can hold, rejuvenated institutions, which can enlist new loyalties and persist through the devotions of the faithful. In this way, an oligarchy may become a democracy, or a worn-out empire a church-universal, or a colony a republic. Effective reform capitalizes on the weaknesses of the old and transforms them through appropriate structures into a new kind of life. There is no state without a government, no religion without a church, no sports without an arena. But these will not be thought up out of the blue, or even maintained by the aid of a strong spirit, unless they are bolstered by external things.

No doubt, the most jolting discontinuities in a society are produced by the introduction of new materials, inventions, and new sources of power—by the "technics" of a society, to use a phrase made popular by Mr. Mumford. The technics of a people —that is, their instruments and machines, the materials from which they are fabricated, and the power by which they can be moved and operated—these limit the conditions of cultural life. "Carboniferous capitalism" of paleotechnics can support social relations that differ materially, say, from those that "hydro-electric mixed capitalism" can support in neotechnics.[5] Whether a people lead basically a rural life or an urban life, where their cities may be located, whether on seacoast or inland, whether they will necessarily be congested or may be roomy—these and countless other characteristics depend in a major way on the kind

44

of technics that is at their disposal. Not only their physical settings and their economies, but their art and their politics, their manners and their amusements will also reflect their technics.

None of the technics of civilization, it seems, commits man to values which are tawdry or elegant, even though there may be some predispositions towards one or the other. Rural, agricultural life would appear to possess a wholesomeness, a self-sufficiency, a colorful ease that could not be matched in the city. But this need not be so. Dreariness, monotony, stupidity, intellectual and artistic poverty may just as easily characterize it. Neither must the city be gaudy, raucus, perverted, and dirty. Dense populations do, of course, make for both intimate cliques and impersonal cosmopolitanism. Disturbances and discontuities are likely to be more ubiquitous, but the ingenuity of man is likely also to be more concentrated, so that his capacity to cope with them may actually be greater than that which can be relied upon in the less intense life of the country.

In either case, emergence of new technics for the support of life, whether arising from novel agricultural processes or altered ways of producing material things, requires new social relationships, since at the very least labor is upset and calls for some more or less radical rearrangements. Dislocations attendant upon technological change punctuate the need for new evaluations of social life and consequently cry out for timely criticism in order to aid in re-establishing such continuities as can once more make life reasonably satisfactory. The genius in such criticism is not that of a single man, of a leader, but that of a people who can, through their native perceptions and concerted intelligence, come to new fulfilments in their social urgencies and at the same time to profounder achievements in their personal lives. Although the stimuli to such results are external, the kind of criticism on which they must rely is internal to their needs. The purpose of immanent criticism is, accordingly, to make that which is alien and disruptive once again germane to their mores. It is, in short, to extend the cultural process.

Finally, there is a third kind of disruption, which is the most challenging of all and is very likely to end in ruin rather than in fulfilment. When two cultures come together, there is, according to the law of culturation, a borrowing of each from the other.[6] Even though we may be sure that each will borrow, there is no precise way of predicting just what each will actually borrow.[7] What is assumed in this reciprocal process is, of course, that each culture has stamina strong enough to maintain something of its own identity. Conquest and subjugation of a people is not an instance of their borrowing, but rather of their being overcome and destroyed as a culture. Disastrous as it is for those overcome, the difficulties for the conquerors are also serious. Their way of life, too, requires drastic change. Whether they can emerge with a culture at all will depend upon whether the conquered can be so incorporated into a new life as to realize their humane ambitions along with a new life for the conquerors. The magnitude of the task is such as virtually to foredoom it.

The foredooming of the culture of a people has been frequently observed in modern times. Colonization in the new world, in Africa, and in Australia and Asia, as well as in innumerable islands, has shown clearly that, at least as far as industrial societies are concerned, their power has been to reduce other cultures to skeletons, if not to destroy them entirely. Unable to absorb the new, incapable of preserving the old, primitive peoples, for example, the American Indian, are likely to half live in the culture of their ancestors and half die in that of their conquerors. The old cultural foci are gone, the new incapable of being formed. Theirs is "a spiritual hybrid of contradictory patches" (Sapir), a life poor in promise and even poorer in the living.

What little hope there is in this debilitating condition is, according to some moralists,[8] the new realization of the condition of man as belonging to the community of all men. This is irrealism even though it contains a present-day touch of realism. The effort to preserve primitive peoples intact, to keep them from being contaminated by the industrial world, is something like trying to keep youth intact, even though it requires the sophisticated art of cosmetics to accomplish its end. A sentimentalism set on preserving the old ways is like preserving an eighteenth-century home with fireplace and copper pans, plus adding central heating and a new kitchen with built-in thermador. We cannot forsake the old, and we dare not neglect the new. Whether there is sufficient realism in proposing that the new context of culture must be a kind of universal context provided by a state of the magnitude of the world itself is an enticing thought, even if it suggests some cultural inadequacies. It is nevertheless a proposal which, in the face of the disturbances characteristic of contemporary cultural crises, deserves more than an uncritical relegation to limbo. I wish to return to this proposal in a later context where I think we can deal with it more adequately. Meanwhile, I wish to pause to consider the course of our immediate discussion.

When we look to the broader results of our discussion of cultural discontinuities, we seem to encounter a conclusion, a problem, and (derivatively) a suggestion. The conclusion is that discontinuities can be counted on constantly to arise in the course of cultural life and that only through internal criticism which proposes a realignment of institutions appropriate to humane needs can the necessary continuities of social life be re-established. The problem that confronts us is: how are we to conceive of humane needs; or, differently put, what is the character of the ends by virtue of which we can rightly judge the satisfactoriness of institutional alignments, or realignments? The suggestion is that we cannot properly sustain the conclusion without satisfactorily answering the question. I wish to clarify this somewhat enigmatic point by proceeding directly to what I regard as the normative character of a genuine culture.

From at least the time of Plato, there has been an unending attempt by philosophers to appeal to a universal in the belief that only in this way is it possible to ascertain the worth of any action, individual or social. Nor is it likely that the impulse to seek for universal criteria is wrong, however difficult it may be to reach agreement on what the criteria should be. In this matter, man's loves and hates bear directly on his perceptual acuteness. As it has been said, for example, only one who loves liberty can come to see its value. Apparently, it requires a generous nature in order to come to recognize the most general criteria for measuring the worth of things. And certainly there is nothing puny in Plato's appeal to the Good itself as the only standard sufficiently universal to provide an adequate measure. In some important sense, surely,

Plato is right, for only what is good is good.[9] The question is whether this is a mere tautology, and therefore true, or a synthetic proposition requiring a substantiation far beyond anything that is immediately evident in the terms themselves. How to construe such propositions in connection with the cultural life of man is the problem directly before us.

Somewhat rephrased, the problem is: what measure is there by which we can mark the change from worse to better, or vice versa; or, slightly differently, is there some means we can employ to measure progress? Any affirmative answer to these questions will in some sense lead us to a universal. Since universals may be construed in such different ways, I propose that we break the discussion down into three parts, and discuss, first, the likelihood that there is any universal institution by which we can satisfactorily measure progress; secondly, whether there is some unique process itself by virtue of which we can satisfactorily measure it; or finally, whether there is some principle we can properly employ, and if so, what, how, and by what right?

Men are easily led to believe that that institution which commands its supreme loyalty has about it a kind of universality which deserves the loyalty of any right-thinking person. An institution conceived as being the condition of the realization of man's highest ambitions is one that a person is duty bound to bend every effort to bring into being. In the Western world it was the Greeks who first became conscious of their institutions and who attributed highest esteem to the city-state. The orthodox Greek view, contrary to that of the modern world, regarded a man's first obligation to the state. Citizenship consequently came to be conceived of as man's highest office, since in order to become a man at all he must first become a citizen. Consistent with this conception, it was thought that no more bitter punishment could be visited upon a person than to banish him from his native city-state. Ostracism was thought to cut one's most important ties—his ties with a common life. Accordingly, to participate in the common life of the city, to cultivate the virtues of a citizen, and to be regarded with honor were held to be the very essence of becoming a civilized being and a man.

Plato (and Aristotle, too, in his own way) perceived the

limitations of the particular virtues characteristic of actual, historical states. Critical of them, he nevertheless purified the ideal of the state and, making a utopia of it, he remained true to something of the spirit of classical Greek life.[10] Although as a measure of progress one can make a better case for the idealized form of the city-state than for a slavish imitation of an actual state, yet the limitations of the former are still present inasmuch as its modification over the latter is of the nature of an "or-something-like-this." Even when the specific particularities are dismissed, there remains the provincial infection characteristic of any institution.[11] Since the virtues of a life are indigenous to that life— what we previously called its mystique—they cannot be simply transferred from one institution to another or from one epoch to another. It is no mere accident, for example, that the cardinal virtues of the Greeks became subordinate in the medieval period to the trio of faith, hope, and love.

A whole new orientation of ideals as well as of institutions is involved in passing from the Graeco-Roman world to the medieval world. In this case there is the explicit avowal of the Church as the institution universal. All-encompassing—and for Europe (and beyond) it was—the Catholic Church became for millions what the city-state could be only for thousands—the institution in which and through which man could alone realize his individuality by becoming a member of a universal organ of life, material and spiritual. As long as the Church could maintain its superiority to the State, it could present at least the façade of making good its claim. When this disappeared, its theology still buttressed the spiritual claims of the institution. Yet, however extensive the claims and however widespread the institution, neither the claims nor the institution could withstand the onslaughts of Protestant reformations and of secular innovations. The great medieval synthesis could not maintain itself in the face of the unsanctioned forms of mysticism and the undercutting commercial activities, both of which required the promulgation of new institutions for the emancipation of a new kind of social life.

One of the engaging questions of this new life is whether the state or the economic institution of the market was becoming the primary focus of men's new loyalties.[12] Although it was true

49

that the two often coincided—even to such an extent that they could be confused with each other—it is an error not to observe the oppositions as well as the coincidences. Capitalism did find, for the most part, an ally in the state, and the state often found in capitalism an instrument so indispensable that the end of the state was even defined, in a curiously paradoxical way, as the preservation of private property. The strength of capitalism, however, has been not its sanctity but its resiliency, even if in a somewhat non-capitalistic form, in coping with some of the serious problems of economic existence, and by virtue of this, operating, not as a universal institution, but rather as a tough one in the fabric of industrial life. To regard it as the measure of the good life, however, requires a reverence that even the businessman questions in his sentimental moments or on Sunday.

Nor can we today subscribe with insouciance to the belief that the nation-state is—or can be—constituted as the container in which alone the amalgam of the good is to be found. Little of what we know of Western social life could have become solidified without the state, but as with all institutions it too must include an admixture of the base along with the precious. The indictment of the modern state has become so insistent that it is no longer necessary to regard it as an unmitigated good, as the supreme object of loyalty, or even as the hope of continued security—much less as the meaning of history itself. No chauvinistic view, whether of the nineteenth-century variety, such as Fichte or Hegel adopted, or of a twentieth century variety, such as one hundred per centers would have us adopt, can survive critical scrutiny.

The final argument of the devotees of universal institutions may come from those who believe that the world-state provides the supreme context for the good life. The effectiveness of this argument resides in its analysis of economic and military concerns, rather than in any inherent universality of a world-state. So contemporary is the nature of the problem that it cannot even be adequately conceived in, for example, Stoic or Grotian or Kantian terms. The universal peace that is said to be the crying need today is, negatively, the peace which comes out of the potential of contemporary military power, and, postively, the peace which is related to this potential—that is, an industrial world possessed of atomic energy, jet-powered machines, and other space-instruments, together with their biological, psychological, and social correlates. Kant's universal peace has as much relevance to the issues debated in the United Nations as Democritus' conception of the atom to quantum theory. The predicament being unique, the solution must be equally unique. Any approach to the reorganization of institutions which fails to take into account the peculiar role of science and technology in the problems of our world is doomed to failure as a bit of fancy.

I cannot believe that we require today any very decisive criticism that an institution of any nature whatsoever can be regarded as a universal measure of progress. Surely we are not so provincial, unhistorically minded, or so blinded to the nature of social requirements as to seriously think that any institution could contain the comprehensiveness and the relevance and effectiveness to provide the kind of life which is indispensable to modern society. At best, it would have to be a utopia. But the significant difference between modern and traditional utopias consists precisely in the recognition that the modern utopia relies on means rather than ends. It is concerned with consent or the use of intelligence and persuasion, rather than force and conflict, and it regards communication and the conditions for communication as of greater significance than any particular institutional arrangements. Communities, we have discovered, can be so varying in their nature, and yet self-justifying, that we have been compelled to look beyond the institutions themselves to find what it is that makes them self-justifying. May it not be something in the process itself which constitutes the real measure of worth? A challenging answer in these terms is given by those who assert that it is in "the scientific method," or perhaps better, in "the experimental method" that the very stuff of progress is contained. This theme is too impressive to be ignored.

In a statement at once provocative and arresting, John Dewey once wrote:

Science through its physical technological consequences is now determining the relations which human beings, severally and in groups, sustain to one another. If it is incapable of developing moral techniques

51

which will also determine these relations, the split in modern culture goes so deep that not only democracy but all civilized values are doomed. Such at least is the problem. A culture which permits science to destroy traditional values but which distrusts its power to create new ones is a culture which is destroying itself.[13]

Dewey's point of view may be regarded as a culmination of at least one significant aspect of modern thought, namely, that philosophy can never be extricated from the quagmire of hopeless befuddlement and dogmatic pronouncement until it relies on method, rather than on substantival assertions. Coupling this with the actual success of science in achieving "warranted assertibility," he seized upon science as the most adequate embodiment of method. His whole philosophy, one might say almost without exaggeration, is an attempt to show how the experimental method is the solvent of the problems of man.

There is no need here to rehash the well-known steps which Dewey has detailed for arriving at a conclusion through reflective thought. The business of formulating hypotheses and of testing them is monotonously repeated by nearly every schoolboy. Yet, although the elements of reflective thought have become part of our intellectual folklore, the significance of the method has been appallingly poorly understood. Sometimes the misunderstanding is traceable to a confusion between science as process and science as result, sometimes to an inveterate tendency to separate inner and outer, or subjective and objective, and to assume that the method is applicable only to things external to us. Thus, there is the deep-seated habit of regarding the scientist as an observer of things, who in his objectivity can dispassionately record nature, himself remaining quite unaffected by the processes he is describing. His task, it is thought, is to remain aloof from the subject matter of scientific investigation, and to look at nature as through a window which separates him from it.[14] According to Dewey's instrumentalistic point of view, nothing could be further from the truth, for, paradoxically, nature comes to be known only by changing it. Rejecting the "searchlight" theory of knowledge, the instrumentalist, as the name suggests, believes that knowledge is the result of employing instruments which, by affecting things, in turn become affected. Through the interrelations, we come not merely to know but also to be able to control things.

I am not interested in urging the adoption of this point of view but only in recognizing its claims as a solvent of the problems of man, and especially as providing a criterion for the measure of the worth of anything. We need for this purpose to bear in mind at least three aspects of the instrumentalist's conception of scientific method, each of which is crucial to his definition of method. First is the insistence that the essence of a scientific law is to assert relations which hold between events; secondly, that the assertion of these relations is tentative and subject to the self-correcting processes inherent in the methods of science; and finally, the results of science are continuous with the problems of man and are indispensable to any satisfactory solution of human problems. A word of clarification of each of these is in order.

However much theory may enter into science, an ineradicable minimum of observations is indispensable to the process. In science we must acknowledge in William James' famous language "the stubborn, irreducible facts." Without this, science is not empirical. Moreover, without empirical foundations, it can tell us nothing about the world. Dewey acknowledges the hard, stubborn facts as "events." These do not come into being through any magic, nor is there any magic by which we can make them disappear. They are the "given" in experience. But events come at least in pairs, if not in triplets, or other multiples. What the scientist searches for, then, are the relations that obtain among events. This search, which taxes all his ingenuity, is by no means an easy one. Scientific explanations, it follows, exclude all appeals to occult qualities or essences for conjuring up appearances. There is nothing "behind" the events themselves in the way of "forces" or hidden productive capacities through which explanation of observable events is made intelligible. Explanations in terms of forces, whether in the physical or psychological or social world, should be spurned. They are at best verbal duplicates of things. They can never explain them.

Equal in importance to the fact that science describes the relations of events is the fact that it is nevertheless a self-correcting process. This is because the "given" in experience is also a "taken." What is given is so by virtue of the scientist's taking it in through the use of instruments, both ideological and physical. The theories he employs and the palpable tools he manipulates make him a better or worse investigator as he uses them skillfully or not. Since his aim is precision, his achievements depend on the aptitude and refinements of his techniques. The genius displayed in this process is such that science becomes ever-increasingly more adequate and more precise. Loose qualitative formulations are displaced by more adequate quantitative ones, testable by ever more refined precision instruments. This constant ingenuity in the use of means involves a constant correcting of results—so much so that it is only commonplace that the conclusions of science are but tentative and interminably subject to modification and correction.

Both the beginnings and ends of science are, from the instrumentalist's point of view, obscure in the sense that science gradually emerges out of common sense and the practical arts and that it is continuous with technology and industry. Although science is more highly theoretical and more systematized than common-sense knowledge and the practical arts, there is no clear-cut line of division between them. At the other end, too, the instrumentalist insists that the interplay between technology and science is so intimate that they cannot (and should not) be separated. Science can no more be confined to the laboratory than technology can be confined to the factory. Technology and industry are not just the testing ground of science, but they react upon it and help to define it. Significantly, the instrumentalist points out that the applications of science are *in* rather than *to* the world. From his point of view, it is accordingly a mistake to try to separate science and technology, for the principal consequence is to distort both of them, with the added objection that narrowly conceived agencies exploit science for their own purposes and to the destruction of its full potential for human progress. In this case, science as institution interferes with the development of science as method and, consequently, of science regarded as results. By dislocating the contextual bonds of the scientific method, the problems of man become more taut, even reaching a breaking point.

From a consideration of these characteristic factors of the

54

experimental method, the instrumentalist concludes that there is a kind of modern folklore that can be fatal to any satisfactory resolution of man's problems. The roadblocks placed in his way are none other than the sanctities of modern life. These sanctities are constituted as emotionally engendered beliefs, dogmatically held, and by their nature incapable of being corrected or subjected to intelligent criticism. They are, in Professor Clarence Ayres' expressive language, the "legendary-ceremonial systems of values" as opposed to the "scientific-technological system of values."[15] The legendary-ceremonial values arise in man's attitudes which turn him to his static past. He looks for support to those institutions which he has inherited and which have provided habits of life for him and his ancestors. Some of them he regards as supreme institutions, and it is they that he is willing "to die for." In contrast to the legendary-ceremonial, the scientific-technological institutions are those which have come about as a result of the scientific method. They are under constant scrutiny and criticism in the light of the facts which man has been able to garner by means of the scientific enterprise. They give to life a flexibility appropriate to the changing circumstances of men's problems, and they cater to his life needs rather than to his emotional adhesions. They are, in Professor Ayres' words, not the "values men die for," but "the values men live by."

The conclusion to which Professor Ayres comes directly supports Dewey's instrumentalistic conception of the good life. Both insist that it is in the freedom of men's minds that we come to understand the good. But freedom is possible only as there is, first, liberation from the fetishes of dogmatic ritual and parochial superstition and, secondly, capacity to grasp new facts and new relations by unhampered access to the study of nature and the enlarging of one's world by "moving about, venturing into unfamiliar regions, and meeting with strange peoples." To penetrate deeper one's world and to enlarge one's outlook—this is to inculcate new attitudes of mind and through the experimental method to bring to fruition truer values in place of old and false ones, which are tied to moribund attitudes. The indictment of older cultures, including our own, is serious, and the proposal that knowledge, not superstition, is the measure of the virtues of a culture is impressively contemporary, despite its deep roots in the philosophical tradition. By centering knowledge in science and the experimental method, the instrumentalist may be granted to be in touch with what is most progressive in the modern world. Is it not also fair to assume that what is most progressive is best taken as the measure of progress?

The question may, and probably should, cause some uneasiness. This uneasiness increases even further for those who would limit science to the sphere of investigating factual things, rather than values. And although Dewey, for example, constantly inveighs against the separation of facts and values, does not even he suggest that there is a fundamental distinction between what we commonly think science to be and what we think moral judgments are? We may recall in our earlier quotation, Dewey said not merely that science is determining through its physical and technological consequences relations which human beings sustain to one another, but also that "If it is incapable of developing *moral techniques* which will also determine these relations . . . not only democracy but all civilized values are doomed." The implication appears to be that science is one thing and moral techniques something different, however closely related they may be. The question we want to pose is, of course, what is the nature of "the moral techniques?" And are they such that they imply some kind of universal by which we can measure the worth of a culture?

The question suggests that there is something lacking—or at least an oversimplification—in adopting the principle of the experimental method as that which provides a proper standard for measuring progress or the worth of a culture. *Prima facie,* the object of science is to detect relationships among events, regardless of whether they are liked or disliked, approved of or disapproved of, or thought to be good or bad. Yet the relationships which we have been concerned with in commendable cultures are special kinds of social relationships. Even though these may be required for the promotion of the scientific enterprise, it nevertheless behooves us to identify as precisely as we can the nature of the relationship itself. I wish to suggest now a first approximation to what I regard it to be, and then to develop its ramifications at length in later discussion.

56

However closely science is connected with morality—and we need not doubt either the fact or the intimacy of the connection—we should not confuse the two. Science is not morality, and even though the practice of it may involve moral considerations, we still should not confuse them. The plaguing issue then is what is it that is distinctive of morality? How are we to recognize morality if we should come across it? To answer these questions without begging them has come to be regarded as the most anguishing problem of ethical theory. Admit even one assumption as to the nature of moral action and the whole superimposed theory, with whatever factual considerations that may be brought to its aid, comes tumbling down as a barn in the path of a cyclone. Nor is it any more defensible to adopt a position of ethical skepticism and simply deny the possibility of defining morality, for this, too, involves its own kind of dogmatism which is in the end self-defeating. In the face of such a quandary, does not any road lead to a dead end, whether it attempts to follow the direction of "ordinary language" or that of any other language for which we may ourselves have some predilection?

Although there may be no ultimately satisfactory way to avoid the impasse, my suggestion is that we temporarily adopt the criteria that are implicit in the conception of a genuine culture, making such use of them as we can in answering questions about the evaluation of cultures, and adducing some considerations to uphold the plausibility of adopting them. Thereafter we may more profitably look to some of the knotty issues of value theory in our attempt to learn whether or not we can further bolster them and provide them with a greater measure of justification. In any event, this course should disclose some important points in value theory.

By his insistence upon culture as the context in which to study human life, the anthropologist clearly asserts culture is revealed in a context of social relationships. Whether it is their way of eating, of making love, of worshipping, of providing sustenance, or what-not, men's conduct and their attitudes toward the world are socially engendered. Although enculturated actions surely do have biological and psychological roots, these roots are so overgrown as to be scarcely discernible. And in any event, they can never explain the distinctive qualities that appear in enculturated persons. What clues are discoverable as a starting-point for the study of morality are suggested by the centrality of the social as indispensable to an understanding of human life. Yet, from the very outset, one must cope with an ambiguity contained in the concept of the social. It can, of course, signify that which men undertake together for their mutual well-being—that which they can share in common and which unites them as joint partners —or it can signify anti-social responses which are geared to the actions of one another for the purpose of gaining an advantage over another, for the end of dominance rather than for that of mutual well-being.[16] The above distinction calls attention to two normative aspects of the social, concerning as it does both ends and means: it concerns ends as fulfilments and it concerns means in the sense that care for persons in the process restricts both the kinds of ends that are acceptable and the ways of reaching them. Ends which unnecessarily involve injury or destruction to other persons become on this view wholly unacceptable. The other conception of the social imposes no such restrictions on the agent. Whether it is wanton destruction, a bit of sadism or lechery, rapine or murder, the relations are social, even if they look to an end which eventually destroys the social connection.

There is no real paradox that arises from this double meaning of social. It has, in fact, been recognized from time immemorial. The one kind of relationship is called "moral" and the other "immoral," and there seems to be no good reason for changing that meaning today. Both morality and immorality involve relationships of persons, but in the one case there is promotion and fulfilment in those relationships; in the other case, deterioration and frustration. On the cultural plane, we have designated the one as the kind that is characteristic of a genuine culture, and the other, which leads to unjustifiable wantonness, cruelty, sentimentality, and hypocrisy, as characteristic of the spurious. It looks then as though we are on the verge of being able to identify the one—suppose we call it "the positive social relation" as opposed to the other, "the negative social relation"—as constituting precisely the kind of universal principle which is required if we are to be able to distinguish between good and bad, and derivatively between better and worse. Adopting these distinctions, we can then say that a culture is better or worse as it maximizes the positive or the negative social relation, or as it minimizes the negative or the positive.

Because of the nature and complexities of ends, they may be realized to a greater or lesser degree. This is only the commonplace that ideals are never fully realized in action. How staggeringly difficult it is to realize ideals in conjoint conduct that involves massive populations provides some nice questions we need not enter into. Actions can and do fall short of realizing their ends; they can also be degraded by reason of the means employed. To use other persons as means can be a matter of more or less. Consequently, actions can be better or worse in both ways combined. If we regard the positive social relation as one which aims at ends in which persons can share and as having a care for how these ends are achieved, we regard actions as moral in what appears to be at least the minimum that need be insisted upon, if not the maximum. We ask for achievement of positive value and we ask that it be done in a way that is mindful of human beings and their welfare. To ask for more appears to be asking for something more than human—and, we might well say, more therefore than moral.

The positive social relation is just such a universal as we have been looking for. Actions, institutions, processes are always particulars, limited and circumscribed. Only as we can discern the universal which transcends particulars can we evaluate them and possible alternatives to them. In the case of morality, a principle is required to bespeak the very function of moral action—to achieve and to achieve well. Its office then is to be a standard of content, and not to prescribe content. A standard is no substitute for that which it measures, and a moral standard is no exception to the role played by a standard. What morality requires in addition to its standard is intimate knowledge of proposals for action, together with the context in which these proposals are made. Consequently, there are two aspects of moral action, both of which are indispensable. There is the knowledge which is intimate and internal to action itself, a knowingness without which action can be only stupid and uninformed. But secondly, there is that which is external and yet to which an action must measure

59

up—the standard which is neither created nor destroyed by the action. The very function of a standard requires that it have an independent standing. Otherwise there can be no appeal from the particular itself, which in being its own measure can measure nothing else—or, in other language, is unique and therefore without measure.

To put the matter more accurately, even if seemingly paradoxical, what we require in order to measure a thing is something which is both external and internal to it. If we think of it for a moment in the crude terms of a measuring rod, we observe immediately that, first, it is an effective measure because it is separate and apart from the thing measured, but secondly, it is a measure of length, and this can be possible only as the rod and what is measured both display the character of length and thus become *com*-mensurable. Length is not measured by color or sound or heat, unless we can discover some transformation formula by which it may be translated from one set of terms to another, since only as there is some definite correlation, say, between length and temperature can we use a thermometer to measure temperature. In any event, we insist that whether we actually measure length by a rod, a thermometer, or a spectrum, such measurement is possible only inasmuch as the thing measured has the property of length and an appeal may be made to something beyond the thing itself as an independent standard of measurement.

The same would appear to be true of the measurement of values. For if a thing is wholly unique and self-contained it is *ipso facto* incomparable, and we can at best stand in awe of it or, at worst, shudder at it. Neither reverence nor fear, however, constitute measuring rods, for neither reverence nor fear is the value to be measured. The dilemma which faces us in regard to cultural values is whether we can accept both the theory of immanent criticism and the theory of progress. If the only reliable and meaningful criticism is that which is internal to a culture itself, then we seem really to be in possession of no measure at all. And if, on the other hand, the measure is external to a culture, is it not irrelevant and impertinent, just as if we tried to measure the virtues of Balinese music according to the standards of occidental counterpoint, or were to raise the ridiculous old question, was Beethoven greater than Rembrandt?

Progress is significant when it engenders processes relevant to the dilemmas of a people and resolves them in a satisfactory way. Proposals for change that do not arise out of a clash of interests are irrelevant and useless. Cultures are not exportable commodities, and to attempt to impose a way of life on a people can end only in frustration and anger. The reason for this is not far to seek. As we have seen, institutions and processes are always particulars; they exist in specific contexts and their particularity is a matter of time, place, and circumstance. Being relative to surrounding conditions of life, they must be fitted together as mortise and tenon. Even science and industrial technology are exportable only as laboratories, manufacturing processes, and educational facilities can receive them. And in the final analysis, the test of their satisfactoriness consists not in science and industry but in whether they can further a people's ends and provide a richness that would otherwise be absent from their lives.

To express this in terms relevant to cultural processes, we may define progress as any social movement by which a people transforms a spurious into a genuine culture, or, assuming that there are degrees of spuriousness and authenticity, we may say that progress consists in a people's moving from a less genuine to a more genuine culture, or, obversely, from a more to a less spurious culture. The criteria for this movement we have already noted: the achievement of ends and care for persons in the process. Without achievement of ends, a society is impotent, and without caring for persons, achievement is suicidal. The dynamics of the process will no doubt involve cultural focus, as providing tentative direction, even though in the process the focus may come to be entirely redefined.

Progress cannot be realized without immanent criticism. This form of criticism now comes to be revealed as a process which, though it cannot proceed without an intimate knowledge of the clashes, quandaries, and vexations in a society, neither can it succeed without an appeal to a standard which supplies a moral quality necessary for success. The moral quality, that is, "the positive social relation," is universal, not in the sense that it can stand

61

alone as that which men seek on its own account, but in that it stipulates conditions in accordance with which any action must be undertaken if it is to be moral—that is, if it is to prove satisfactory, or, we might just say, civilized. Progressive criticism is immanent in the sense that any significant proposal for action is a response to particular dislocations within a society and advocates specific courses of action for reform. Only to the extent to which these dislocations are similar for different people will similar proposals for reform be effective. Even science, if we follow Dewey, will be applied in actions rather than to actions; otherwise, it is an abstraction out of context which defeats its primary purpose—criticism.

Having analyzed in considerable detail what is involved in immanent criticism and its relevance to a genuine culture, we may conclude this discussion by briefly suggesting some major consequences for ethics and social theory, especially as related to present-day controversy concerning cultural relativism and absolutism. Since much of the controversy—as in most controversies—depends on definition of terms, we should aim at as much precision as possible in order to reach the highest degree of agreement. I turn first to cultural relativity.

If by cultural relativity we mean that cultures do as a matter of fact differ from people to people, the question is essentially one of fact and is verifiable only by empirical study of the beliefs, attitudes, customs, and institutions of peoples, including the varieties of tools, instruments, and other artifacts which they employ. No one, I assume, cares to substitute dogmatic assertions of how peoples live for what is revealed by actual study of the social facts themselves. We may as well even further grant that there are good reasons for believing that lives of people will vary considerably because of conditions relevant to them—climate, topography, soil, vegetation, animal life, and any other environmental conditions that set limits to feasible forms of action. The controversy arises not from the fact of the relativity of customs or of environment, but from judgments which in essence assert that the customs of any one culture are as good as those of any other.

I am not aware of any simple name for such a theory, but if

we want to invent a descriptive barbarism to designate it, we can somewhat appropriately call it "anti-ethnocentric relativism." Negatively, this theory feeds upon the assumption that judgments of superiority and inferiority of cultures employ (wrongly, of course) one's own culture as the measure of the worth of any culture. Positively, its insistence is that dignity inheres in every body of custom and that since all bodies of custom are conventions, we should be tolerant of them all. From the combined assumptions of dignity or equal, intrinsic worth of all bodies of customs and the necessary arbitrariness of them, the conclusion for tolerance of all cultures (a culture being defined in this case as the total body of customs of a people) is well founded.[17] In adopting this "anti-ethnocentric relativism," one would seem to have included in it the requirement that any such culture is a genuine culture. Although the conception of relativism appears quite satisfactory from a purely normative point of view, it is absolutely false from the point of view of immanent criticism.

In the first place, from the point of view of immanent criticism, any one who believes that his own culture provides the correct standard for all ways of life would be not only parochial in outlook, but also a fool. This would be so because a consistent belief in the relativity of values is a belief in the requirement that values are relative to needs, and that only as they are truly responsive to needs are they values at all. If needs change and customs remain permanent, they are not only not dignified, they are stupid. In fact, the only dignity that a custom would seem to possess is that which can stand the test of the most rigorous criticism of those who have to live with it. From the point of view of immanent criticism, consequently, one is most truly critical of his own customs, not of those of other peoples, for he knows his own customs best and is therefore better prepared to criticize them in all their fullness and detail. Knowledge and imaginative creativity are thus the basis of this criticism, not dogmatic, parochial ethnocentricity.

If "anti-ethnocentric relativity" provides no adequate basis for criticism of cultures, neither does the extreme absolutism, which is its opposite. The extreme absolutistic point of view is one from which it is asserted that moral values are independent and not definable by means of cultural context and that the discovery of a moral dictum (truth-telling, for example) is such that it constitutes an obligation for all peoples at all times. In this extreme view, moral dicta are alleged to be just as independent of personal desires, wishes, or inclinations as they are of varying customs and social approvals. Neither institutional forces nor those which arise from man's appetitive or irrational nature can make an action right or wrong, for rightness and wrongness are matters of moral perception, which, once recognized, ought to hold for any person at any time. When a person acts contrary to what is right, such action must be attributed to moral myopia—and the same is true even if it is the vast majority who so act.

This extreme absolutistic position is philosophically interesting because it evolves a special kind of apparatus for the apprehension of moral virtues. These apprehensions are attributed to peculiar characteristics of mind and are invariably apotheosized under the banner of reason. To differentiate such reason from that which is characteristic of the discursive, logical processes, it is designated as practical reason in contrast to the theoretical. In any event, its mode of perception is that of an intuitive or direct grasp of the rightness or wrongness of an action, as well as of the obligatoriness to do or to refrain from doing something or other. This point of view is commonly regarded as a form of deontological ethic. Its most marked opposition to all forms of cultural relativism resides in the fact that it takes simple, isolated, or isolable, self-evident judgments as final and ultimate judgments of moral actions. Following MacBeath, we may say its method, in contrast to that of cultural relativism, is the "method of isolation."[18]

I suppose the most serious criticism that is launched against this absolutistic point of view is that because the judgment is isolated, there can be no recognizable procedure for correcting it. In this case, the truth being immediate, there is no reliable test or check of any judgment except that of immediate certainty. In the light of superior certainty, one might acknowledge his earlier mistakes, but only as he himself happens to reach the superior stage of enlightenment. Although the test of maturity can be urged, it does not prove to be very reliable, for the simple

64

reason that no satisfactory standards of moral maturity are provided. An even more serious objection resides in the fact that one may question whether the method of isolation is calculated to yield moral judgments at all and consequently whether this view does not make morality defeasible. For the attempt to single out a moral faculty and to make moral action dependent on it is to slice human nature, it may be argued, in such a way as actually to divide morality from the rest of man's nature. And this divisiveness, it may be concluded, is precisely what defeats morality and thereby makes alleged moral dicta quite unintelligible. If truth-telling or honesty or frugality or modesty is important, does not its importance lie in its impact upon persons rather than in anything intrinsic to its nature? Is not its importance found in reasons beyond it? And thus may we not, taking lines out of context, quote T. S. Eliot against himself and say:

> Now is my way clear, now is the meaning plain
> Temptation shall not come in this kind again.
> The last temptation is the greatest treason:
> To do the right thing for the wrong reason.[19]

The question concerning importance may be regarded—and no doubt many do regard it—as improper. To insist upon importance is to insist upon asking questions about relations when this is just what is being denied. Therefore, it is to beg the question. This retort, however, is double-edged, for if questions of relations are irrelevant, then there is also a denial of the pertinence of moral judgments to life. And this leads us back once more to the criticism we made of customs *qua* customs elevated to the level of morality—they may be stupid. So, it seems, moral judgments may be stupid, irrelevant, and impertiment. This is what absolutism comes to—not that truth-telling, for example, may not be good policy and relevant and pertinent, but simply that there is no way of telling from the isolative, absolutistic moral point of view whether it is or not. And even if one could tell, according to the absolutist, one should ignore such considerations. The moral sophistication involved in such a standpoint leaves ordinary mortals incapable of knowing whether they are ever morally right and it makes them helpless in knowing to whom they can properly appeal for guidance. It is, moreover, entirely at odds with immanent criticism, which is in essence an appeal to the relations of an act to other acts a person may engage in, as well as to the impact it may have upon what other persons may or may not do.

There is a form of absolutism, however, which is indispensable to immanent criticism—that which invokes a principle, rather than specific moral dicta. The virtue of such a principle resides in its being relevant to all human actions, not just to some (that is, those that are alleged to have imprinted on them the stamp of rightness or wrongness). Accordingly, such a principle can be appealed to as a measure of all human actions inasmuch as they all possess potential, if not actual, ties which bring persons together in distinctively human relationships. According to this view, all men's actions are grist for morality, not just a few or not just certain kinds of dramatic (melodramatic?) ones. Sincerity, kindliness, and courage, for example, may better be expressed in a way of life than in a single action. In the former there can at least be some solid evidence of their expression, whereas the latter is always subject to irresoluble doubt. The playwright, the novelist, and the epic poet understand this, even if the moralist does not. And the method of immanent criticism is one which would rather rely on the sensitivities of the writer than on the obtuseness of alleged moral dicta, incorrigible in practice, rigid in theory, and unenlightened by the sensitivities that can be shared only in the contextual vitalities of life. Such are the consequences of divisive absolutes.

What I have tried to show in this discussion is that only by combining principle and cultural context are we capable of arriving at satisfactory answers to our original questions pertaining to what is culture-bound and what is supra-cultural. Our conclusions can now be briefly gathered up. Not all cultures are estimable—some may be essentially sordid, suffocating, and insufficient. Only a genuine culture is liberating, full, and rich. Consequently, it is not fitting to be slavish to the life of any society, primitive or literate, nor to emulate what is focal in any society. Tolerance has its limits, and is mostly irrelevant when cultures collide and call for changes of focus in each of the clashing societies, when peoples once independent become interdependent and need new institutions to carry on their lives, and when new creativities can fire human imagination and give rise to new kinds of human intercourse.

Secondly, I have argued that to distinguish the genuine from the spurious we must have a *principium divisionis*. By its nature, it must be a universal and should not be confused with particulars, whether as a whole culture, an institution, or a process. A prime virtue of a universal principle is that an appeal can be made to something apart from the urgencies of life itself, for without such an appeal life is impoverished by its incapacity to do anything but yield to them. In order to redirect them, to mold them in harmony with social requirements, to humanize what would otherwise be blind forces, actions must be principled and institutional relationships structured in accord with the potencies of social need.

Finally, although principles do not change and may be regarded as absolutes, it is from the wedding of principle and practice that civilization is born. Civil life is precisely that which is guided by principle and stabilized by institutons. The genuine culture which is its outcome is one which taxes the capacities of man in achieving distinctive social ties and in overcoming unnecessary alienation of man from man. The agonies of civilized life are those birth pangs which give men dignity in their joint undertakings and in their mutual respect; they are not the agonies of lone souls destined to suffocate themselves in their inner privacies. The process of bringing together principle and practice is the unending process of immanent criticism, which in a genuine culture is carried on in every area, whether politics, art, domestic relations, religion, recreation, industry, or education. Immanent criticism is the vocation of man.

PART TWO

On Values

"*Human life is—and has to be—
a moral life (up to a point)* because
it is a social life."

A. L. Kroeber and Clyde Kluckhohn,
Culture, p. 177

Chapter 3

NON-MORAL AND
MORAL VALUES

How, BASICALLY, DOES MORALITY DIFFER FROM OTHER
values? Why does it appear to have priority over them? What are
its sanctions and justifications? These questions, I think, no serious
philosophy can quite avoid. But the range of answers lead to a
whole series of controversies never capable, it seems, of finally
being put to rest. My reason for reconsidering them lies in the
belief that our preceding discussion of culture provides a strategic
approach that makes these problems more resilient to analysis
than those approaches which avoid the cultural context. This
approach is one which tries to avoid abstracting morality from
the concrete context of human actions. Even so, it collides, of
course, with contrary preconceptions of what concreteness should
be taken to mean. Although we wish to follow the advice that the
closer we come to recognizing the realities of human life the more
adequate is the account of what morality is, unfortunately there is
no test of what the realities are. Under the circumstances, there
are bound to be wide divergences of opinion, which can be only
partially corrected by criticism. Regardless of the final results, the
most feasible procedure appears to be to set forth as boldly as
possible what we regard the realities to be and to disclose as carefully as possible the grounds that support them, in the hope that
correction through critical insights and analysis may lead to increasingly solid agreement. Seeing no more promising alternative,
I proceed accordingly.

Although values, it seems, are chiefly a function of social
relations, there is a class of them that appears to be non-social. It is
best, therefore, to treat of the latter first and then turn to the ways
in which values manifest themselves in social life. The best case
for non-social values has traditionally been made by those who
call attention to the satisfaction of wants as constituting the very

essence of value—or what in the tradition has been called the principle of utility. It may well be that all values do trace back to utility. The ineradicable truth of the utilitarian principle resides in the fact that man is an animal and that most, if not all, of what he prizes is intimately related to the satisfaction of his wants. I wish to make only two observations about the theory of utility and then to pass on to the bearing of this upon the theory of social values.

The first is that the theory of utility seems to be basically correct as far as it goes, but that it seems to go scarcely beyond a few obvious biological needs, and that even these are likely to be so modified by social life that a simple biological description is a gross falsification. Nevertheless, when wants are concerned with immediate drives of hunger, thirst, and sex and are reached by goals that are independent of prestige or further concerns of human life, their satisfactions may be regarded as values belonging to the animal nature of man. Any adequate description of the factors involved is tremendously complex. Although biological factors are at the root of complex cultural patterns, their cultural modifications so completely metamorphose them as to render them incapable of providing in themselves a satisfactory theory of values.

The reason why the principle of utility falls short of being adequate is not difficult to see. It is because the principle—and this is my second observation—cannot provide any distinction between wants and needs. The simple, elementary, biological wants are needs of the organism—needs for its continuance and well-being. Wants, however, may be multiplied—and in the human organism certainly are multiplied—to such an extent that, instead of being constituted as needs, they may be trivial, capricious, or even self-destructive. If, for the sake of clarity, we designate the class of wants and needs both as desires, we immediately perceive that there is nothing in the nature of desire as such by which we could distinguish what is needful from what is only wished for or wanted. It becomes imperative for value theory, however, to distinguish the two, or, to employ a somewhat equivalent distinction, between the desired and the desirable. Desires may, by being satisfied, create either positive or negative values and thus cannot be taken to be the criterion for either one alone. This is the elementary, but extremely difficult, problem of value theory, and unless it, or its equivalence, can be solved, no genuine problem of value theory can be solved.

The same problem, *mutatis mutandis*, is involved in the hedonic formulation of the utilitarian theory. In this form, good is equated with pleasure and bad with pain. The hedonic interpretation is seen to contain serious limitations by virtue of the obvious instances in which pleasure may be regarded as bad, as, for example, when the younger Mussolini took great delight in dropping bombs on defenseless Ethiopians. It will not do to appeal to the simple hedonic principle that it is bad because and only because the amount of pain produced was preponderant over the amount of pleasure (actual and potential), for even were the amount of pain very slight in comparison with the amount of Mussolini's pleasure, no doubt we still would say it was bad. Evidently, bad does not mean preponderance of pain over pleasure. This criticism of hedonism underlies the argument which is used by those who advocate the necessity of avoiding the naturalistic fallacy. From their point of view, both the utilitarian and the hedonic principle commit this same fallacy. Rather than regard it this way, I prefer, for reasons soon to become apparent, to regard it simply as failing to distinguish between two kinds of values.

Combining the utilitarian and hedonic point of view into a single theory, I suggest we regard them together as constituting the principle of felicity. Let us define the principle of felicity as signifying that course of action throughout the life of a person in which he passes from one satisfaction to another without intervention of pain.[1] Were the life of man one of felicity, it would no doubt be an impertinence to suggest that any other course of action were appropriate for him to follow. But the real question is whether, in view of the manifest infelicity of life, the principle of felicity could have any widespread application. To tell a person to seek pleasure is, first of all, not very helpful, because it does not tell him what to do; and secondly, it is misleading, because it ignores the conditions which make different kinds of lives possible and which generate the profundities that give human life its unique character. It appears evident, then, that there are values

73

of two distinct orders—those of felicity and those which we may at least temporarily call moral values. The hard problem for value theory is to make a convincing case for the priority of one over the other.

Assuming, as we commonly do, that moral values have priority over felicity, we would still want to know what in mature life is the reasonable place of felicity. One view is to regard the values of felicity as an ingredient of moral life, even though they do not satisfactorily characterize that life. Another is to regard them somewhat apart from that life, though hedged in by it on both sides—that is, as a moral holiday. Lastly, it may be regarded as sheerly independent of morality—as a kind of Arcadia that is without any concern for, or premonitions of, moral life. Each of these views has something to be said for it; and just because pleasure and the satisfaction of desires can never be quite excluded from the good life, nor can they be entirely incorporated into it, therefore, because of this paradox, they may be hedged by morality. No doubt, the question of the place of felicity admits of radically divergent answers for the reason that it is not couched in terms of man's actual predicaments. This may be illustrated by referring to one of the most variously characterized of all fairylands— the state of nature.

Hobbes's characterization of the state of nature is the most interesting of all, precisely because he first pictures it in the positive language of the principle of felicity and then proceeds to draw from his analysis of the state of nature the exact opposite conclusions, in which it turns out to be a hell on earth. In other versions, such as Rousseau's, when he is not talking politics, it remains the most idyllic of habitations where, apart from the contaminations of social regimentation and restrictions, human life comes to its supreme flowering. Other contract theorists variously describe the state as partaking of both good and bad in various proportions. Interestingly enough, as soon as the state of nature is related to the human predicament, the essential antagonism necessarily brings out its ugly aspects, in contrast to what might be hoped for in the civil state. It is not surprising then that

Hobbes's phrase about life being solitary, nasty, and so on, should be the most often repeated phrase of all.

Seen in this light, the significant element that is introduced in the contractual relation is precisely the element in which a person is forced to take account of other persons. This is just what spoils all the fun, and this it is that reveals the life of felicity as a hopeless abstraction. It turns out, then, that not even the biological needs are assured of being met in the state of nature. On the contrary, wherever a man turns, he must contend with other men in his attempt to siphon from nature the minimum to support himself. The picture is one of complete despair. Not only does it not befit man, but it is impossible to maintain. Hobbes knew this, and that is why, clearly, he did not intend to picture the state of nature as an actual state in which man could live. Secondly, he clearly did not mean that there was any actual historical contract by which man by some magic propelled himself into the civil state. The state of nature is a device, not a kind of life.

The implication for value theory is unmistakable. Felicity is a self-contained value only in abstraction from the tough problems of life. It can maintain itself only so long as it is not threatened by moral ends. Once the questions of morality are injected into human life, then man must concern himself, not just with the question of things that will cater to his desires, but also with other men who also are contenders for the same things. This requires a whole new orientation of life, for now there are overriding considerations. One might argue that the "peace and security" which Hobbes suggests as the values of the civil state are just other *desires* to be satisfied. But this cannot be so. Peace and security signify a kind of life and not kinds of things to be attained. They present superior claims to *any* others, and thereby they call for the *evaluation* of desires and aversions in a way which makes them justifiable. The charm of felicity consists in its irresponsibility, the power of morality in its responsibility. Perhaps regrettably but necessarily, the charming loses its innocence when confronted by its parent, morality.

Maturation, it may be worth pointing out, is continuous with youth and not a brutal rejection of it.[2] So morality and the civil state may be regarded as salvaging much from the life of felicity, and there is a good deal more in the civil state than the apotheosis of political power. It is, in fact, a grave mistake to confuse the two. Hobbes came close to doing this, but he saved his theory by insisting that arbitrary political power is never the worst of all possible states. This, of course, he could do only because it always turned out that political power could never be entirely arbitrary, even though his reasons were sometimes confused.[3] Basically, it seems to me, Hobbes gave the reason that there is a kind of life in the civil state that makes morality important just because of the enrichment and extension of it that is possible through the recognition of others, in contrast to completely self-directed pursuits aiming at felicity. And these values, moreover, cannot come to fruition if man regards others simply as things to be used for his own benefit, no matter how subtle the cunning powers he exercises for using others. The difference is not one of subtlety; it is one of basic values themselves—in fact, just the difference between felicity and morality.

It is instructive to look to Hobbes's own words in his description of the civil state, the most pungent of which are found in the negative form when he is detailing why man should repudiate the state of nature. When a man is without other security than what is furnished by his own strength and invention, then:

> In such a condition, there is no place for industry; because the fruit thereof is uncertain: and consequently no culture of the earth; no navigation, nor use of the commodities that may be imported by sea; no commodious building; no instruments of moving, and removing, such things as require much force; no knowledge of the face of the earth; no account of time; no arts; no letters; no society . . .[4]

When we read "peace and security" in the light of the above quotation, it is clear that morality is to be equated with civilization itself, and not just that stern kind of puritanism which insists upon the renunciation of the goods of life. We can begin to see good reasons why felicity is a vain ideal: it is incapable of giving man what he mosts wants, because his needs are so much more urgent, and their satisfaction so much more rewarding, than what is contained in the life of felicity.

Another way of expressing this is to say that man's animal

nature, the biological drives, can be expressed in the state of nature, but that human nature is expressed only in the civil state. Bluntly, the works of man—his industry, his technology, his communications—are a function of his nature, and this nature is social, not solitary; rich, not poor; elegant, not nasty; human, not brutish; and long-lived, not short. We may say, then, that either it is this or it is not civilized, leaving unsaid whether the not-civilized is just innocent or is anti-civil. Whatever may be said for felicity, it may not be said that it has any concern for the commonwealth, that is, for those values whose essence consists in their being shared.

Civilization creates the commonwealth; felicity could never create it. What is involved in civilization is extremely complex, and it is certainly not created by a contract in any usual or legal meaning of that term. Communication and some fellow feeling are inevitably part of the process, but there are no forces in the life of felicity that could impel man to move from one to the other. And this is because there is no communication or fellow feeling which is intrinsic to felicity, nor is there any necessity in the progression from one satisfaction to another to provide a basis for intelligible criticism, since by definition there is no trans-individual property capable of making such criticism possible. Also, since there is no genuine contract in passing from felicity to morality, one should not take literally Rousseau's identification of the personal will with the General Will, though there is some sense in which this may be properly construed. What Rousseau, more than Hobbes, was alert to as being intrinsic to the conception of the civil state were that utility (now definable as satisfaction of needs) was the prime consideration of the civil state and that moral conditions (liberty, in a positive sense, and equality) were indispensable to the definition of utility. Both of these were accordingly included in his conception of the General Will.

Apparently, a prime motivation among the contract theorists was to reveal a bipolar set of values. And however ugly they described the one as belonging to a state of nature, the ugliness was not its principal feature, for this is clearly implied in Hobbes's having recourse to the principle of felicity and Rousseau's rather contradictory attitude toward the state of nature depending on whether he was talking politics or education. The picture could be painted as ugly as one would have it, and it nevertheless, when domiciled in the state of nature, has charm. It had to have charm because it was unrelated to anything else. Let it once approach the realities of social life, such as it did during the French Revolution, and then it can become the enemy which menaces everything dear to civilization. Then the choice becomes unmistakable. There are no grounds for defending felicity; there is every ground for defending morality. Although felicity may be counted as a value, it is of a different order from morality. Separate and apart from morality, it enjoys status before moral claims come to be advanced. In morality, it becomes metamorphosed in the sense that utility must, for all its transformations, become an integral part of moral life. After morality, it lives to defeat the claims of noisy pretensions that are groundless forms of etiquette or arbitrary injunctions that one submit to the will of a special interest, individual or collective. Some further explication of this may be helpful.

No doubt the strongest case which the hedonist makes consists in the insistence that pleasure—or perhaps better, pleasurable experiences—are reasonably regarded as good in and of themselves and without reference to anything else. Accordingly, it is the "now" of experience to which value is referred—not to some far-off goal which may never be realized and which if not realized may reduce all the effort expended not just to the useless, but to tragically painful, and therefore to a negative wastefulness. The delights that man can enjoy give him assurance and meaning in a life that could otherwise be only vacuous. The charming and the alluring are what give life tone and provide a liberation of energy that is immediately recognized as good. Or, looked at the other way around, there is something wrong with a fellow who is constantly morose. Other things being equal, one who chooses pain rather than pleasure is not only queer but cannot make any sense of the alternatives open to him.

When the claims of hedonism are not countered by those of morality, there is no logic to oppose their own counsel for ever-increasing enjoyments. But once moral claims are advanced, the siren of pleasure "must" give ear to the demands for recognition by others than the self. New principles are involved even if an attempt is made to preserve hedonism by altering it from an egoistic to an altruistic form. I do not wish to rehash these questions so minutely covered in virtually every textbook in ethics. It is interesting to note, however, that when Bentham, for example, adopts the altruistic form, he begins to exploit the language of "utility" and his fundamental interest shifts from the allure of pleasure to techniques for achieving social reform. What appears evident in this shift is that Bentham, like Hobbes and Rousseau, is seeking for an amalgamation of utility and social responsibility. Bentham's ideal fell short of a complete moral outlook—no doubt because of his driving interest in social reform. Had he developed more fully his conceptual framework, he might have conceived the amalgamation of utility and responsibility as constituting a moral outlook, invigorated by effective technology, enhanced by a consciousness of excellence, and consummated in the satisfactions shared by those who, through these processes, have established an authentic community of interests.[5]

Morality is vacuous to the extent to which any of these conditions is wanting. Without its accomplishments, life is ascetic and sterile; without its excellence, it is tawdry and not fit for human consumption; without pleasure, it is pedestrian and merely depleting; without the community, it is suffocating. Yet the claims of morality are not automatically self-validating, and when these claims are spurious, the beckoning of felicity will be welcome and its consummations unassailable. Only just authority can make an effective appeal to a person to submit to the strictures of moral life. Any other is a sham and deserves his cynical and complete rejection. Under the circumstances, there need be no cause for wonder that morality has been one of the least satisfied objectives of human life and has given way to all kinds of aberrations, including those of felicity itself. Regardless, however, of the extent to which moral claims have found adequate place in the history of mankind, there is a theoretical point I wish to make, extremely important in the interpretation of value theory.

The data of human experience point unmistakably to the fact that there are at least two orders of value and that neither is reducible to the other, although they may be related to each other in very complex ways. This, I think, our discussion has already

79

revealed. If this is actually the case, then we must reject the charge that this position involves the naturalistic fallacy, such as it has been alleged by G. E. Moore and others. Upon the assumption of the irreducibility of kinds of values, it follows that "good" cannot be interpreted as a simple, unanalyzable quality, analogous to "yellow." Since there are two different orders of value, there cannot be one quality which they have in common and which makes them into values, for then there would be only one order and not two. There is a sense in which we may equate pleasure with good—namely, the sense in which we speak about hedonic values. Hedonically, pleasure is good, and pain bad. When the non-naturalist asserts that there is a single quality, *he* begs the question by insisting that "good" does not mean "pleasure" and by intimating that pleasure may not be good. I hesitate to coin another counter-fallacy in the face of the plethora of them that continue to be urged against Moore's most provocative "naturalistic fallacy." Yet what appears clear from our analysis is that Moore may be said to have committed "the moral fallacy."[6] If pleasure is said to be not good, that is, bad, surely it is meant not that it is hedonically bad, but that it is morally bad. Hence, the non-naturalist assumes that there is a single type of value and that it is moral value. But in truth he has proved merely that there is another type of value, not that all value (that is, positive values) possesses some quality in common.[7] I do not wish to extend this debate, exciting as the sheer logical problems are. It seems only fair, however, at least to point to the serious questions raised by our insistence on two orders of value instead of one.

The two serious and interrelated questions that are raised by separating out two orders of values are, first, how is it possible to make comparisons of two separate orders? Secondly, how can a person make choices between two incomparable orders of things? I am not certain that we can give complete answers to these questions. I shall, however, offer some tentative suggestions and hope in subsequent discussion to arrive at more fully explicated and satisfactory answers. The second question may actually provide a better clue to what is involved in appropriate answers.

The fact of the matter is that we do constantly make choices between two orders of things in economic matters as well as in moral matters. The economist has a simple answer—in some ways, much too simple. When I choose between purchasing a hat or giving my children their allowance, the decision is made on the basis of "utility," or the degree of satisfaction I expect to derive from the one as compared with the degree I expect to derive from the other, the economist would have us say. Since there are degrees of utility, all I need to do is to maximize what I believe these utilities to be. There is, moreover, a way of measuring comparative utilities, and that is by the price I am willing to pay for a commodity in comparison with other choices I might have made. What I purchase, then, are "commodities" and the measure of them is "price." What is most interesting about all this is not the mechanisms, not the fact that I may speak of all goods as commodities and that I may measure their comparative value, but rather that I am capable of making any choice at all. For despite the gratuitous assumption of calling all things commodities, as if thereby there were some common quality which makes them comparable, the fact still remains that we do actually make choices. The agonizing processes involved and the reasons for the choice other than the superfluous appeal to "utility" are of no concern to the classical economist, since he has ways of measuring utility.

Nevertheless, there is a further question that plagues both the plain man and the moralist: Is the choice an "intelligent" or "wise" choice? This is a question which, however answered by the plain man, haunts the moralist. Essentially, it divides those who believe in rational conduct and those who deny its possibility and conclude, with varying degrees of skepticism, that all choice is arbitrary, a function of the will, and insusceptible of rational decision. This arbitrariness is inexpungible, some believe, and even though reason may come into play to enlighten us about conditions involved in it, the choice is itself ultimately non-rational.[8] One may even argue that some decisions may be rational in the sense that some things are comparable and therefore evaluatable, but any actual evaluation depends on a priori decision or commitment which is not rationally determinable.[9]

The special problem we encounter by virtue of separating the hedonic and the moral realms may thus be rephrased as to

81

how we may rationally choose one of the frames of reference rather than the other, even though once a frame is chosen, decisions within it may be rationally comparable. The appeal one would like to make—and may ultimately have to make—to resolve this question is to human nature itself. Actually, this is the answer foreshadowed by our preceding discussion. If it is true that felicity is a hopeless abstraction, then it is so precisely because it ignores the realities of human life—even despite the fact that it is an abstraction from that life. This impasse suggests that we must rephrase our question and seek proper answers by considering regions of relevance, rather than a comparability which simply does not exist. In this way alone can we raise pertinent, rather than impertinent, questions. We don't ask how loud is the smell of smoke, or how sweet is green, or how yellow is middle C. Why then should we ask how pleasant is it to prevent one person from wantonly kicking around another person or how moral is it to savor the ecstasy of catching a rainbow trout or how right is it to enjoy the taste of a pickled pomegranate.

The formal answer to our first question is implied in the answer to the second. Comparability of values is not a requisite. If it were, and if we still tried to maintain that there are separate orders of values, then we would be committing the naturalistic fallacy. The fact seems clear, however, that hedonic values are hedonic just because they are not moral. They do not require nor can they provide an accountability. To expect them to do so would be as absurd as to expect to find out how salty is the warmth of the sun. Once we ask for the accountability of pleasures, we are asking for something for which we know that pleasure itself can never provide the answer. Nor can hedonic values maintain themselves—certainly they can't maintain their independence—if what we are requiring is responsibility. Pleasures may belong, as we have already indicated, to moral holidays, to escapes, to states of innocence, or to revulsions from pious vacuities, although the latter are probably self-defeating because they know too much. But felicity is too frail to contend with morality when the issues of human existence are calling for satisfactory answers to the searchings of the human spirit.

The formal answer carried us some distance in seeing what

the nature of values is, the kind of existence they can possess, and their relevance to the affairs of men. We still want to know, however, whether moral values involve in the center of their being something arbitrary, something so irrational that they carry no weight beyond the fortuitous choice of an individual, and that although he may regard his choice as important, there is no reason in heaven or on earth why anyone else should so regard them. To come to grips significantly with these matters, I think it is better to turn back once more to the occasions in which moral choices seem to be made.

Our discussion of the role and nature of the non-social and the social values has reached the point where we can observe morality to be a function of the latter. Only the social can reasonably be expected to display a sense of responsibility—that is, an inherent and effective regard for the well-being of persons. The dividing point between felicity and morality thus turns out to be that in which either there is no relevance of a person's actions to others or else the degree of relevance is so inconsequential or unpredictable that it may for all practical purposes be ignored. The social is, on the contrary, that for which one may justly be accountable to others either for his actions or his inactions. In the one case, there is a sphere of autonomy in which a person may be guided simply by his propensities and act as he will with thoroughgoing irresponsibility. In the other, it is right that his passions be tamed and his actions channelled according to patterns which advance mutual well-being and the life of the community. In each case, the aims, the methods, and the results are different. Whereas both look to the liberation of the human spirit, the one finds it in the Dionysiac loosening of the passions, the other in the Apollonian harnessing of the power that wells up from the appetites and that is guided by the dictates of compassionate understanding. When the totality of these powers is expressed in the patterned life of a people, we may call it a civil state.

The civil state may now be recognized as nothing more nor less than what we previously found to be the genuine culture. By verbally identifying the two, we may better appreciate the civil state to be the total pattern of values, and not just a form of government or a source of political power. The contract theorists made this very necessary distinction, sometimes described as the distinction between the social contract and the political contract, sometimes as the distinction between the social contract and the fiduciary powers of government.[10] Hobbes was clear on this when he employed the theory of the commonwealth as the basis for creating sovereignty, however confused he might have been about the virtually unlimited rights of the sovereign once it was created. Rousseau was even clearer by virtue of his insistence that the civil society represents the advance of man from the condition of a limited and stupid animal to that of a moral being. His own words may be worth repeating. It may be recalled that he wrote:

> The passage from the state of nature to the civil state produces a very remarkable change in man, by substituting justice for instinct in his conduct, and giving his actions the morality they had formerly lacked. Then only, when the voice of duty takes the place of physical impulses and right of appetite, does man, who so far had considered only himself, find that he is forced to act on different principles, and to consult his reason before listening to his inclinations. Although, in this state, he deprives himself of some advantages which he got from nature, he gains in return others so great, his faculties are so stimulated and developed, his ideas so extended, his feelings so ennobled, and his whole soul so uplifted, that did not the abuses of this new condition often degrade him below what he left, he would be bound to bless continually the happy moment which took him from it for ever, and instead of a stupid and unimaginative animal, made him an intelligent being and a man.[11]

This conception of morality cannot be satisfied with moral dictates about truth-telling or bearing no false witness or paying debts, and the like. It can be satisfied with nothing less than a morality which is expressed, not just in personal relations, but also in the whole range of institutional life. Hence, it includes political morality, man's economic relationships, his legal practices, art, the family, religion, and whatever else may belong to the structured character of social life.

However all-inclusive morality is, we may nevertheless single out from it a part which is uniquely significant for exercising a kind of formal control over the lives of a people. Part of what is demanded of a people is too important to be left to their whims of discretion—and especially that which touches them primarily in a collective capacity, rather than just in an individual one. This we may call the general welfare, and we may speak of it as that part of the social which is of such importance to the community that it requires public institutions for its care and promotion.[12] The general welfare is commonly thought of as involving only a part of human values—the public in contrast to the personal In spirit, this distinction is correct, even if the personal is likely to be formally confused with the "subjective," or, as I would prefer to say, with the "felicitous." The latter would be in error because the personal is moral and has its own accountability, even if a person is not formally accountable to any other specific person or persons or to any agency representing a person or persons. Yet the personal, like the idiomatic character of a work of art, has a logic of its own, a kind of responsibility in the absence of which it would not be personal—or, to carry out the illustration farther, it would not be a work of art—even though a person who acts in a personal capacity is not, and no doubt should not be, responsible to any specific board, bureau, agency, or government. The subjective is essentially irresponsible; the personal is not.

The general welfare, however, both in common language and in what seems to be technical usage, refers to those common needs of a society which are such that benefits and responsibilities can ordinarily be effectively proportioned only collectively, not individually. The goods, moreover, are such as to be thought to be good for all persons or almost all, either directly or indirectly, and are not of a kind that can be reasonably bargained for in the market.[13] On this account, formal agencies prove to be useful to the conduct of those enterprises that are essential to the maintenance of public services, services in the absence of which a society would not get on, or would not get on at all well.[14] The classical conception of such services includes primarily the armed force necessary to defend a country, the police power to maintain internal order, and the courts of law to administer justice. What particular agencies or institutions are required in addition are, of course, matters of time, place, and circumstance. Primitive societies may possibly be able to dispense with any of the above services. Today, the list for an industrial society would have to be indefinitely extended, and for the Marxist it would include all agencies of production of goods that flow through the market, as well as other regulative agencies needed for the "dictatorship of the proletariat."

There are serious ambiguities in the notion of the general welfare that need to be cleared up if it is to prove useful for either theoretical or practical purposes. Sometimes the notion is meant to express an ideal end which might or might not be capable of realization; sometimes it is meant to refer to actual practices and institutions which constitute the good; and sometimes, especially for political and for moral theory, there are unique means that are regarded as intrinsic to the processes by which the general welfare comes about. A word concerning each of the first two and a somewhat more elaborate explanation of the third are called for.

The "general welfare" may signify a normative principle which refers to ends that are not in existence but that are regarded as good, whether or not they are actually realized. The conception is likely to be vague because the means by which they can be realized are neglected. If it turned out that there were no means possible for the attainment of the ends, they could be finally interpreted only as a kind of wish, not realistic political or moral concepts. Opposed to this view is that which defines the general welfare as the established and approved institutions of a society, such as are constituted, for example, by the army, the courts, the schools, libraries, and the like. Whether or not they are for the general welfare, however, depends upon whether they actually meet the authentic needs of a society.

The most perplexing question of all is that of how the criteria of need are to be established—in fact, so perplexing that many writers believe there is no way of establishing them and regard all statements of criteria as insufficient or groundless or, at best, arbitrary agreements, with limited applicability. Whether or not the applicability is limited, there are those who insist that the method of agreement is essential to the establishment of any institutions in the realization of the general welfare. This insistence is, of course, at the base of those theories which require

86

consent as the only acceptable basis of government. It certainly underlies contract theories of government, even if in a somewhat aborted form, and no doubt it constituted one reason for speaking of a General Will as the agency for creating the civil state. And in certain contemporary theories we have seen a reinterpretation of this in which a "leader" is supposed to be the very incarnation of the will, more reliable in his intuitions of its requirements than any that are possessed by the masses or the *Lumpenproletariat*.

None of these theories is insignificant. Each has in one way or another been instrumental in actual political states, and the issues are certain to be debated as long as men are interested in the secular or religious affairs of the community. However different the methods for discovering the general welfare, there is agreement that actual public policy may enhance or detract from the life of the community and that the agents who devise policy have a responsibility for securing the better rather than the worse. Without prejudging the knotty issues, we nevertheless seem to be on firm ground in suggesting that the formation of public policy is inadequate unless it can reconcile two quite divergent ends of government: it must satisfy the practical requirement of providing a substantial service and it must have a concern for the integrity of persons. The former looks primarily to efficiency. The latter, although presumably preoccupied with morality, often provides an excuse for inaction, vacillation, and procrastination. A government which neglects either performance of service or morality is one which is precariously balanced, if not headed for outright destruction.

These preliminary considerations should suffice to remind us of the need for regarding the general welfare as an integral part of civil society. In fact, it looks as if the major controversies pertaining to the reality of the general welfare arise just because of the failure to take into account the civil society as the necessary context in which the term has application. Moreover, it is important to remember that, given the civil society, both morality and utility are in some degree and in some proportions already present. Consequently, the kind of issues that arise pertain really to the extension of one or the other or both. Or to put it slightly differently, the principal question is how to transform the institutions of a society in order to make them express a more genuine form of culture equal to the requirements of changing circumstances as revealed by immanent criticism. To understand more clearly, however, the ground for the traditional indictment of the term we may profitably first refer to some historical statements and then look to the formal indictment, to which we hope to provide at least the outlines of a satisfactory answer.

One of the very interesting chapters in the history of political states is that in which the various brands of political leaders vie with one another in oratory as to how his own brand is required for serving the authentic interests of the people. Authoritarians as well as democrats, Tories as well as Whigs, may be of one voice in this regard, and the claims which appear, even though clothed in a language appropriate to the issues of the day, are otherwise independent of time. James I, no less than Adolph Hitler, speaks in the name of the welfare of his subjects, be it in the language of theology or in that of racial characteristics. James I says, when he writes in 1598 *The Trew Law of Free Monarchies,* that the Christian monarch will:

> procure the weale and flourishing of his people, not onely in maintaining and putting to execution the olde lowable lawes of the countrey, and by establishing of new (as necessitie and euill manners will require) but by all other meanes possible to fore-see and preuent all dangers, that are likely to fall vpon ciuilitie among them, as a louing Father, and careful watchman, caring for them more than for himselfe, knowing himself to be ordained for them, and they not for him; and therefore countable to that great God, who placed him as his lieutenant ouer them, vpon the perill of his soule to procure the weale of both soules and bodies, as farre as in him lieth, of all them that are committed to his charge. And this oath in the coronation is the clearest, ciuill, and fundamentall Law, whereby the Kings office is properly defined.[15]

The Hitlerian version is at least partially rendered in these terms:

> It is thus necessary that the individual should finally come to realize that his own ego is of no importance in comparison with the existence of his nation; that the position of the individual ego is conditioned solely by the interests of the nation as a whole; that pride and conceitedness, the feeling that the individual or the class to which he belongs is superior, so far from being merely laughable, involve great dangers for the existence of the community that is a nation; that above all the

88

unity of a nation's spirit and will are worth far more than the freedom of the spirit and will of an individual; and that the higher interests involved in the life of the whole must here set the limits and lay down the duties of the interests of the individual.[16]

A Thucydides speaking of Athenians, a Jefferson speaking of rural Americans, or a Franklin Roosevelt speaking of industrial Americans—each echoes a faith in a people's achieving its own best interests whether it is in judging a policy, freeing itself through farming and education, or being capable of overcoming the state of being ill-fed, ill-clothed, and ill-housed. I am not at this point interested in trying to assess the claims of the superiority of either authoritarianism or democracy (however fixed my personal beliefs are on the matter) or of attempting to decide whether a reconciliation between the two is possible, but rather in recognizing a crucial question of value theory: In view of the wide divergence of belief as to what constitutes the general welfare, and in view of the divergence of the means by which it is to be known, and further, in view of the universality claimed for each of these beliefs, can the general welfare signify anything realistic enough to be of use in morals or in politics?

The indictment of the term may be made quite particular. It is first of all said to be mere words. It is empty of content and signifies nothing. Consequently, it (a) can provide no direction for human actions, (b) can be of no use in establishing criteria by which institutions could be known to be for the general welfare and, accordingly, (c) can justify any action or institution which anyone pleases, even though it may be contradictory to what another justifies by what pleases him. If these allegations are true, they render the term a menace to serious inquiry and suggest that it be relegated to the lumber heap of political oratory. Moreover, these allegations are not just made thoughtlessly or superficially or by those who are simply interested in advocating ethical theories whose implications deductively cause them to repudiate the term. They are often made by those who are alert to the political realities and who are led to a justifiable skepticism induced by observation of practices. Professor Kelsen, for example, on serious reflection about such problems observes: "Since there is no objective criterion of what is called the interest of the people, the phrase 'government for the people' is an empty formula apt to be used for an ideological justification of any government whatsoever."[17] These are measured words, which ought not lightly to be cast aside. The burning question comes to be, then, whether the term may contain sufficient precision to be used in deciding whether a policy is for the good or ill of a society.

Basically, the question turns out to be how to discover what the needs of a society actually are, together with what is required to meet them, and how to distinguished them both from the desires of special interest groups illegitimately put forth as if constituting the needs of a society and from majority opinion or even from total, ill-founded consensus. Thus, even though we may say, for example, with Rousseau, that the General Will is always right (which is a tautology), we may not say with him that it is ascertainable by the cancelling out of free votes unhampered by the pressures of special interest groups (which, of course, is not a tautology). The second part of the statement is indispensable to a democratic ideology by virtue of its implicating the consent of the people. Yet it would be faulty to neglect to observe that there is more than consent involved in the use of referenda. There is also the implication that the people *know* their own will, not just by reason of the will itself but by reason of their intimacy with the anxieties as well as opportunities inherent in a society. This direct acquaintance, it seems to assume, does not guarantee that the interests of a people will be served, but it does provide a plausibility that their common involvements *may* serve their interests. This plausibility further assumes, of course, that the will is not just arbitrary but that, on the contrary, it is a fundamental expression of a considered response to a human predicament. Such considerations lead us to take account of the substantive issues in context, not just formal actions out of context.

It does seem reasonable that some of the mystery of the problem evaporates when it is seen in context. The general welfare is not necessarily obscure. In fact, some of the goods—and it may actually be that in the final analysis most of them—are rather simple in nature. Life-giving things are good. Sickness is not good; destitution is not good; decrepitude and the loss of human faculties are not good; hatred of self and of others is not good.

Whoever denies these propositions refuses to take seriously the meaning of welfare—which, of course, simply means faring or doing well or living in a state of well-being—or else he denies them in a specific context in which in a particular instance it is well to incur these evils but only in order that one may otherwise fare better or cause others than himself by virtue of that incurrence to fare better. The questions become more complicated but, however complex, they do not necessarily lead to insoluble dilemmas. To be sure, if we cannot advance beyond old saws about the goodness of health, prosperity, and peace, we might very well relegate the principle to limbo. But are we so limited to platitudes in our beliefs about life-giving substances, peace, and the like?

Recalling what was earlier said about culture, we may suggest that to cope with the complexities of political life one must recognize the technologies which are inherent in a culture and upon which a people depends if it is at all able to fare well. If the Ponape depend upon yams, without any feasible alternative, and the Todas likewise upon dairy products, their general welfare may not neglect the means for the effective production of yams or diary products, consistent with the fuller expression of other life-processes. The principle is no different in industrial than in preliterate societies, and sacred cows of the one are no better than those of the other.[18] Whatever the fundamental system of technology within a society, it actually provides a base from which it is possible to anticipate the general welfare, even though reforms lead to consequences contrary to expectations and therefore must be reconsidered in the light of more mature experience.

We know, for example, the criteria we wish to use and how to apply them (whether or not we actually do) in order to make the automobile an effective "institution" for the general welfare. We can make specifications for "safe automobiles;" we can order systems of inspection, not just of the vehicles, but of the operators as well. We can devise reasonable laws and regulations for the operation of the vehicles. We can provide the necessary and calculable services that are required if automobiles are to be used. I call attention to those aspects which are clearly for the general welfare, that is, those which involve services, licensing, and regulations. In a further evaluation, one could, and many do, call attention to the "sacred cows" (the chrome, the disparity between horsepower and utility, the functionless fins, etc.) which, though not officially regulated, are nonetheless false and insulting to human sensibilities. These are not just matters of "subjective judgments." They are matters of use and function, which can be judged with the kind of rigor with which we can judge the worth of any tool.

Even though a critical person may well accept these judgments concerning the automobile as an institution, he may object nevertheless to the extension of such judgments to all social values. For, after all, may we not still raise the question, is the automobile a *good* institution? To such a question we must reply, I think, with the same kind of plain answer. We are committed to the automobile because we are committed to an industrial form of life, of which the automobile is, so far at least, an indispensible part. Horses are nice and so are water buffalo, but for Western man, they are for recreation or for the zoo, not for the serious business of living. The "industrial commitment" has in many ways proved itself in life-giving properties—in health, in longevity, in freeing man from a bare subsistence economy, and so in permitting him to promote intellectual and artistic affairs, sensitive social relations, and to educate himself in ways not conceivable under harsher modes of existence.

No one alert to the barbarities that still remain in the industrial world can overlook also the many evidences to the contrary. Anyone can readily counter with the well-founded facts of the fiendishness of modern industrial warfare, the reckless killing of tens of thousands in automobile accidents, the inhumane monotony of the assembly line, the pent-up eroticism of a half-neurotic population, the nightmares of "artistic productions," the diabolical persecutions of persons for no other reason than the color of their skin, the starving of the emotions in an intellectual world, the atrophy of muscles unused in man's workaday world, congestion and megalopolis, smog and tawdry amusement, insufferable propaganda and cults of religious hatreds, urban delinquency and suburban snobbery, the disrespect for laws of the state, graft, corruption, and malice of every sort—one could easily extend the list indefinitely. But this is a cheap victory, which doesn't at all prove that the crying need is to go back to a simple society with non-industrial technologies such as we find among primitive peoples. What it really proves is that we know with some precision how to evaluate these matters and something of what is required of a complex industrial society if it is to suit human needs. The point should be now made somewhat more systematically and theoretically.

It becomes increasingly clear that the general welfare is not an idyllic end, independent of the means by which it is attainable. It is, on the contrary, the actual creation of new institutions which better human relations rather than worsen them. Hence, sufficient attention must be paid to the processes by which they are created to make certain that the intended ends are not defeated by the processes themselves, or, at worst, that we take a calculated risk that the ends will prove sufficiently advantageous to overcompensate the disadvantages of the means employed. Harsh means, we know, are sometimes (although probably less often than we might suspect) necessary for highly important ends. This is indispensable to administrative office, for administration is, after all, the exercise of power, however subtly or wisely it is exercised. To justify administration, nevertheless, is to ascertain that power is used only for the general welfare. This we have already seen to be a tautology capable of being a menace to a people unless there are reasonable criteria for evaluating administrative acts.

Those who would have us devise criteria out of the blue will necessarily conclude that the general welfare represents an empty formula incapable of reasonable use. We should conclude likewise. But real issues do not arise out of the blue. If they did, their resolutions would be, as in Plato's Forms or Santayana's essences or Whitehead's eternal objects, infinite in number and such that no choice would be possible. It happens, however, that no choices are ever required save from a background of interests and in the presence of limited alternatives. This is true of rats in a maze, a person in a quandary, or a people coming to terms with its food supply. We do not have a choice of setting up a yam culture or an industrial culture—simply, I suppose, because cultures aren't "set up"; they are inherited. Our choices may be to use new tools, new inventions, to modify institutions here and there, devise a more satisfactory system of courts, to change marriage ceremonies, and to alter various prescriptions. We can do this intelligently because we have "commitments," which in truth are the inherited background of interests. This inheritance we can change only partially and in piecemeal fashion. We can effect changes only because we have knowledge of what they entail. The less our knowledge, the less capable we are of choosing, and in the absence of relevant experience, we can make no choices at all.

Applying these principles to the general welfare, we see that choices are actualized when there is a compulsion and an opportunity and the two are related. The compulsion for the general welfare is most intense when it is related to the cultural focus, since the mightiest powers within a society are by definition concentrated in its focal matters. Compulsory focal power is ordinarily released in patterns such as have been created for its expression— that is, in the institutions of a society. When these patterns are blocked, however, energy is pent up, controversies are rife, and the need for modified or new patterns becomes increasingly evident. Yet necessity does not invariably mother altered patterns. Energies may be spent in fruitless controversy, spelling the decline of a culture, or they may be rechannelled into new patterns which redefine the cultural focus and which re-establish a continuity of social action, thus making for new harmonies within a culture which genuinely faces up to its needs.

The connecting link between compulsion and opportunity is imagination or "genius." There are, to be sure, no rules for producing genius, whether in politics, science, art, or any other field, although there may be conditions which either promote or hinder it. In politics, the name we give to it is statesmanship, and a statesman is a man of imagination, character, an eloquence sensitive to political needs and capable of attracting popular support for ends generally recognized as releases from widespread frustrations of social life. He is an innovator, not from the power of oratory or of threat, but from that of imaginative projections of ends which arise out out rich experience that can stand the test of collective criticism insofar as this is possible in advance of innovation. An architect of policy, his plans can, of course, be modified, not only by the foresight that comes from analysis, but also by the realities that are encountered in concrete practice.

The preliminary tests of statesmanship in advance of actual practice are of two interdependent sorts: feasibility and desirability. Of a policy, one may ask whether, regardless of its social consequences, there are the technical resources at hand for its implementation. This is largely a matter of expertise—that application of available knowledge to the particular matter at hand. Whether the matter pertains to the construction of pyramids, temples, roads, dams, the creation of courts, kings, legislative bodies, demes, commissions, the establishment of school systems or religious practices, or the declaration of war, one wants to know precisely the materials and labor involved, together with the likelihood that the venture can succeed. This test belongs to the technology of a culture, and, in the absence of a body of technology or expertise, the question of ends cannot even be seriously entertained. When on the basis of available expertise, conditions seem to be favorable for the technological success of a venture, one of the tests is concluded, short of the crucial evidence of actual technological success, including that of public acceptance.

The second of the two tests is that of the desirability of a venture. This test is more difficult to make; it involves a degree of education and imaginative insight that a people may lack and which consequently predisposes them to oppose anything but the old ways of doing things. Nevertheless, in the presence of crises and through the medium of public debate, it is possible for a vast majority of a people to come to see the desirability or undesirability of a particular innovation. What is crucial to the debate is the criterion which is appealed to in evaluating the desirability of putting a proposal into practice. This criterion is none other than that of morality itself—that is, whether or not the enactment of the proposal promotes or hinders the social relationships of the community. If the building of dams and the erection of canals promotes economic relationships, relieves the farmer of distress, and makes available educational opportunities for his children, without at the same time destroying the integrity of positive social relationships already established, then it would clearly be desirable to build dams and erect canals. The same principle applies whether the question is that of building pyramids, regulating the practices of trade, establishing compulsory education, controlling marriage practices, enforcing sanitation laws, defining crimes, or any other proposal pertaining to the control of social life which is to be administered by agents of the community.

Decisions pertaining to social relations can no more be made in a vacuum than can any other practical matters. The same practices in different societies can one be undesirable and the other desirable, just as contrary practices in different societies may both be desirable. Although there is a criterion of the desirability of social practices, there is no formula which can mechanically be applied for automatically achieving social well-being. There are, however, symptoms by which it can be judged whether or not the practices of a community are desirable. Widespread frustration deriving from social discontent and issuing into violence, reigns of fear and terror, the prevalence of deceit, lies, intimidation, and threats, along with other unregenerate forms of social life which deteriorate humane relationships and the processes of communication, are the marks of social undesirability. In other words, the criterion of the desirability of institutional practice is the degree to which it makes effective "the positive social relation." The highest actualization of this is the integrity of man in a society of integrity.

The judgments which are derived from the application of the criterion of desirability may at times clearly prove a course of an action to be either desirable or undesirable in varying degrees, or to be genuinely controversial. If desirability were the only test of social practice, one would favor the first, disfavor the second, and withhold decisions pertaining to the third. The problems of practice, however, are further complicated by the fact that the test of desirability must be coupled with that of feasibility, which similarly may lead to conclusions of the feasible, the unfeasible, or the problematic. Combining the two sets of criteria but ignoring the matter of degree and thus, because of its irrelevance, the possible state of indifference according to the criterion of desirability, it then turns out that there are nine possible combinations, of which only six have practical political meaning. The three grades according to desirability combined with what is not feasible are for lovers, dreamers, artists, and mathematicians. What is feasible and undesirable is for those with a diabolical bent of mind; what is feasible and good is heaven on earth. What is problematic on the scale of the feasible and either bad or good or controversial on the scale of the desirable is for gamblers, vile or courageous or desperate and given to tempers choleric or sanguine or mercurial, respectively. Practically, the most interesting combination is that of a proposal which is feasible but controversial. Those who assert this as the only alternative and who further assert that all political proposals are indefeasibly controversial mean to say that the general welfare is an empty formula, that there are no other alternatives, that the controversies are incapable of rational solution, and consequently that morality, other than the profession of individual preferences, has no place in politics. Curiously enough, the motivation behind it often appears to be a democratic belief in the necessity for individual consent. Yet this belief seems to be misplaced, however indispensible the need for employing means for eliciting individual consent in a democratic society. If, on the other hand, the controversial is not indefeasibly so, then by definition it turns out eventually to be either desirable or undesirable, and leads to consonant practical decisions. Classical democratic practice breaks the impasse by use of the referendum. This need not prove the correctness of the decision. But then classical democracy also insists upon means which allow persons to change their minds. Of course, by this time the opposite decision may no longer be desirable. But such is one of the quandaries of democratic practice, which, along with alternatives to it, we can consider in a later context.

Before concluding our explicit answer to those who deny that there are objective criteria for determining general welfare, I would suggest, even though it seems to beg the question, that first of all there clearly are practices in a society which are feasible and desirable and that clearly there are others which are rejected as feasible but undesirable. Those public services which are patently recognized as aiding a people in its necessary business or which add to the amenities that heighten the sensitivities of a people and bring them to a consciousness of life, not aimed at its destruction, belong to the former class. In contemporary industrial societies this has become commonplace to such an extent that wide-scale planning, even in nations quasi-officially opposed to it, has become the rule rather than the exception. And even when the debate does rage, it is not carried to the extreme of eliminating what are by conservatives themselves regarded as required services.[19] Secondly, those prohibitions which are necessary if people are to live together at all are bound to be constituted as repudiations of undesirable forms of action. Kroeber and Kluckhohn find, for example, no culture which "tolerates indiscriminate lying, stealing, or violence within the in-group." Further, they assert that "No culture places a value upon suffering as an end in itself; as a means to the ends of a society (punishment, discipline, etc.), yes; as a means to the ends of the individual (purification, mystical exaltation, etc.) yes; but of and for itself, never."[20] Although universality of belief is not a sure test of worth, these cultural prohibitions are such as clearly protect the life-processes that are reasonably signified by the "general welfare," once it is understood what is involved in "indiscriminate lying," "suffering as an end in itself," etc.

It would, of course, be an egregious error to assert that there is some simple technique for resolving controversial issues, and I would not be understood as having made any claim that all controversies are rationally soluble. Because of the nature of the public, there are questions pertaining to the general welfare which may not be desirable to raise due to the antagonisms their translation into public policy would create. Others may be, and no doubt are, of such importance that the matter of antagonisms is so minor in proportion to the necessities that they can for practical purposes be neglected. Still again, the costs on the scale of feasibility may be so burdensome and the social relationships improved so slightly or unpredictably that a prudent person could recommend only abstaining from action.[21] Yet even in those cases where there appears no way out of social dilemmas, the moral principle is still available to remind one of necessary conditions of acceptable solutions. The matter is parallel to an artist who fails in his painting. His failure can be measured only by artistic standards, and it will not do to suggest that he use some other to make his painting a success. Likewise, those who propose that, because an appeal to the general welfare as a moral principle will not succeed, we should appeal to some other principle. The analogy to art may suggest further fruitful parallels.

Our formal answer to the critics of the "general welfare" can now be given. The expression is, of course, words, but not merely; it carries meaning partly as a generalization from social life, in which not only are there common purposes but there are even some, like the common defense, for example, whose meaning is essentially collective and which requires special agents entrusted with authority for its function. The contingencies of social life are such that the general welfare cannot be predicted in the absence of concrete knowledge of the life of a people. Hence, to say that a people have needs but we don't know what those needs are is, to be sure, in itself an empty formula. It is like asserting that health is good but not knowing what to do in order to produce healthy states. Fortunately, however, it is also like "health" in the sense that concrete knowledge of a person's condition and generalizations from experimental data may be used to produce a state of health. So with the general welfare. Diagnosis, prognosis, and connecting knowledge are indispensable to its realization. The needs of a community, like the needs of an individual, change in varying circumstances. In matters pertaining to health, there are useful generalizations, which constitute the minor premises, so that it is possible to assert that under such and such circumstances vitamins, or spinach, or more oxygen will correct the deficiencies of the patient. Similarly, it may be said of a society of which we have intimate knowledge that it requires old-age pensions, unemployment insurance, schools, libraries, cheap sources of fuel or fertilizers, improved transportation, more responsible courts of justice, etc. The social disorders arising from poverty, frustration, unused creative talents, are the symptoms of the deficiencies that need correction. The "general welfare" as a term is empty only in the absence of specific knowledge or of minor premises which, when connected with the major, do lead to conclusions.

The major premise—namely, that to promote the general welfare is the necessary collective business of a society—can give direction to social action only as it is combined with the tough empirical content of the minor premise. Universals become effective in providing direction for concrete action only as their relevance to particular situations is established. The test of relevance is the connection of proposals with the deficiencies of institutional life. The signs of the deficiencies may in varying degrees be manic conflict or depressive apathy. When either of these seriously affects the cultural focus of a society, radical treatment is called for. We have already seen that the difficulty may be in the focus itself, either because it confines actions overnarrowly or because altered circumstances make it inappropriate to the vitalities of social life, or both. Ballot boxes, for example, may come to be seen as insufficient instruments for the expression of common interests; such additional instruments as free public schools and novel ways of making actual opportunities for the expression of talents may very well be required to make the general welfare into a living reality. At least, it would seem to be the case in a democratically oriented society.

Direction is a matter of social needs ascertained in context. Newborn infants are capable of making but the most primitive kinds of choice. As they develop habits and acquire experience, they are increasingly capable of ascertaining needs and of choosing effectively. In society, people can collectively desiderate needs and plan courses of action because they inherit cultural patterns and institutions which are capable of being modified to suit their requirements. The pressures that break out in institutional life are the clues to the needs of a society, but whether the proposed remedies will actually meet the needs depends upon (a) whether they can be made to fit into a cultural pattern, and (b) whether the pattern as so modified is capable of being sustained without destroying the society of which it is an expression and, consequently, the pattern itself. If the needs require a more radical remedy than this, anticipation and intelligent choice of action are of no avail, and the society will be torn by forces beyond the control of human knowledge and traditional cultural pattern.

The principle of the general welfare may be employed to direct cultural change only as there is, first, compulsion, which is an expression of cultural forces, and, secondly, the interrelated criteria of feasibility and desirability, by which imaginative proposals can be tested. Feasibility is, of course, a function of natural knowledge, through which man comes to know about things, organic processes, persons, and institutions. The state of the practical arts pertaining to these matters limits man's effective control over his general welfare. There is, however, no society which does not possess some degree of expertise available for this purpose. The criterion of desirability is more difficult to apply. Basically, it is incorporated in social habit—the institutions of a society— and is present in the positive social relationships embedded in them. When, however, new proposals are made, the tug of habit is a serious obstacle to the formation of new habits and limits facility of change. Moreover, since desirability pertains to actual social relationships, they are the expression of common social feelings, not easily purviewed by experts. In such matters, the common feelings must usually be trusted. Since, however, these feelings are notoriously difficult to change and not readily capable of imaginatively anticipating new positive relations, education together with great social pressures are usually required to bring about far-reaching innovations. To bring about the general welfare is even further complicated insofar as a synthesis between feasibility and desirability must be achieved. Little wonder is it that authoritarians from Plato to Hitler have advocated supreme rulers to make the decisions, whether philosopher-kings or *Fuehrers*. The point is, nevertheless, that within limits positive social relations, as well as the feasibility or unfeasibility of actions, are capable of being known, and capable of being predicted and of being controlled. On this account, the general welfare is viable. The culture in which it is present, the social forces on which it relies, arbitrary as they are, when coupled with knowledge, imagination, and human understanding, all of which can be shared and tested—these are the ingredients of the general welfare.

Welfare does not consist, then, in the creation or promotion of whatever institutions one pleases. The arbitrary culture cannot be tampered with simply to suit one's fancy. My dear old banker friend, Mr. Jones, used to propose that we return to an age of handicrafts. Mr. Jones was honest but mistaken. The pains, the suffering, the heartaches, not to speak of the inepitudes, the frustrations, the incapacities, would be intolerable, because man knows something better. Since he does know something better, even though it contains evils, he cannot go back to the worse. There are no means to go from a complex industrial society to a handicraft society, for there are no compulsions to carry us in that direction. The compulsions are those which cry out for a realistic attack upon our indigenous cultural maladjustments, not upon our unrealistic dreams to escape them. Our crucial instruments are only the knowledge we possess and the moral standards which apply to any society whatsoever. Our knowledge changes, and with it our institutions and the particularities of life; the standards for measuring them do not change. A complete realization of values can come about only as utilities are subjected to moral standards. These standards become effective determinants of social action, however, only as sanctions make them so. To the important question of how sanctions become operative I now turn.

Chapter 4

ON MORAL SANCTIONS

ONE OF THE MOST VEXATIOUS QUESTIONS OF MORAL theory is that of how moral standards can come to be effective in the life of a people. This involves the very troublesome question of moral sanctions. Various writers have answered it in a variety of ways, sometimes in ways that are beside the point, sometimes in ways that defeat their own theories of what constitutes morality, and sometimes in arbitrary ways that cannot be inquired into and validated. Although I am certain that there are aspects of the problem I shall not be able to penetrate, I do hope to be able to focus upon them sufficiently clearly to be able to avoid the errors mentioned above.

To bring order to this discussion, I wish to do two things. First, I wish to criticize two different notions of sanctions, each of which involves in a different way the error of confusing morality with something else and consequently of making for untenable notions of sanctions. Secondly, I wish to develop a general theory of moral sanctions in which both "internal" and "external" sanctions will be seen to be indispensable complements within the moral situation. I proceed to the first of these tasks.

There is an "obvious" kind of answer to the question, why should morality be sufficiently appealing that anyone would want to act morally? The answer is that it "pays," that it is in one's interests so to act. Felicity and morality, it may be said, are not opposed to each other, and a person who pursues his own best interests at the same time pursues those that are for the well-being of society at large. No doubt, there is some well-founded truth in this simple answer. Certainly it was at the basis of the classical eighteenth-century view. And in one of its most important formulations, namely, as it applied to a simple kind of competitive capitalism, there seems to be some empirical data to support it. The theory of the "unseen hand" where "private vices" constituted "public virtues" was not only attractive but also turned out in fact to be a great liberating force for vast numbers of persons. Little wonder is it that philosophers as well as political economists should have identified public well-being and private wish, for through this identification a person seems to achieve a greater measure of liberty and power than if he were limited to his own devices in a somewhat uncongenial state of nature.[1]

Based as it was on an over-simplified conception of natural law, the eighteenth-century theory began already in the nineteenth century to reveal serious shortcomings, and has come to be virtually discarded in the twentieth century. Professor Hayek and some others would still have us save it by distinguishing between the "rule of law" and "substantive rules," but even they indicate the need for making exceptions when men find themselves placed in dire circumstances.[2] It is more than questionable whether the general welfare, as our previous discussion has already disclosed, can be limited to the procedural function of maintaining "rules of the game" designed to preserve competitive enterprise. This nineteenth century version of the job shop, as we shall have occasion to discuss later, is scarcely appropriate for understanding the conditions of the giant monopolies and oligopolies that are everywhere apparent in, if not necessities of, modern technology. But we need not force this question here, for the real issue remains, regardless of whether we insist upon limiting the general welfare to regulatory procedures for controlling a kind of economy or whether we include within it substantive public services as well.

The procedural conception of the general welfare insists upon appealing to, and enforcing principles of, fair play, justice, equality, honesty, and the like, even though it leaves the substantive choices of actions to "individuals" to be implemented privately as they will, subject only to the rules laid down in advance. It requires no very great sensitivity to observe that there is a radical difference between the ends which are dictated by the arbitrary choices of individuals and means which may or may not be hindrances to those ends. There is, in other words, no inherent necessity between felicity and morality. Although they need not be opposed to each other, they may at times actually be opposed, and consequently they cannot be regarded as being necessarily in harmony with each other. The relation is contingent. In miraculously lucky times it holds; otherwise, not. It cannot, therefore, serve as a foundation for a general theory of moral sanctions.

The denial of any necessary connection between felicity and morality is to be found in the reasons for which we already discovered the need for distinguishing between them. Felicity has as its end pleasure or the satisfaction of desire, depending upon whether we interpret it strictly in hedonic or in utilitarian terms. The internal sanctions for it then are the psychological feelings of anticipations of pleasure or pain, which are said actually to govern human conduct—"the sovereign masters," which, according to Bentham, "point out what we ought to do, as well as . . . *determine what we shall do.*" Since, however, the dictates of morality may actually differ from those of felicity, the sanctions too must differ. The appeal for morality can be only that which attracts man to the moral relation itself; otherwise it may be a contributory appeal of some sort or other, but it is not a moral one. If there is something distinctive about morality—the positive social relation, or however it may ultimately be characterized— something which appears to be unique to human life, it is this to which the moral sanction *qua* moral must appeal.

The simple attractiveness of the theory that morality is enlightened felicity places such a burden on the adjective "enlightened" that it cannot support the weight of meaning. According to an oversimplified interpretation, Hobbes is thought to have advocated this theory. Man desires many things, and the continual successive attainments constitute felicity. But there is something else he desires, and that is "peace." If the desire for peace were like that for meat pie or whiskey or shoes or a warming fireplace, it could strictly be regarded in terms of felicity. But obviously it cannot be so regarded, first, because it may override any of these desires, not just in the way that one desire is more pressing than another, but in the sense that it takes precedence, whenever it is relevant, to *all* desires, save possibly those pertaining clearly to self-preservation; and secondly, as we have already noted, because it is a desire for a way of life rather than for particular things. It is not just a stronger desire than for things, for it feeds not so much on strength as it does upon discrimination. It desiderates, therefore, something of a different order—one which pays attention to what brings men culturally together in a society, rather than dividing them or making them indifferent to one another. "Peace" signifies not just the industrial arts but the "peaceful arts," which relate men in ways that make culture possible. The extension of "desire" from things to a way of life is a disservice to the term, for by being extended to anything and everything man does, it cannot but explain nothing whatsoever and thus lose all significance. Being psychological in origin and in effect, it can never reach beyond responses to the more responsible activities which are man's peculiar lot. And for similar reasons, such sanctions fail to relate realistically to institutions, which are characteristic of human societies.

Eschewing the more psychological interpretation of moral sanctions, some there are who boldly insist that the only effective sanctions are those which are lodged Machiavellian-like in institutions, and especially in the police power, which is absolutely indispensable to any state whatsoever. Accordingly, moral appeals can be regarded only as a kind of sentimental weakness, womanish and ineffectual. "Covenants without the sword," it is said, "are but words and of no strength to secure a man at all." The elaboration of this theory of sanctions is commonly called "political realism," but in principle it could equally well be cast in other terms, whether theological, military, economic, industrial, legal, or even geographical.

The essence of this kind of realism is that it selects a single factor of social life as the controlling one. In its typical political form, then, it seizes upon the police function as that which alone can guarantee order within a society. Men do not effectively respond, it assumes, to blandishments but only to punishments, and derivatively to threats of punishment. The methods which have been developed to enforce order in a society stagger the imagination. They vary all the way from simple confinement to incarcerations involving an endless variety of deprivations, including conversation, food, drink, light, warmth, sound; and they vary from deprivation to an ever-increasing number of tortures from the simpler bodily ones and mayhem to the most diabolical use of medical or psychological treatments for causing debilitation up to and including death. The use of force may be directed primarily against some few selected individuals or it may be directed against rather large populations, involving purges, pogroms, and persecutions of one sort or another to the end that a homogeneous pattern assures a ruling body of virtually absolute control over political life. In theory, the employment of force should not exceed what is necessary to attain the end; in practice, it invariably exceeds this requirement. Modern totalitarianism may, and in the case of Nazi Germany apparently did, place this end as the rendering of its subjects as agents whose only will was to obey what was requested of them by their superiors.[3]

There is a basic similarity in the employment of force, whether it is done by the agents of political or religious, financial or militaristic, bureaucracies. The Inquisition was quite as capable of employing refined methods of torture as are political governments. A ruling military clique is not necessarily superior in wielding power to one whose supreme devotion is to financial ends. And those who suffer do not have their suffering minimized because torture is used in the name of religion rather than in that of politics, in that of the manly spirit rather than in that of economic self-sufficiency. The various forms of "realism," whether religious, social, or geographical, have in common the singling out of some one factor that is alleged to be the determinant of social organization. Whether it is the will of God, economic geography, manifest destiny, or some variation on these themes, the advocates believe that there is some one power which determines the totality of social manifestations and through which alone these manifestations can be controlled.[4]

As involving "mystiques," these theories cannot but lead to the apotheosis of an elite kind of society. Inevitably, they implicate sacerdotal rule for those who would preside over a people's destiny—or what the rulers would no doubt prefer to call a civilization. The employment of force under such circumstances is actually for the brutalization of persons rather than for their civilization. The hypocrisies, the divided personalities which come about by dealing with an elite, on the one hand, and the *hoi polloi,* on the other, the failure to achieve basic loyalties, the vacillation between saccharine sentimentalities and bitter brutalities cannot but be a mark of a spurious culture. The quality of the sanctions employed in such a society can have no higher integrity than that of the society itself. Those who suffer under this kind of rule can be expected to act only from a sense of personal prudence, for only fools or the mentally sick could feel bound to any external sanctions beyond those necessary for calculated self-preservation.

The conclusion is unambiguous. The sanctions of realism are effective only as long as the use of force or the substantial threat of its use is a fact. The are not moral, even though in the necessarily spurious culture in which they exist they are dressed up as if they were. God's will or the Aryan race, for example, are appealed to in order to bolster a persecution which is no more in the interests of the persons addressed than is the grafter to those who are compelled to make the payoffs. The will behind the sanction is a partial one; it belongs to a special interest group and imposed on others through coercion, it can only disrupt their lives. As alien, it can be recognized only in the most external of ways—through force, violence, and fear. It is self-defeating and incapable of appealing to anything that liberates or moves one as a person. Such a being can therefore only listlessly respond to it as something he can neither understand nor have any will to understand, save perhaps as it becomes transformed into a cultural life which overcomes the alien in a new synthesis.

The paradox that confronts one in interpreting moral sanctions is double: How conceive of sanctions which effectively control human actions and at the same time allow for moral agents, that is, persons capable of making choices? And secondly, how conceive of sanctions which, although they promote the well-being of persons other than the agent, may promote his well-being only trivially, or not at all, or even negatively? The first pertains essentially to external sanctions; the second, to internal sanctions.

Part of the paradox of sanctions is removed if it is true that one is born into a society of moral relations. On this assumption, the molding forces of a society that constitute its external sanctions are such as to bring new members within its sphere of influence and to perpetuate it. How these factors operate are no doubt very subtle and complex, but the fact itself is no more debatable than that of enculturation itself. No one can grow up in a society without taking over habits and attitudes that can be traced back to its structure. Patterns ranging from the language a person speaks to his attitudes towards love and play, work and leisure, respect or disrespect for authority, habits of eating, moving about, making friends or enemies—these along with countless other ingredients of life are ordinarily taken over with appropriate modifications of personal idioms from the customary patterns of social life. However wide the divergences, they are not such as to conceal the basic patterns which underlie them. And these patterns make it impossible for a person not to have regard in certain respects for other persons.

If, for example, a child grows up in a family, he unavoidably incurs demands made upon him. It may be that he has certain household duties to perform, the performance of which frees him for other activities; or failing this, he is punished in some way. If he is not to grow up as a neurotic, he will know with some precision what these duties are and the circumstances under which he is expected to fulfil them. Again and more precisely directed to his relations with other persons, he will be expected in all probability to maintain certain more or less consistent attitudes to other members of the family, more or less amiable, respectful, and co-operative. And however subtle or harsh the means used to bring about these attitudes, they are certain to show up in patterned actions that will normally, and at times even at great pain, favor sympathetic understanding of, and willingness to help, other members of the family. Even when there are substitutes for family organization, the relations are never so impersonal as to make sympathy and assistance for another irrelevant.

Cultural patterns, of which family relations are only a part, are systems of actions in which there are reasonable expectations of how a person may fare in acting either in accord with them or contrary to them. Associations of all sorts reinforce a respect for others. Schools, clubs, churches—in short, all kinds of group activities, even gangs—are predicated upon there being common ends in which persons may share, as well as some division of labor for securing these ends. Such division lends itself to the defining of a system of rights and obligations which invariably causes one to have regard for others with whom he is commonly associated. Such a system becomes effective by virtue of the sanctions or rewards which attach to the rights and the disabilities suffered by those who refuse to abide by the correlative obligations. But sanctions essentially external may become internal, so that eventually the system itself comes to be regarded as its own reward and sanction for those who have once become familiar with it. Right and wrong consequently come to be derived from a cultural system and thus, because of the social relations that are involved, one comes to know his obligations as being those of a son, a worker, a club member, a church-goer, a citizen, etc. The very nature of social life requires systems of obligations and thus, formally or informally, recognitions of other persons.

Moreover, these relations guarantee that no culture can in fact be wholly spurious, for, if there were such a culture, the approved ends would be only those of self-seeking and the only effective means of attaining other ends would be through sheerly external compulsion. In such a state of affairs, no agreement on ends would be possible, whereas in actual states the spurious is capable of being overcome in virtue of the potential for agreement even if at the expense of some who may have to forego their personal felicity. If the spurious did not contain elements of the genuine, morality would truly be impossible. Under these circumstances, a spurious culture could not develop into one less spurious, nor *a fortiori* could it develop into a culture more genuine, save by a miracle. This is to say that it requires a miracle to pass from the state of nature to the civil state, unless, as Locke conceived it, morality were already characteristic of the state of nature.

The sanctions of morality are approvals of it, but morality is also capable of being approved because it is approvable—that is, because it makes human beings accountable to others. Cultural life entails responsibilities. Its members, therefore, must accept their responsibilities—that is, they must perform their functions conscientiously. What needs to be explained, on this theory, is not a person's willingness to perform morally sanctioned functions, which are ubiquitous in social life, but rather his rejection of the morally sanctioned ways and his refusal to play a significant part in the life of a culture. Such a person is an egotist, who, through some quirk of circumstance, refuses to accept responsibility. What makes him a curious specimen is not the fact that he seeks felicity, since this is actually beyond his comprehension, but the insistent acclaim for self when there are absolutely no personal qualities that justify such acclaim. As a bully, this character is a case for the psychiatrist, preferably before he seeks through demagoguery to become a dictator of men. Too removed from his world to find his fulfilments in it, too close to it to seek more complete liberation through imaginative reconstruction, the egotist belongs to no world, and unless he awakes from his quixotic dream can only arrogantly tilt windmills.

From the assumption of the functional moral relations within a society, we can come to a way of seeing how external sanctions induce internal sanctions. Being moral in character, the external sanctions induce internal sanctions that partake of the same nature. Since they are moral, the external—and derivatively, the internal —are reasonable, genuine, and approvable. They are reasonable in the ends which are sought; they are genuine in that the persons involved, together with the relations among persons, exhibit integrity; and they are approvable inasmuch as a person conscientiously plays a part which is complemented by others who are equally conscientious in their ways of acting. As the systematic relations become perfected, persons thus act as co-agents in a genuine culture. Aristotle was on the track of this when he asserted that morality is induced by habit. Unfortunately, he found no reasonable way of converting habit into morality save by the addition of the internal sanction of pleasure taken in action. No doubt Aristotle intended pleasure as a sign of the acceptance of morally sanctioned ways. But the sanction itself must be moral and should therefore be traced back, not to individual habit, but to social habit. As institutional form, social habits either have or have not integrity, and thus when imposed upon the young, they are responded to, even by very young infants, as manifesting integrity and therefore acceptable, or as manifesting deceit and therefore unacceptable. The corresponding psychological principles involved are becoming better known day by day. A complete psychological explanation will no doubt reveal the very nature of conscience.

If conscience is the internal sanction of moral actions for

agents who are unable to explain "the rightness" of actions other than that they are just felt to be "right," conscientiousness is the sanction for a more articulate morality, capable of enunciating the ends both feasible and desirable and the corresponding obligatory means, including the "proper" roles to be played by the agents of the moral enterprise. It is this fuller meaning we need to give, I think, to John Stuart Mill's most engaging phrase, "the conscientious feelings of mankind." Although Mill regards the sanction as a feeling, which he further believes to be a sufficient urgency to moral action, he nevertheless insists upon an objective counterpart, the principle of utility, which expresses the good at which the sanction aims. Thus he observes that "the sanction will not exist *in* the mind unless it is believed to have its root out of the mind."[5] Mill is, apparently, on solid ground in making the sanction refer to morality itself and in constituting it itself as moral in the sense that it aims at moral action and not at the non-moral. Extending this to external sanctions as well, we may contend that in a genuine culture the same is true of them as well. In fact, by virtue of this similarity, we may trace the origins (as we have) of the feelings to the relationships which exist in the institutions of a society. Accordingly, the conscientious feelings are an adumbration of the integrity which itself is a characteristic of the authentic institutions of a society.[6]

Upon this emendation of Mill's theory of sanctions, we may now assert that both internal and external sanctions have a profoundly moral character and that both aim at the moral principle of the positive social relation. Thus in the consummation of morality, the feelings lead to appropriate action and the institutions are the veritable embodiment of the moral principle. On the personal side, action is assisted by the development of those habits that exhibit character—that is, conscientious fulfilment of obligations. On the social side, the clash of institutions and the predicament of divided loyalties are a spur to the search for more completely harmonious arrangements of social life. In short, the very forces of social life cry out for imaginative creation of those human relations which are approvable in the lives of the people who are affected by them. This is to say that in a system of obligations, the sanctions which exist *in foro externo* can be safeguarded only by the just distribution of rights and duties. External sanctions without justice are abominations; with justice, they are the translation of human compassion into effective social solidarity.

The question of moral sanctions thus brings us back once more to morality itself, which alone can provide justification for them. But in recurring to the subject from the strategic point of view of its sanctions, we can better observe aspects of morality that may have escaped notice or that have been insufficiently characterized. The topics that give promise of profitable re-examination are the interrelated ones of the means-end continuum, justice, and the sense of wholeness.

It was John Dewey who brought most clearly into focus the means-end continuum as central to moral philosophy. He urged it as an ethical principle; he made it foundational in his theory of values; he observed it as characteristic of the aesthetic process; and at least in some formulations, he employed it as central to his theory of meaning.[7] A notion so extensively used in a particular philosophical outlook is bound to take on various colorations from context to context as well as to be virtually incapable of precise definition, but it need not be hopelessly ambiguous.

Dewey tells us that means and ends are just different ways of looking at the same thing, sometimes in a collective sense, sometimes in a distributive sense. He tells us that the one is not different in principle from the other, but only an intermediary. He tells us that there are no final endings in the world, but only ends-in-view, which eventually become themselves converted into means to further ends. Or again, ends are consequences of which the means are willed actions, ends are conditions for further existential occurrences, ends are processes immediately enjoyed, means are ways of instituting a complete situation, and the like. It would no doubt be wrong to assert identity of meaning throughout the various contexts in which the terms are used, even though it may well be that the meanings in context are sufficiently clear for the purposes of the various analyses for which he employs them. Besides the variety of meanings of the related "means and ends," there is also that of the troubling term "continuum" and its related one, "continuity." Dewey's use of the terms bears no identity with the mathematical use of them. The question is whether they are capable of signifying anything helpful for the purposes of social theory. I shall try to answer this in the affirmative, and in a spirit which I believe is one with Dewey's

Abstractly put, the means-end continuum is important in respect to a theory of ends, a conception of direction, and the nature of the process by which the ends are attained. Ends are, in the first instance, the imaginative projection of goals arising out of past experience. They are the realization of meaningful objects, and as such they have precise identity and being only as they are culminations of antecedent processes. One can project ends insofar as they have some qualitative features, but the real identity of ends is to be found in their outcomes as histories. Ends are endings, not quite intelligible except as there are preceding stages of developments leading up to them, such as when a drama leads up to its climax. Taken by itself and out of context, a climax can be appreciated only as strident fury without drama—that is, at best only as melodrama. Seen by themselves, goals, too, must seem melodramatic and not quite worth all the bother. Success is in itself pompous and not very attractive; health is a little too ruddy; peace is ascetic, like a will-less Madonna in the rose garden; and even amiability seems a little empty-headed. The encapsulated qualitative identities never quite ring true and can be only death-masque copies of a reality lost in the quiescence of vitalities.

Ends are correlatives. The "after" is not remarkable without the "before," and both are shocking in their immediate juxtaposition. The question we cannot silence is, how did they get that way? To the shock of birth, man must become inured—or else. But the shock of birth gives way to the recognition of development, to intermediaries which, taken in their severalty, give rise to increased clarity of ends, as well as to a grasp on life, a sureness, which makes for character. Whatever breadth or narrowness may be included in such a life depends upon the generosity or stinginess of the purposes it contains. The realities of existence make, in general, for breadth, but the tautness of persons often cuts their world down to a size commensurate with their personalities. In any event, the ends are a function of the means, and both are continuous with the relations by which the one shades imperceptibly into the other. Means are ends seen clearly from the point of view of consummatory experience. Ends are means seen obscurely from the point of view of problematical, disjointed experience. The perception of the relation between the two is the mastery of meanings such that discontinuity is succeeded by continuity, hesitancy and frustration by certainty and fulfilment.

Meaning thus is the process by which means are converted into ends through their continuous redefinition in unimpeded action, the culmination of which makes sense. This is the process of the "funding of meanings," where the preceding is incorporated in the succeeding, as, for example, when the tensions of a drama become clarified through dramatic conflict, ultimately to be resolved in coming to terms with them and in reaching a solution, whether happy, comic, or tragic. In this process, means are not for the sake of ends; they are ends themselves, though always more or less incomplete, even as life itself. But just as the meaning of life is not death, neither is the meaning of means the end; rather it is means-end as long as imagination and desire and understanding are the moving forces within it.

The importance of the hyphen consists, first, in the recognition that consummations are present consummations, that a mature conception of life requires one compact with immediate realization, that unless there is an amalgamation of utility and desirability, life can only vacillate between the poverty of activism and the twaddle of sentimentalism. Dissociate sentiment, action and intelligence, separate attitudes and knowledge, divide all things into facts and values, and the world becomes an abstraction and life trivial. A mind that acts but finds its consummations elsewhere has unbounded faith in the miraculous, but little regard for the connectivities that make man at home in his world. Values are too precious to be put off, even if their worth can be sustained only in the rough and tumble of forces only partly under our control. This recognition of the moving forces marks a second importance of the hyphen. In the meaningful processes of life, we are able to channel these forces; we cannot destroy them. This is why endings are not finalities but, at best, strategic positions from which actions can be converted into new channels; or failing this, we are at the mercy of the shocks which come from the uncontrollable waves of necessity, in which, lacking all control, we can only submerge our being.

Continuity, then, consists precisely in the capacity to redirect actions so that (a) realization is a pervasive fact of human life, and (b) perception of relations makes possible that control of consequences through which realization takes precedence over lethargy and frustration. Continuity is not the imperceptible shading of one action into another. On the contrary, it is more likely to be a matter of bold decision in which incisive choice is made at those junctures of life where redirection is necessary to prevent the rotten growth of unbridled formlessness as well as of the stale monotony of rigid formalism.[8] Between the two is man's opportunity to make human ingenuity transform a world of flux into one of fulfilment—a world, in short, in which culture is the complement of nature.

The relevance of the means-end continuum in social life is in essence that of the processes which spell out a genuine culture. Antiquated, non-functional institutions are just those that mark the defeat of a people who would achieve a meaningful existence. Paying lip-service to forms once vital to their forefathers, a people who hold on to forms grown stale can only weaken their sensibilities to the realities of their own life. Sooner or later, they will find that they will be thwarted to the point of social crisis. Continuity is established when a person may sensitively pass from one aspect of social life to another without experiencing embarrassment, shock, or insult. If, for example, one cannot fit together his religious and his business practices, if a belief in the dignity of labor is belied by onerous and monotonous conditions of work, or if a people in general acclaim their art but denounce their artists, their culture contains critical discontinuities and demands a reconstituting of institutional patterns and thus a redefining of its cultural focus. When it is out of focus, a culture cannot but destroy the sensitivities, blind its members to the actual relations that do hold, and prevent them from undertaking the decisive actions that constitute the means-end continuum. Functions become buried in ritualistic observances; utilities become tawdry means to an end, usually adorned to conceal their poor workmanship; and the society becomes divided into those who serve and those who are served. The resulting unbalance can only leave man frustrated and exhausted—at least until such time as a continuum of means-end can once more be established.

The conclusion we reach is one that cries out for an imperative of moral action. If, as seems to be the case, there are forces in social life which, when they are understood and directed, are transformed into consummatory as well as useful actions, the resulting culture contains the norms by which its highest good can be measured. If again, as seems to be the case, there are natural sanctions, external and internal, which make it possible to channel actions towards the more genuine, rather than the less, then, by responding positively to these sanctions, the likelihood of achieving the more genuine is increased. And finally, if, as seems to be the case, the genuine is a culture which realizes the means-end continuum and brings about a balance of functions within a culture, there appears to be a law of justice which would apportion obligations in a way that makes social life inherently significant.

The imperative required is one which promotes continuities throughout social life. Its end is to minimize dogma, tradition, and vested interest; and to maximize knowledge, beauty, and utility. Such an imperative may be phrased, "Seek that just distribution of functions and fulfilments that maximizes the sense of the wholeness of things." Morality is a matter of establishing right relations of persons within a culture. Both personal and inter-personal factors enter into the moral situation, and a lop-sided theory of ethics results from ignoring either, as well as from a failure to relate them in a context that makes each complementary to the other.

On the personal side, there is the crucial consideration of a person's talents, potential and actual. There are, of course, minimal talents without which one cannot even act as a person among persons. Imbeciles and idiots would be recognized in practically every society as incapable of effective social intercourse, and morons capable only to a minor degree.[9] Not merely a degree of intelligence, memory, and imagination, along with at least most

117

of the perceptual faculties, but also capacities to move about, carry on the vital functions, enjoy some minimum of good health, and be able to enter into communication, would appear to be indispensable to anyone's participating in social, and therefore in moral, life. Beyond these elementary qualifications, there exists an endless range of capacities and talents from the ordinary to the extraordinary, from the necessary to the trivial, and from the ridiculous to the sublime.

It is fatal to moral theory either to fail to recognize individual capacities and the extent to which they differ from person to person or to apotheosize them to the point of making them the supreme concern of all action. In the one case, a reduction occurs, as, for example, when men are regarded as "hands" and are treated according as they perform just those services. Such reduction makes for a conception of the masses which is blinded to the capacities of men for making moral decisions or in being moved in any way but through external forces, especially through economic sanctions. Invariably it leads to an authoritarian conception of society. In the other case, individual capacities are so prized as to make impossible anything but *prima donnas,* who in their preciosities are incapable of discovering common ground for social life. This kind of individualism is so complete that it leads to vacuous conceptions of both personality and of society. One who adopts this point of view insists upon the development of all of a person's talents. But this insistence is actually preposterous, since it would signify the development of an infinite number of talents. Nor does it aid our understanding of human talents or of human personality to move to the further insistence upon the infinite worth of personality. In the first case of developing talents, the theory is impotent as a guide to practical action, since (a) no clues are provided for a point of attack, (b) the development of certain talents would be mutually self-defeating, and (c) some talents are destructive of either self or society, or sometimes both. In addition, in the case of the infinite worth of personality, by making ends all-important, it leaves no room for means, and renders utility non-operative.

As for interpersonal relations, a theory which requires a man to act from motives of altruism is equally inadequate as one which would require him egoistically to realize his potentialities. Other-mindedness is not just a function of other-regarding impulses. Rather, it is a matter of doing what is believed to be important, whether it is primarily for the agent's welfare or for that of others. Importance is an affair of emphasis and direction, neither of which is supplied by altruism or egoism. In interpersonal relations, it is supplied by the focal elements of a culture, modified and made concrete by the personal dispositions and tempers of mind that form living personalities. In the interplay of institutions and personal choices, there is a meeting of both the cultural and the personal dimensions of social life. The talents which are praiseworthy, and the expression of them in a form satisfactory to those implicated in them, come to be seen in a cultural pattern which cuts across both egoism and altruism. It is compassionate to the extent it is approvable by all who are affected by the agent's actions. Compassion, then, is nothing less than conscientious action undertaken as an integral part of furthering a genuine culture.

Our statement of the imperative of justice may now be seen to reveal an inadequacy of the Marxist formulation of it. Despite the fact that Marx had as a result of his dialectical and historical method as keen an insight into the cultural foci of various societies as any social philosopher has ever displayed, nevertheless, except for the dictatorship of the proletariat, his abstract formulation of it makes the imperative an absolute, out of social context, and consequently insensitive to the particular demands of cultural life. "From each according to his abilities and to each according to his needs" is a momentous insight into the demand for an equation between contributions a person can make to social life and the goods he can in turn receive from it. Implicitly, it takes meaning from an opulent, industrial society, which partakes of, or is a modification of, the capitalistic society from which it evolved. It looks primarily to a factory system of the production of goods and it seeks an equalization in the distribution of products. The modifications are principally those of distribution of products, but the factory system is presumably left intact with only such changes in organization as are involved in the shift from profits to production. In Marxian terminology, this represents a shift from profit seekers to managers, from exploiters to administrative accountants.

Unless "abilities" are construed as contributing to the productive enterprise of the industrial system, and "needs" the goods and services which are its products, both are abstractions and are without definition. Presumably, Marx meant to define them basically in an economic sense inasmuch as he believed the fundamental laws to be economic. If, however, economic laws are only conditions of the attainment of certain ends, rather than determinants of social life, then Marx neither was capable of defining a genuine culture nor of deducing the total consequences of social life from the economic relations alone. From the point of view of authentic culture, Marx may be taken to task for his insistence upon a single strand of social life as its determinant.[10] By virtue of this particular insistence, Marx became all the more effective critic of Western capitalistic societies—and effective to just the degree that the cultural focus has been defined by capitalistic institutions. For in narrowing the focus upon economic life, Western societies have been guilty of virtually making economic determinism into reality and of thus rendering culture spurious. The remedy of this spuriousness is not to be found in the dialectics of economic determinism, of which Marx was indeed a supreme master, but rather in redefining of the focus in order to free human talents from their impoverishment brought about through the unconscionable pressures of economic existence. The ideal of the classless society consequently cannot be defined by the productive enterprise, but rather by the other needs of institutional life as effective means for achieving political, legal, scientific, aesthetic, educational, etc., as well as economic and industrial, modes of the liberation of human talents. The conclusion may actually reveal the necessity of reducing, rather than of expanding, production. At least this point of view frees us from the prejudice of trying to define social necessity in terms of the productive enterprise in almost complete disregard of the nature of the commodities produced. Justice, we should conclude, is not properly defined as a function of industrial abilities and economic needs, but rather, in good Aristotelian fashion, as virtue entire. This ideal will not only lead men to search for equitable relations of rights and duties, but also lead to the freeing of man from the useless, the degrading, and the superfluous that he may achieve in fact utility, dignity, and that husbanding of resources that permits a wide margin of personal undertaking. Otherwise, man is hopelessly bogged down in trivialities and senseless regimentations.

By regarding justice as virtue entire, we are forced to reconsider the ideal of wholeness in which the vocation of man is to achieve a sense of dignity in a society which has integrity. Dignity is itself a matter of completeness, of achieving a oneness of the animal and the human, not by submerging the human, but by making the animal a mode of its expression. Impulses which are animal in origin become converted through human agency into forms socially responsible. Asceticism is embarrassed by bodily functions; vulgarianism is embarrassed by human sensitivities; each is divisive and destructive of human well-being. Although in a theological sense, dignity may be regarded as a gift, in a human sense, it is an achievement, a conquest, which man comes by, and which he may lose.[11] One feels properly insulted to be called half a man or not quite a man. One should feel insulted, because the implication is that one is not a fully responsible agent, and so not a moral being. Yet by disjointing the actions of man into feelings apart from knowledge, and both apart from action, we do in fact make necessary a distinction between objectivity and subjectivity that destroys this conception of morality.

There is much to be said for the Greek view that morality consists in a continuum of beauty in action guided by deliberation and knowledge to the end of the furthering of the life of the community. In this view, the positive element of satisfactions and consummatory acts predominates over a more stringent or puritanical form of ethics. By reason of emphasis on fulfilment, there is sufficient justification to employ the term "morally good" rather than "right" to characterize it. The quality of elegance of action is primary, with that of obligatoriness being derived. This sort of ethic feeds on a humanistic outlook which concentrates upon positive attainment. Its buoyancy results from an excellence which is a function of the balancing of parts to meet the challenges to human disturbance. The more popular mode of value theory reduces to a dreary affair just because it dissipates human wholeness into minutiae and subjectivities in which human excellence becomes no longer intelligible. When, for instance, beauty is regarded as a kind of mute ecstasy in perceiving forms; when action is thought to be an enterprise which is justified by some stated end; when deliberation is conceived of as a species of human cunning, and knowledge a set of propositions confirmable by sense data; and when the community is said to be only an aggregate of individuals, each of whom possesses undisclosable states of consciousness—under this kind of analysis we can see why moral value cannot be believed to be anything very significant. And under these circumstances, we can see how moral theory fails to cope with the urgencies of the day, or of any day. Until moral theory is cast in terms more significant than those of dumb feeling, incommunicable states of consciousness, dissociated actions, and irrelevant knowledge, it will remain in a province of and for professionals.

A somewhat quaint, yet impressive, version of morality was given a nineteenth century formulation by John Ruskin. In *The Two Paths,* Ruskin proposed a theory of morality which, rejecting anything like a moral sense, insisted that man is moral only as his actions display a co-operation of the hand, the head, and the heart. To do, to know, and to feel—these are the ingredients of moral, or we might just say, human fulfilment. This statement is reminiscent of his position earlier formulated in *Modern Painters,* in which he believed greatness in art to depend upon man's capacity to feel deeply and to perceive rightly. Elsewhere he tells us that greatness is a process that calls for "the entire human spirit." When this fails, feeling is morbid because the soul and the body are separated from one another. This morbidity of the emotions brings about what he characteristically calls "the pathetic fallacy."[12] I speak of this version of morality as "quaint" simply because he was so wedded to a system of handicraft and so intolerant of the factory that, for example, he not merely loathed the steam-engine but even blinded himself to the possibility of finding a genuine culture in a world of large-scale industry, division of labor, and the corresponding economic activities of man, including, of course, the concept of "the economic man." What Ruskin saw clearly and what can be carried over into a twentieth century reading of morality is not just the wholeness of man but also the "sweeter symmetries of the human soul," which are sustained by the further symmetries of society itself, and which art expresses.

If doing and knowing and feeling are the indispensable ingredients of morality, and if individual morality cannot be dissociated from society, then it is to the latter, to morality "writ large," that we should look in order to find where the greatnesses or weaknesses of society lie and how well individuals can hope to fare in their world. If, as we have suggested, morality is the convergence of doing, knowing, and feeling, then we should ask ourselves, what are the *institutions* like which correspond primarily to these human characteristics? The macro-institutions which pertain to the first two are clear, and they do indeed provide some clues as to the special character of morality in the modern world.

Technology is the genuine mid-point between knowing and doing. Its translation, however grating to the ear, as "know-how" is semantically quite correct. There can be no doubt that in our society is the closest wedding of knowledge and practice, of science and industry. Despite popular, current criticisms, the development of the sciences—certainly of the physical and the biological—have exceeded the wildest dreams of what a generation or, say, two generations ago scientists thought possible. Their constantly increasing knowledge of both micro- and macro-physics is literally bewildering. Much the same is true of both the studies of heredity and those of biological growth, as well as of the cross-disciplinary studies between biology and physics and between biology and chemistry. Whether the process of significant new discoveries will continue indefinitely or whether, as some have suggested,[13] the "end of science" is in sight in the sense that its principal theoretical formulations are not likely to yield to terms much simpler than those now being employed, the fact remains that we know how to go about getting knowledge and we know the kind of inquiries we must engage in to discover more about our world.

Although science and technology modify industry, and it in turn modifies them, we may with some caution nevertheless consider it as having a quasi-independence. Production of goods in contemporary industrial society is scarcely less impressive than the genius which underlies it, science; and the share of external rewards that go to its organizers is the greatest of all—both in prestige and in material remuneration. Industrial societies have proved themselves capable of providing for every material want a man can have—and even for many that he doesn't have. Material hardships can be reduced to the barest minimum, and poverty itself need extend no farther than to a small margin which for a variety of reasons cannot readily be included in the ambit of the industrial world.[14] What we have seen come about is a complex of science-technology-industry that makes it scandalous not to satisfy the necessary material wants or to provide the necessary public services of virtually everyone living in the industrial world.[15] I am not suggesting that the scandals do not exist, but that, when they do, it is just because of knowledge and the genius that can render it effective that they are scandalous. Also, I am not suggesting that in rendering genius effective, an industrial world will not make mistakes. On the contrary, mistakes, often serious ones, are inevitable; but part of the genius consists, as we have already had occasion to note, in the ability to correct mistakes.

The natural question is, since it is not knowledge and its possibilities for application that render genius ineffective, what is responsible for the failure to utilize it satisfactorily? According to some theories of practical life, knowledge is a sufficient principle of moral action. On the theory advocated here, there is a third term to be taken into account, which must also accord with knowledge and practice: feeling or sentiment. Theory suggests that we should examine this factor of social life in order to learn whether it may be responsible for a failure of "the sweeter symmetries of the human soul." In a later context, I wish to discuss some of the details of the application of this principle. At present, it suffices to indicate the principles involved and what may be expected when they are violated. The general categories that are appropriate are science as the institutional embodiment of knowledge or the intellect, industry as that of action or practice, and the arts as that of feeling or sentiment. What our theory calls for is the recognition of the need for harmoniously interrelating all three, such that the character of each is modified by the others. It was, of course, John Dewey who in modern theory was most insistent upon the urgency for preserving the continuity of knowledge and action. His often-quoted statement about "applied science" being more truly knowledge than what is "conventionally called pure science" rests upon the principle that the former "is directly concerned with not just instrumentalities, but instrumentalities at work in effecting modifications of existence in behalf of conclusions that are reflectively preferred."[16] It may be further suggested, as Dewey and others have, that what stunts the development of science is not any contamination with industry as such but only with that industry which is itself stunted by special interest groups who conduct it in the distorted light of partial benefits instead of in the fuller illumination of more inclusive ones.

Unless there is a suppressed premise, the mutual liberation of both science and industry through a more effective technology does not entirely cope with the moral problem. The suppressed premise contains the aesthetic dimension, so indispensable to the good life. Science is sometimes thought to possess this—in the elegance of its methods and the economy of cutting through myriads of data in the precise statement of scientific law. Industry, too, is sometimes thought to possess this—in its symmetry of organization and economies of effort in bringing to man commodities with gleaming qualities. Finally, technology may be regarded as partaking of the aesthetic—in the balanced harmony of theoretical elaboration and practical anticipation, made in the image of the eternal idea on the drafting board of the engineer. There is in all of this a viable element: the practical arts which gain, rather than lose, by the excellence of honesty in merely being functional. Functionalism is not to be easily waved aside, even in view of all the weighty semantic objections that have been pressed against it. Honesty, and the whole-hearted acceptance it involves, can have a sobering effect upon industrial life, including the kind of workmanship that enters into it. Because of its necessarily close kinship with both theory and practice, a case for functionalism in the practical arts looks as if it were in the strongest position of all. What more can one ask for than production theoretically grounded, practically effective, and emotionally satisfying? No doubt, something like this is the indispensable formula of practice in a genuine industrial culture. In the contemporary world we may very well be on the verge of making it into a reality.

There is, however, a further institutional aspect of the arts, that is, the fine arts as opposed to the practical arts. One may suggest that the former constitute a kind of anomaly, that they follow a pattern of specialization, which is precisely what makes our culture divisive and spurious, and that the sooner we come to realize the arts as the elegance of our utilities rather than of the refinements of life, the better off we will be as human beings.[17] The fine arts may or may not be somewhat moribund, but at least *rigor mortis* has not yet set in. Nor is it likely that this ever will happen, however jaded the arts may become. Song, music, the lyrical, poetry and the episodic, the dance, the human figure, representations in wood, stone, paint, and textures of every sort— these cannot but charm the senses and titillate the imagination, whether or not they are capable of enlightening or profoundly moving us. There are phases of the fine arts which bring out mostly their eccentricities and which cultivate subjectivities out of all proportion to the realities of the world, save as they indirectly underscore the crises of life. It may be that we are presently undergoing one of these crises in which, to use an expression from David Daiches, we have no "common symbols" in the arts by which we may richly communicate with our fellow men. Shortcomings such as these are not necessarily permanent, and artists may yet come to see their task, not as an ornamentation of life, or even as a supplement to it, but rather as a genuine complement which gives meaning to what would otherwise be senseless activity, busyness, and emptiness. That the arts have from time to time played such a role is indisputable. That they might again play it is another of those questions pertaining to the potential genius of a society committed to an industrial technology.

The retribution visited upon a society that fails to realize its genius is inexorable: its knowledge is foreshortened, its action without adequate guidance, and its enjoyments "the tickling and fanning of the soul's sleep." As has been often pointed out, its insistence upon a purity of knowledge leads invariably to an ideal of contemplative life shut off from the vulgarities of the surrounding world. But, and this is the paradox, the surrounding world is necessarily vulgar because it has to rely either on activity itself as its own end (work for work's sake, or production for production's sake) or on improperly related ends (work for remuneration, or production to avoid unemployment, etc.). A utility whose ends are not clear is a senseless thing and a waste, if not brutalizing. The search for ends apart from the contaminating world then may find itself in the foreshortened knowledge, which constitutes the contemplative ideal, or in the subjectivity of an escapist art, whose principles make it virtually impossible to distinguish between opiates and aesthetic enjoyment. The concrete ways in which these various dissociations manifest themselves are nothing less than the inevitable sanctions which man incurs in failing to respect the continuities between nature and his own nature.

It is not the fashion today to picture utopias.[18] There is good reason not to. The magnitude and intricacies of contemporary science-technology-industry, together with the subtleties of their interrelations, require an incredible genius to paint a suitable utopia. Our more modest conclusion leads us to principles and processes, rather than to the more complete blueprint and specifications for the construction of the new society. The principles are only those that recognize the necessity for constantly making the various institutions of society responsive to the relative needs of one another in accordance with a generous cultural focus that respects the range of human urgencies, intellectual, practical, and emotional. They will, moreover, be concerned with reciprocal fructifications of these urgencies, without belittling or starving them. The principles, then, may be formulated as the necessity for constantly re-establishing the means-end continuum, for abiding by the imperative to justice, including its implications for both dispassionate and compassionate action, and, finally, for achieving withal that inclusive wholeness of life in which the personal and the social are recognized as reciprocal aspects of human realization. The processes by which these principles are made concrete are just the civilizing processes at work; their strategy is immanent criticism made effective in human life.

There remains a further question which may be thought to constitute the *coup de grace* of the conclusion stated above. Who, it may be asked, makes the decisions by which these ends are realized? In view of the vagueness traceable especially to the use of the passive voice in many of our statements, the question is justified; and unless some reasonable answer is supplied, the question may be regarded as delivering the final *coup*. I turn to a consideration of what may constitute a satisfactory answer.

Part of the question turns on the implied assumption that only individuals can choose and consequently make decisions. The implied criticism then seems to take some such form as the following: Society is not an agent but an aggregate of individuals. A society, therefore, cannot as such make decisions, but only the individuals who constitute it. The choices that are made are done so on the basis of individual prepossessions, for which we can never fully account; and to the extent to which we can account for them, they are the expressions of personal desires and aim at personal fulfilments. They express, consequently, a kind of personal utility, even though there are obvious cases in which the utility affects others and may under appropriate circumstances further their utilities as well. "Social action," it may then be concluded, is in essence nothing more than a limited and derivative agreement as the result of common purposes and postulates.[19] It should perhaps be added that these purposes and postulates are limited and derivative in part because they are contingent upon similarities of circumstances, physical, biological, and psychological, and in part just gratuitously similar.

The argument, which seems so formidable at the outset, actually outdoes itself. Commencing as it does with a healthy skepticism and a buoyant principle of sheer contingency or arbitrariness of action, it ends up having to account for those agreements on common ends which provide at least some verisimilitude to social life. We do well, however, not to accept the cheap, dialectical victory of the argument and not to commend ourselves upon recognizing the self-contradictory conclusion to which it finally leads. This is too easy a victory when we observe what goes into decisions and how they are made either by particular persons or not at all. But although we do observe this, we are still entitled to observe the crucial factor in the analysis of the existence of common purposes. From this we may be able to discern the common ground which makes them effective.

Let us grant that every decision that is made is made by an individual. Hence, if there are "common decisions," these are such as can be made only by a number of persons in their severalty. Even though we assume that only individuals make decisions, there is nevertheless a distinction to be drawn between decisions that are public and those that are personal. A public decision is one which a person makes as an agent of a public institution—that is, one which is formally recognized as pertaining to the general welfare. Usually, he will act as an agent of government, but it may be, under certain circumstances, of a church (when official cognizance is taken of it, as in a theocracy), of a family as, for example, a parent who may be held officially responsible for his children's conduct), or of any other institution which has official, or perhaps even quasi-official, responsibility for his actions. Or, simply put, an act is public whenever it is subject to legal sanctions. Any other decision is personal.[20] Personal decisions may have consequences, and even important ones for others, but insofar as the sanctions are unofficial or non-legal, they may better be regarded as falling outside the realm of the public. What is especially relevant in this distinction is the sense in which all public decisions *essentially* involve common grounds for the expression of common purposes. Our discussion of the general welfare need not be repeated except to observe that welfare functions may apply in either a distributive or a collective sense or both. Postal rates are primarily an example of the first, the common defense primarily of the second, and education of both. The public does not manage the post office or the army or the schools, although decisions made by the public agent may reflect a consensus of opinion gained through referenda, or other statistical means, or, on occasions, just through the agent's own intuitions. That an agent can make decisions is clear. What may not be so clear, and what I wish to discuss presently, is how or in what sense there may be said to be "consent" of the people and how, accordingly, the public agent may be said to be responsible to the people.

As for personal decisions, they too may express, even if unofficially, common purposes resting on common grounds. The chief differences are, first, the kind of sanctions they involve, and second, their relation to the well-being of a people. The actions being informal and unofficial, the social sanctions, too, are informal and unofficial—relying as they do upon the initiative and responses of other persons. The sanctions may be absent, mild and inconsequential, or disastrous, depending upon a multitude of factors not readily foreseeable; but they, too, can be interpreted also as individual reactions to a single person's conduct. Official actions by agents of the public are always intended to be for the general welfare. This constitutes their *raison d'etre*. Personal actions may or may not be for the well-being of either the agent himself or anyone else. There is always a moral sanction that it should promote well-being, even though there are no official sanctions that apply to it.[21] The difference between personal and public may be seen as differences of formal organization for carrying out purposes and for the differences in justifications of them. These are important differences, but they are not such as to make implausible either the making of decisions or the assessing of responsibilities. Social action may be difficult to analyze and its agents not always easy to spot, yet there are in it no intrinsically impossible answers to the questions, who acts? or how are we to understand that conjoint activity by which massive social effects take place? The passive voice is an evasion only in the sense that in principle there are no insuperable difficulties in maintaining this position, however challenging and difficult actual empirical analysis may be in particular cases.

In discussing the nature of external sanctions, I attempted to show what the common grounds are for realizing common purposes. The fact that the patterned actions of persons that constitute the institutions of a society clash is sufficient reason for many persons to seek to reorient their actions in more satisfactory ways, for it is they individually that suffer from the clashes. Newly created patterns may come about through "consensus," through external force, or through planning that may involve consensus, force, or both. These various processes of patterning are somewhat known to the social scientists. Taking the clue from this kind of knowledge, we do better to look to the processes and principles by which cultures become more genuine than to try to evolve utopian states, which, in truth, can have no more solid grounding than what derives from the processes themselves. The principles of utopia are in reality no different from those of a genuine culture—the establishment of a seamless web in which institutions harmonize with other institutions and none of them seriously thwarts the range of the intellectual, practical, and emotional needs of man, but on the contrary each assists him in bringing about a synthesis which provides the maximum of liberation consistent with the principle of justice. A grounded utopia, in other words, will be that concatenated pattern of institutions which satisfies the social needs of man, as well as encouraging meaningful individual pursuits fulfilled in personal felicity.

The burden of our discussion has been to find the meeting of social life and moral principles. The embodiment of such principles is a process of satisfying the demands of social intercourse. It includes the indispensable utilities and it does so in a way that makes the undertakings sensible and equitable and confers upon them an integrity which comes from continuity and fulfilment. An undertaking is sensible when it answers a felt need; it is equitable when the tasks are shared according to principles of fair play, honesty, and respect for persons (of their capacities and limitations); it has integrity as it fits in with the totality of sensible actions such that fulfilment rather than frustration is the rule. Anything short of this constitutes a deficiency, which, unless it is overcome, invalidates morality to the degree of that deficiency. Sensible needs may be reduced to a minimum, equity may be strained, and social fulfilment enjoyed at a low level, but in each case there is a point below which society becomes dissolute and morality inoperative. Moral principles may be abstracted from the whole, but to identify morality itself with anything less than the functional whole is to abstract supervenient qualities from what sustains them and gives them substance.

How these principles may be applied to various aspects of life, and what difference they make to life, remains the basic challenge. The challenge belongs, however, to a culture, not to an individual. For although it is the individual who participates in a culture and who alone makes decisions, institutional patterns are the result of the conduct of large numbers of persons and of a vast number of decisions, which by their very nature are such that an individual or a few individuals cannot conclude them for the rest. If they did, the vast majority would not participate in a culture, but would only be subject to it. Under these circumstances, there is doubt whether we should use the term culture in any but a pejorative sense, since the principles of the genuine culture would be inoperative.

The further task which remains is to ascertain what the major types of institutions are that constitute the stuff of a genuine culture. We shall want to know how they may be expected to fare if they are guided by the principles we have now set forth. There is, of course, a grave danger in treating various institutions separately. Yet some separation of treatment is inevitable. What I propose as possibly being the least offensive procedure is that we treat first the institutions which use primarily the language of power, and second those which use primarily the language of expression. By appropriate cautions and by indications at crucial points of reciprocal modifications, I trust that we need not blind ourselves to the need for recognizing the meshing of the institutions of both power and expression, without which a culture cannot but be spurious. To provide direction for the discussion, I shall consider these institutions in the context of the complex industrial societies of our times.

Part Three

The Institutions of Power

"And individual happiness does not only require that men should be free to rise to new positions of comfort and distinction; it also requires that they should be able to lead a life of dignity and culture, whether they rise or not, and that, whatever their position on the economic scale may be, it shall be such as is fit to be occupied by men."

R. H. Tawney,
Equality, p. 112.

Chapter 5

LIBERTY, SPURIOUS AND GENUINE

A SALIENT FACT OF HUMAN EXISTENCE IS THE constantly increasing power that man is capable of exercising over nature, animate and inanimate, and over other human beings, if not always over himself. Every schoolboy knows this to be the case, and he knows that the sources to which this power may be traced are science and technology. Whatever the many problems that science and technology raise, they nevertheless make possible controls over our world that are somewhat bewildering. There is no need to try to detail the various kinds of energy man has discovered, the ways in which they can be converted from one form to another, as well as their effects upon various materials ranging from the inorganic to the organic. In part, this cannot be detailed; in part, it is common knowledge shared by virtually everyone alert to advancing civilization, whether pertaining to invention, means of communication and transportation, instruments of warfare, or to peaceful manufacturing, health, and nutrition.

The burden of our preceding discussion has been to show, not that this "advancing civilization" is any better than earlier forms, but that it carries with it its own kind of responsibilities, which contemporary man must face if he is to achieve a satisfactory kind of existence. It is commonplace that man has lost much through this advancing, impersonal technology—mostly, of course, in the loss of personal relations. He has, in effect, become committed to a mass society. The burning question turns out to be whether it is possible to achieve within it a mass culture, viable, authentic, and satisfying. The balance is one as delicate as ever faced mankind, one which, slightly tipped, can mean destruction or bestial slavery, and in either event, unparalleled suffering. For all its comforts, present-day life is fraught with danger, if not with catastrophe. There is only human intelligence and good will, made even feebler by gross impersonalities in a world committed to hygienic compassion and doctored technology. Under the circumstances, a system of checks and balances may ironically promote the very results they are supposed to prevent.

It is abundantly clear that our predicament is one that presupposes a machine-technology which must be reckoned with in our political economy. The advent of machine-technology gives man an advantage today: the resources at his command are immeasurably increased over yesterday. At the same time, it complicates immeasurably the organization of society which relies upon the use of these resources. Industry grows big, and with it government, too, grows big. He who would destroy big government must also destroy big industry. Since such a course of action is not very appropriate, the obvious alternative is to understand the institutions of power (especially the economic and the political), and to fashion them as far as possible into forms suitable to the human estate.

I do not regard it necessary for our purposes to attempt any elaborate description of machine-technology. What we need to know is something about science and something of the way in which knowledge is built into machines and recording devices so that man can exercise control over the world in which he lives. The first pertains primarily to methodology; the second, to techniques for manipulating forces and bringing about desired results. Precise definition of either one is incredibly difficult, and the results, even when attained, may unfortunately prove to be sterile. Yet some characterization of each of them, together with some of the interconnections, is called for.

Science has two rather opposed characteristics which make it difficult to be simply defined. In its modern form, it is ineradically empirical in its content; but at the same time, it is systematic and organized in its form. Sometimes the empirical element seems to dominate; sometimes the systematic; but except in a purely mathematical science, both must be present to some degree. An adequate account of empirical science needs to supply a satisfactory answer to one of the most perplexing of all questions:

How arrive at dependable correlations of events? Or, to phrase it in a somewhat different form, how make predictions of a precise nature? The underlying problem is commonly thought of as that of induction, and in essence it relates to the difficulties of asserting, without begging the question, what future occurrences will be on the basis of past observations. Although the disputants in the controversy have no authentic doubts about the efficacy of scientific knowledge, they are nevertheless as far apart philosophically as extreme skepticism, on the one hand, and extreme dogmatism, on the other—with a variety of theories of conventionalism and modified realism in between. With such an array of qualified disputants, we shall fare better by leaving the problem to them and by assuming with them, as practical persons rather than as philosophers, that the results of science are sufficiently valid to justify fulsome confidence in its methods.

The awkward questions do, of course, in a sense break out again in any attempt to answer definitely, what *are* the methods of science? We seem to be reduced to a position of saying something about science without having an adequate theory of it. Paradoxically, the awkward position may turn out to be the least embarrassing one to take, since its pretensions are not very great and therefore agreement increases proportionately. In this way, we may avoid, without prejudging, the more perplexing questions about the bases of inductive knowledge.

Empirically, science has got far away from "the picture conception of the world." Although knowledge apparently arises from the rough data as they come in crude experience, science does not really arise before the discoveries of less obvious similarities, like those, for example, of the burning of a candle and the rusting of a nail. It is, moreover, a fortunate fact that once noted, similarities can usually be confirmed by those who are endowed with only a moderate intelligence which they are willing to use in following the explicitly stated techniques of checking experiments. Although the methods of science may be passed on from one generation to another, this is not to suggest that moderate intelligence is enough to advance science in important ways. In truth, the more radical discoveries appear to involve ingenuity and indirect methods that belong essentially to genius. Genius then becomes commonplace as its disclosures become "obvious" to those not ingenious enough to have made the discoveries themselves.

There is, however, one advantage in regarding science as employing "the picture conception." That is the advantage of analogical reasoning in which a segment of the world is thought to correspond to a model. The model being complex, the mind, ranging over its relations, attributes similar complexities to nature. Clearly, there is no necessity that the two should correspond at all, or even that if they do correspond in some respects that they should correspond in others. There is, however, the ready occurrence of suggestions for looking for parallels between the two. And perhaps even more important is the inevitable belief that events occur in contexts. To the extent that this belief is correct, we may fruitfully employ reason to explore these contexts and to rely upon unifying concepts instead of being forced to regard science as a totality of descriptive statements or presences of events. For example, we could, with Kepler, attribute elliptical motions to planets instead of just dating their successive positions. The economy of this sort of assertion and prediction goes far beyond direct observations. And the systematization that results makes a theory of predictions more plausible, although by no means infallible, for the assumptions entail consequences which must be true if the assumptions themselves are true. Occurrences thus can be better understood, and for similar reasons technology may be more clearly understood.

If there is a difference between science and technology, surely it is the difference between theoretical formulations and practical applications. And if we wish to hold with a current view, we may assert the difference to be one of emphasis rather than of kind. The weaker distinction is strong enough and has the virtue of allowing to knowledge an element of manipulation as well as one of intellectual comprehension. If we regard the inductions of science as being abstract formulations of guides to action, the genius of manipulation can still carry over into its discipline the power of organized theory. Its fundamental technique can thus be thought of as the creation of contrivances which are the embodiment, and therefore the test, of science-at-work. And the work is literally the conversion of forces to bring about intended effects. The genius is thus the double one of actually making the devices and, in case of failure, of having to decide whether it is traceable to the device itself or to a faulty knowledge of principles which are supposed to be embodied in it. For these reasons, one can justly say that in a superlative degree technology is the meeting of theory and practice.

Surely, however, it is a mistake to confuse the two aspects of knowledge, or to try to assimilate one to the other. Both the formal part of knowledge by which the intellect moves by necessary steps from one part of a system to another and the devices by which events are brought into being in specified ways are indispensable to knowledge. Hence, a mathematical realism that attempts to dispense with manipulative techniques is just as much at fault as an operationism that attempts to define concepts through the empirical data which result from actual operational procedures. By its alliance with the abstract, modern technology is capable of achieving power incomparably greater than that which is tied to common sense knowledge and therefore applicable to a much more narrow range of problems.

There is, as we have before had occasion to observe, a sense in which technology is abstract, for, in being midway between science and industry, it partakes of the wider scope of science rather than of the ultra-concreteness of industry. By knowing how to produce consequences, it liberates itself from the more specifically motivated ends of industry and leaves it as a ready resource for effecting a great variety of consequences, of which some particular ones may be regarded as important to realize at some particular juncture in society. It occupies a position of neutrality that industry cannot assume, for whether this knowledge of how to do things is for man's well-being or ill-being or a mixture of the two, it involves human decisions which go far beyond technology itself. Whereas in industry, the decisions are already made and men are committed in its organization to an economy that for better or for worse limits, and therefore gives a clue to, many of the other decisions that they may make.

Through technology and its liberating potential, we have come to see increasingly evident in our day another dimension of science. This is science as institution. Science has content in the gathering together of corroborated statements which supply us actual information of what our world is like. It has method in its way of going about getting reliable information. In addition, it has an institutional base which makes it a regular part of social life. As institution, science can become integral to society, because its methods and the resources for actualizing them are sufficiently understood to incorporate them within public policy. The building of laboratories, the founding of libraries, the training of personnel, the support of expeditions, and even the creation of scientific bureaucracies—all these contribute to science as a going concern in modern industrial societies. Major undertakings in the fields of industry, communications and traffic control, the military, planning and resource development, are unthinkable without an array of experts to seek specific information and to advise in multitudinous ways. The expertise which is the upshot represents a way of thinking about our problems that is as much a part of our lives as fashions in dress, family life, and baseball.

The difference between modern scientific expertise and that of other societies is that it is intellectual to an unprecedented degree. Other societies have been respectful of age for the experience and wisdom it is supposed to carry with it. They have prized muscular dexterity for the handicrafts that require it. And they have accordingly sanctioned virtues that are relevant to the skills and human intercourse of their society. But none of them has, as has modern machine-technology, devoted the serious, sustained, and concerted effort to exploring the forces at work in the world and their conversion into utilizable forms for the promotion of human ends. These results are made possible only as there is a devotion to intellectual pursuits uncontaminated by prejudice, dogma, or conscious obfuscation. The price modern man has had to pay for his commitment to this intellectual pursuit is the ever-increasing degree of impersonality in human relations, an impersonality which paradoxically looks for emotional stability in a world calculated to deprive man of emotional expression because it deprives him to such a great extent of face-to-face relations. I am not suggesting a picture of the scientist impassive and as cold in his interior life as his exterior, white coat. Although his excitement may reach a pitch, the results of his scientific investigations, we are constantly reminded, must nevertheless be judged by their testable content, not by their enjoyable accompaniments.

The scientist may find adequate rewards in work, prestige, and remuneration. So may the engineer, the industrial organizer, and possibly many of the technicians, whether on the side of the engineer or of the organizer. Their intellectual stimulation, their conversation, their sense of power, understanding, and fulfilment all promote a good life. Their kind of society has never quite been known before, and its many elegances can make for an enviable human existence. The grimier picture is in their alter-egos —the life organized by the machine and regimented by the assembly-line. Here the impersonal pursuits stimulate no conversation, they silence; they give no power, they deplete. The tragedy of life is the purification of it, which nevertheless renders helpless its vast dependencies. It promotes understanding of nature while atrophying most men's power to enjoy their work; it produces goods which make communication increasingly tenuous; and mostly it harbors subjectivities in the recesses created by inexorable pressures to an activistic life. These are a new kind of suffering for man. His institutions of power have exercised controls over it. The burning question is, are they capable of liberating man in a way consonant with dignity and morality? We have traced the question back to the complex of science-technology-industry. Can we similarly discover the answer in this same complex? I suspect the immediate answer is, "No," the proximate answer, "Yes," and the more thoughtful answer, "No and Yes." We may as well consider them in turn.

As we read modern political economy, it looks as if man's deepest concerns are with his freedom. From the founders of modern philosophical thought to Rousseau, Kant, Hegel, Dewey, and Jean-Paul Sartre, the emphasis has been upon the liberation of man. The concern is not a simple one, for we want to know *from* what shall man be freed and *for* what. Unless we are reasonably precise about the objects of these two prepositions, our conceptions are likely to be rhetorical or otiose, and in any event unclear. Freedom has meant so many different things that it seems advisable to note something of the range of the concept before concentrating on that which is most appropriate to the conception of morality already developed. Besides this "moral theory of freedom," there is that which may be called "dreadful freedom" and that which may be called "felicific freedom."

"Dreadful freedom" has been most elaborately explored in existentialist philosophy. The existentialists have sought to clarify their conception of man and his ineradicable alienation from the world of existences. His is an essential kind of being, and, although his external life is constantly entangled with existences, he can and must extricate himself from the external, the unintelligible, the "in-itself," and contend with the "for-itself." Man's essential nature cannot even be suggested without this distinction, which in Sartre's phraseology is the distinction between being and nothingness. Being is composed of those existences which are the "facts" of experience, the dumb givenness of things, their materiality, to which we become inured. Although man is confronted with being, he is also concerned with change, alteration, or the bringing about of new effects in the world. Consciousness gives him a prevision of what this world might be. "Might be"—this is non-existence or "nothingness," which can come into being only through a "nihilation" of that which previously existed. The new, in turn, becomes a subsequent existent.[1]

Man's freedom is observable as a struggle between being and nothingness. It is "a pure wrenching away from himself and the world," the condition through which he possesses "the permanent possibility of this [nihilating] rupture" with the world.[2] Thus, man is able to escape existence by constantly realizing his essence. Existence is determinate; it is capable of being characterized; it precedes essence. Essence, on the other hand, is uncharacterizable, nameless, anonymous. It is intentional act, and, although acts are preceded by motives and are interrelated with causal sequences, they are neither determinable by them nor definable in terms of them. "I am," says Sartre, "condemned to be free."[3] This it is that we may speak of as the *dreadful* freedom.[4] It cannot rely on precedent; it cannot rely upon others; it can only surge up from the depths of man himself. Recognizing consequences, this freedom cannot be validated by consequences nor indeed confined to any existences whatsoever. Little wonder, then, that it is the mark of pure anguish in man—a search for the unknown or, in Jaspers' terms, for "the nameless."[5]

Being an ultimate in existentialism, freedom is not formally definable. Any criticism of it runs into the difficulties, not only of illusiveness within a single philosopher's writings, but also of the variations from one to another. For these reasons, there is serious question whether any good at all can come of criticism of the concept. Yet since there does appear to lurk some common elements in the principal versions, critical discussion of them can have the virtue of defining more clearly our own position, even at the expense of possibly unwarranted blanket criticism, part of which may even conceal similarities between it and our own position.

A major strength in existentialist philosophy, and probably that from which much of its appeal stems, is its tenacious insistence upon disclosing the dilemmas of the human condition, together with all its anxieties, and upon resolutely condemning the realm of the trivial to that of triviality. Looking to the depths of intentional acts, to the inevitable choices that man cannot surrender, since surrender is itself a choice, and to the cruciality of consciousness, the existentialist cannot but find arid the busy world of gathering information and of regarding superfluities as if they somehow contained the essence of human life. Theirs is a heroic world in which only man is responsible for his condition, not science, not technology, not impersonal forces, not even the subjectivities of emotional life. Freedom is an ultimate; exercising it, man constantly stands on the brink of the unknown, of the unnamable. His is a life of anguish. He and he alone makes himself, whatever that self turns out to be. If a mass society appears to be one which cultivates the average and the commonplace, it is not because man is average or commonplace, but that he chooses, whether from envy, the carnal pleasures, or what-not. And in so choosing, he acts in "bad faith"—that is, with an intent to deceive himself. The man of authenticity—and in an important sense all men are such—knows that he cannot deceive himself. His impulsion is therefore to make his life for himself; not in the image of others.

A man's freedom consists sheerly in his own transcendence of his own present. Others can neither support nor direct his own freedom into channels of their wish. One's knowledge of another is, at least in Sartre's formulation of the theme, knowledge of bodies, knowledge of them as objects. Their consciousness, and consequently their freedom, ever flees me. He insists that "I shall never touch the Other save in his being-as-object. I shall never be able to accomplish anything except to furnish his freedom with occasions to manifest itself without my ever succeeding in increasing it or diminishing it, in directing it or in getting hold of it."[6] Associations among persons, then, come from oppositions, from "the look that transcends the look." "The look" makes another into a body. It makes him regard himself as he appears to my look, which is, so far, destructive of his own consciousness. Sartre concludes that the essence of the social relation consists in conflict and that its norm expressed in sexual terms is "sadistic-masochistic," unfortunately a relation in which consciousness never meets consciousness, but only body, in all its varieties of shame, pride, fear, conquest, and slavery. Only in an attenuated sense do persons regard themselves as belonging to a community of subjects—namely, when there is a third subject which threatens the others and creates for them a "we-community." The experience of the "we," however, is said to be psychological, not ontological.[7] The sense of solidarity derives from the threat which comes from the image of an alien third person. Accordingly, class consciousness requires an oppressor class to account for a class of the oppressed.

What appears so attractive in this view is, I think, the genius of a dialectical criticism that exploits freedom *from*. The stupidities of life, the contradictorinesses, the banalities—in short, the spuriousness of it—these are explored with consummate skill, both in existentialist philosophy and in existentialist literature. The existentialist possesses a rare ear for detecting the various reductions of human pathos to naturalistic noisiness. Freedom is man's capacity to escape from what is inhuman and factitious, no matter what the external circumstances may be. Human assertion lies inescapably with man. He can therefore always free himself from what is beneath the human estate.

"Freedom from" rings clear in this philosophy, but "freedom

for" is annihilated in the sound-proofing of the nameless, the characterless. Freedom without realization is an empty thing, a vacuity. In Sartre this becomes a thoroughgoing nihilism. Although I certainly do not rule out nihilism, a freedom which has it for its outcome deserves at least the adjective "dreadful," and, probably better, we should not call it freedom at all, but just leave the activity to die out in the "anguish" from which it cannot be dissociated. In regard to Jaspers' form of existentialism, this criticism should be toned down, but is not, I think, entirely ill-conceived. His Godhead, his "nameless powers" provide a less nihilistic point of view, but, like the Kierkegaardian spiritualism to which it is akin, it so removes the ineffable from anything knowable that its supreme act of faith cannot be grounded in anything intelligible. To ask man to seek his freedom in this is to ask him to turn his back upon all the human powers that have been traditionally associated with human freedom—reason and the cognitive powers of man, imagination, memory, and the power which comes from human understanding and the covenants of men, not to speak of their power over things.

If the existentialist becomes somewhat inarticulate concerning "freedom for," he is simply blinded to the freedom that derives from the agreements among men. He has apparently no comprehension of how a "meeting of minds" may come about, whether it is of the untutored variety of sympathetic understandings which persons arrive at through conversation and intercourse or of the more sophisticated forms of communication and expressions which are characteristic of the sciences and of the fine arts. This kind of liberation can never be found in philosophical analyses so devoted to the inner recesses of the inner consciousness that they are congenitally incapable of recognizing either a ground for the existence of other minds or the ability to arrive at fundamental agreement.

The existentialist has thrown the searchlight on recesses of consciousness too little investigated by philosophy. But in doing so, he has neglected to illuminate varieties of the consciousness which thrive less on conflict than on a community of ends. Sartre, for one, emphasizes a point of view in which the individual constantly struggles "to appropriate" another's freedom—this in contrast to, say, Rousseau's advocacy of the increment of freedom that persons can enjoy by cultivating together the peaceful arts. For the former, the cafe waiter is a function. He is, the author says, "nothing but the function of serving the patrons." This is preposterous. Even though I may regard the waiter in this light, clearly my judgment is more a commentary on my own limitations than on the objective facts. The egocentrism that Sartre suggests here is even more starkly expressed in his essay on *The Republic of Silence*. In suggesting that "total responsibility in total solitude" is the very conception of liberty, he asks that we forsake the community as the locus of men's liberation and that, instead, we cultivate the austerities of withdrawal and solitude. Man needs a measure of solitude, to be sure. Even Alfred North Whitehead, in defining religion as what man does with his solitariness, nevertheless insists that religion cannot come to fulfilment until man leaves his solitariness and returns to society. To fail to see that the life of aloofness is a truncated version of human life is to fail to recognize what I should regard as an elementary truth.

The more interesting question, I think, is that which asks, what are the truly productive relations between solitude and society? Karl Jaspers comes closer to recognizing a need for man's participating in a world of fellow men. But even his version falls short of a human ideal. He writes: "Participation in the community of interests and of labor of all those who pursue the same occupation or practice the same means of earning a livelihood, a participation that will safeguard one's own life subject to externally imposed purposes and conditions, is now unavoidable." This participation, however, is not one of *com*passion. And even the tenderness which he urges for the teacher or the father is not one of compassion, but rather of avoiding the cruelty of snatching "the ground from under the feet of others without showing them the ground on which he himself stands."[8] For all its devotion to the super-reality, the essential egotism of this point of view is one which makes freedom so much an affair of inner preciousness it misses the obvious freedoms of a common humanity. And it regards inevitably their commonalty from a superior standpoint, degrading it at the same time it upgrades itself. And thus, for all its protestations, as well as sincere actual actions by its advocates, for democratic practice, it remains at heart anti-intellectual and predisposed toward an elite form of society. Its anguish and its preciosity render it incapable of being otherwise.

In contrast to the elite form with which dreadful freedom is associated, felicific freedom is historically associated with the birth of bourgeois democracy. It shuns not so much the trivialities of life as it does life's oppressions—and especially those traceable to feudalism and the arbitrary monarchial forms which grew out of it. In a way, it had a strategy for transforming the world to make it conform to the heart's desire and thus to bring about an intimacy between the subjective and the objective that the existentialist regards as suspect. Felicific freedom, at least in its optimistic phase, assumes that man can become the captain of his fate. It assumes, without too much worry about consistency, both that the world is an orderly one and that it responds, under appropriate circumstances, to human intervention. Thus, because it is regarded as being lawful and because specific knowledge of its lawfulness is thought to give one power over its occurrences, there are said to be no ultimate mysteries of life, and he who would assert otherwise simply magnifies his ignorance into an obscurantism that creates mysteries out of his own deficiencies. The matter is well characterized by a member of the old Hippocratic school of medicine in answer to those who believed epilepsy to be an ununderstandable visitation from the gods. This writer answers:

> It seems to me that the disease [epilepsy] is no more divine than any other. It has a natural cause, just as other diseases have. Men think it divine merely because they do not understand it. But if they called everything divine which they do not understand, why, there would be no end of divine things.[9]

There is in this refusal to multiply mysteries a robustness that stems from a belief in the efficacy of knowledge if man is only willing to employ an appropriate strategy.

The Hippocratic belief is one with Bacon's that man is capable of gaining knowledge and that knowledge is power. According to this formulation, knowledge is no mere contemplative act of intuiting some eternal form of reason. On the contrary, it is a product of the manipulation of things, the careful, precise collation of obtainable data, and the gathering up of results in a way that permits them to be comprehended in a relatively simple form. The process is the laborious empirical one of putting questions to nature and of possessing sufficient genius to understand the answers which nature gives. The experiments are of light and are always such as to teach us something about nature and, consequently, to enhance our power. On this view, there cannot but be an intimate connecting link between knowledge and freedom, and that link is to be found in power.

Knowledge is power, it is said. But this is not quite so. In addition to knowledge there must be, besides a capacity to act, both an end towards which action is directed as well as freedom from impediments which would thwart the end. There are, accordingly, in the classical theory of freedom two foci around which discussion most generally revolves: the utilization of natural knowledge and the absence of impediments. These are, of course, the postive and the negative factors with which classical liberalism had to contend in the development of science and technology and in the rejection of outmoded social forms inappropriate to the activities built upon these newer foundations. In a sense, science was the destroyer of the older religion, as the eighteenth century Enlightenment began clearly to reveal.

Although new secular forms of social life were slowly coming into being, the new advocates of freedom were more conscious at first of the impediments to action than they were of what new forms would best promote the liberation of man. Absolute monarchy, the Church, feudalism, the *ancien regime*—these held little promise for liberation. Little wonder was it that the entrenched theological orientation began to shift from the divinity of the Church to the divine right of mankind, however inappropriate the supernatural blessing might be. In this elaborate process there surely was substance in Sir Henry Maine's famous observation that the modern world represents a shift from status to contract. Freedom came more and more to be regarded as the absence of restraining power for man to accumulate property and to enter into contracts at will. Whoever interfered with those processes was regarded as an officious tyrant, the sooner disposed of the better. In the most extreme form of the doctrine, the only impediments consisted in the use of direct force, not even including threats of force, to compel one to act contrary to his will.[10] Otherwise the determination to act lay with the individual to do as he saw fit.

The directive factor in action, according to this view, thus turns out to be the will. Freedom consists in doing whatever one chooses. In this stark form the doctrine is elliptical, since choice, it turns out, is not entirely arbitrary. One chooses to do that which is for his best interest—or, at least, what one regards to be for his best interest. There is—and must be—some hedging on the doctrine. This is suggested by the assumptions that (1) man is a rational being, (2) that he knows best what his own interests are, and (3) even if he doesn't, the only way for him to learn is by making his own mistakes. The Achilles heel is, of course, (3), since, on the one hand, it raises serious doubts as to the extent to which one is rational (besides excluding children who, it is assumed, are not of the age of discretion) and, on the other, actually invites the contradictory principle that, at least in those cases where the consequences of mistakes are likely to be disastrous, supervenient judgments and external interferences are warranted. This consideration suggests à la Rousseau that man may be "forced to be free." Ordinarily, however, the classical doctrine is one in which reason is curiously individual and requires no extra-individual justification other than the assertion of the will itself.

Nevertheless, the external manifestations of the will are to be found in the creation of new relations which implicate revolutionary forms of social life. The political and economic consequences of felicific freedom historically were nothing less than the birth of modern democracy and the extension of capitalism so as to make it the dominant economic feature of the growing industrial world. Freedom of choice came to be regarded as having a sort of ultimacy in the institution of the ballot box and in the representative government which the ballot box was supposed to insure. No excuse, apology, or justification was required in voting for the candidate of one's choice, and the majority vote carried with it the presumption that the will of the majority would become the effective policy of government. Although the political decisions theoretically could be made to serve any purpose whatsoever, the practical matter of fact was that the political decisions gained stability by virtue of widespread agreement on which economic institutions were to be secured. Hence, a reciprocal relation helped to produce further stability in both the political and the economic realm.

The expression in economic terms of the individual will came unmistakably to be the institution of private property and the market in which contracts could be made and exchanges effected. The potency of these new institutions is most easily seen in its rendering the feudal system totally obsolete. Service gives way to accumulation of property, oaths of fealty to contracts and bills of exchange, protection to competition, birthrights to civil rights, fear of death to fear of life, security to happiness, sin to injustice, and other similar changes too numerous to specify. Little wonder is it that the Renaissance should be full of premonitions of a new world and that the Enlightenment should formalize the liberal doctrine which was to free man.

The ultimates which felicific freedom contains consist almost exclusively in maintaining the conditions for freedom of enquiry, including speech, movement, associations, as well as religious beliefs. These were the primary freedoms, which R. H. Tawney, following Lord Beveridge, so nicely distinguishes as constituting principles in contrast to the more narrow and less crucial ones that may better be considered to be expedients or devices.[11] The freedom which is especially prized is the freedom of the mind, for this is indispensable to all other freedoms. To make up one's own mind on the evidence available, and to assume that seldom, if ever, is all the evidence available—this is fundamental. And this is ever opposed to the cant, the obscurantism, the arbitrariness, and the brutalities that some, in their demagogic ways, would substitute for the mentality that appreciates the humane ideal, the heightening and intensification of the spirit. In contrast to the anti-rational activism and mindless oportunism of only half-human impulses, the liberal philosophy urges the cultivation of thoughtfulness, of sensitivity to the myriads of qualities of the world, and of action which is humanly motivated, even in its less austere irresponsibilities. Cant and dogmatism are regarded as a menace to these freedoms.[12]

Felicific freedom is less strident, more hopeful, even if less dramatic, then dreadful freedom. It has also a peaceful quality in making man germane to the world and in finding, although not guarantees, yet real possibilities, of fulfilment in the world of things and men. Many human expectations are regarded as reasonable and capable of achievement without frantic exertion. The ordering of human life can be supported by the order of nature itself, if only man is willing to allow his inherent curiosities to lead him to discover the inexorable laws which reveal the workings of things. The awakening of the intellect, the sharpening of the faculties, the ranging of the imagination—this, along with the fortitude to maintain their integrity, is the equipment man needs to cultivate the good life. Except for those who demand a more heroic and irrational conception of man, this ideal of felicific freedom is apt to attract all who are not muscle bound by lethargy or cynical disillusionment. Yet however attractive the ideal, its flaw has increasingly come to be realized to be an incapacity to cope with a destructive activism, which is opposed only by the counsel that we outsit it. The counsel does, of course, have merit, for to combat the evil, we all too often discover, is to enshrine precisely the evil which is being combatted. Yet, on the other hand, to sit it out while the world is on fire is to counsel a fortitude that only the most resolute can possibly sustain.

What has ironically undermined the liberal philosophy has been the inexorable development and application of a technology which liberalism itself favored. This technology, we have noted, became the co-operative institutionalization of natural knowledge. As institution, it took its toll on persons as it did on the exploitation of nature. In order to make effective use of this knowledge, large-scale production came into being, together with a shift in fact, if not in name, from the personal to the impersonal and from the private to the public. The fruits of industry were no longer to be had by the cultivation of one's own garden, for the corporate form of life was placing its stamp upon every field of activity from manufacturing to finance and from expertise to salesmanship. The world was becoming too complex and knowledge too vast for a single individual to be an effective agent apart from many others, who had somehow to co-operate in a machine-oriented society, even to produce the barest necessities of life. The fiction of free, private enterprise might continue to be the language of business and of the law, but the way business encroached upon every aspect of life from diet to entertainment and from toilet habits to club affiliations, including working and sleeping habits, education, and religion, made it of concern to the common conditions of social existence, and not just to judgments of individual taste. Under the circumstances, co-operative action is prefigured as a means of livelihood itself, and a consciousness of the concerns which unite persons in their common tasks appears to be the only alternative to the default which permits dictatorships to make the public decisions.

Words are easy to express the predicament, but to achieve a result appropriate to the necessities of life and human dignity too creates one of the profound perplexities of contemporary civilization. Without a corporate form of organization, life simply is not possible in a complex industrial world. Even with all his balderdash, Mussolini was for once right in asserting that the twentieth century is the century of the corporate society. But does this imply also uniform dress, concentration camps, castor oil, the silencing of free speech, and the refusal to permit men to search out new truths together with their validating conditions? If this is so, the future of liberalism is nil. What the eighteenth century could enjoy that the twentieth century cannot was an enlarged sense of irresponsibility—since the consequences were wrought mostly on the individual himself. Today this is changed, and irresponsibility means privilege for a few and tyranny for the many.

If technology is the source of this tyranny, economic domination is its immediate manifestation. *Laissez-faire* makes sense when the typical means of production is the job shop. It is sheer folly when, with the advent of the assembly line and increased automation, the typical form of business organization is monopolistic or oligopolistic. When one-fourth of the industrial output of the entire world is the work of 135 corporations,[13] then business is everybody's affair, and political safeguards are required to cope with what would otherwise be economic tyranny. Unless liberalism can devise an appropriate strategy to give an effective voice to the vast majority, freedom will be for no one—including the outspoken liberals who may not even be able to sit it out while the majority is being directed in everything they do, to the last moment of their waking life.

There is no need today to belabor the issue of collectivization, for every industrial society is collective whether we like it or not. The challenging question is really, what can we do to make it responsible and to make it possible for man to act with dignity? Once the question is phrased in these terms, the pressure to re-interpret felicific freedom becomes irresistible. The doctrine was formulated in the face of a tyranny long dead and when commerce and industry were in their infancy and before the consequences of machine-technology could be understood. Felicific freedom was freedom *from* the oppressions of privileged status, stagnation (religious, mental, economic, and social) and the virtual domination by rural oligarchies. It was a freedom *for* independence, mobility (in belief, in thought, and in action) as well as a liberation that could come from urban life with its vast consequences for freeing workmen, expanding commerce, and promoting the cultivation of the intellect.[14] The emphasis on privacy and the almost unrestricted rights of the individual were matched by a profound belief in the social harmony regarded as having its source in centers of initiative. This belief is best expressed philosophically in Leibniz' conception of the way in which each monad mirrors every other monad in the world and thus realizes a pre-established harmony reflecting God's own beneficence.

Appropriate as felicific freedom was for its time, the question is how much of its time was particular and how much universal. Perhaps none of it was truly universal; and perhaps there is in liberalism a basic incapacity for universality, an incapacity which makes it necessary continually to redefine the term. The freedoms from and the freedoms for are matters of time, place, and circumeance. We know tyrannies today, but they are not the tyrannies of yesterday, and likewise with beneficences. When freedom is defined in terms so broad as to fail to capture the relevancies of a time, it does, of course, become a universal, but of a sort which is more of a platitude than of the sort which can supply a key to an understanding of people's loves and hates and the kinds of activities to which they will passionately devote themselves. The closest expression of a true universal in classical liberalism is the freedom to search out truths, to communicate, and to associate freely with persons of one's choice. This freedom appears to be a matter of principle such that exceptions to it need to be justified—justified as constituting exceptions or modifying conditions rather than as undermining the principle of freedom itself. Yet even the freedom of mind, it appears, belongs more to civil societies which are literate and which have leisure to make something of the distinction between knowledge and superstition, and can thus extend the former and curtail the latter. Nevertheless, since making new discoveries is, in a residual sense, always a matter of an individual person, a society which consistently denies these freedoms to persons obviously denies itself the fruits of discoveries as well as of the intellectual ferment which is integral to civilized or moral life.

Felicific freedom becomes suspect today because of the attempt to reduce the many dimensions of freedom into a single one, the freedom to be left alone, as if encouragement (in proper proportions), external conditions of life, preparations for developing intellectual capacities, emoluments of various sorts, and the like, were entirely foreign to freedom. And of especial concern today is the necessity of redirecting freedom *for* into such channels as to maximize the distribution of the freedoms of the many instead of limiting it to those who, either through personal gifts or social arrangements, are capable of restricting the freedoms of others. The twentieth century has rediscovered another dimension of freedom—what we may call the social, or moral, dimension.[15] This realization is one that refuses to accept a definition of freedom which is universal in form but restrictive in fact. It is a realization that education and various social arrangements do in fact exercise considerable influence over the freedoms a person may enjoy. Hence, although felicific freedom promoted the kind of liberation necessary for talented and semi-talented individuals from the oppressive forces of a worn-out culture and for the creation of new secular and religious forms, at the same time it unwittingly came to favor, by virtue of its emphasis on individualism, a new kind of oppression in the creation of economic forms it could not have foreseen. The new institutions of power could bring whole peoples to their knees through the colossus of cor- porations, abetted by the governments under the flag of which they operated. It is an ironical fact that the very corporations which were spawned under the ideology of felicific freedom and became prime beneficiaries under it have themselves been largely responsible for the need for conceiving of freedom in social terms. Where freedom exists in the industrial world today, it is social freedom that has in fact, if not in name, supplanted felicific freedom.

Social freedom, just because it is social, has a moral quality that felicific freedom can have only in an attenuated sense. Felicific freedom is essentially irresponsible, and, even though it is often spoken of as being rational and as pertaining to man's reason, it is basically a freedom which is meant to make a person not ac- countable for his actions. Social freedom is just the contrary.

The crux of the difference between felicific and social freedom consists in the fact that the latter does not share the early opti- mism that private vices are public virtues. Neither the doctrine of the "invisible hand" nor Leibniz' more cosmic doctrine of the "pre-established harmony" is consonant with the economic reali- ties that economists have now for many years already disclosed. And since the Great Depression there is no doubt that classical economic theory requires drastic modification if it is to come even close to revealing the facts of economic life. The alleged automatic mechanisms of the market are apparently outdistanced by the business cycle, and, moreover, the modern temper is not one which permits people quietly to suffer while the mechanisms catch up with lower levels of economic equilibria. However ele- gant the systematizations of the older, pure economic theory, they can no longer fruitfully serve as the model for contemporary economic phenomena.

In the light of the abundant inadequacies of classical eco- nomic theory, the question they raise for our purposes is, then, what are the factors which require the rise of a new theory of freedom? In the broad, it is not difficult to point to them, even though many of their details are extremely puzzling. There are, first, the economico-technological factors and, secondly, the sociomoral factors. The first have been prefigured in our earlier discussion. Modern machine technology requires a meshing of processes from raw materials to finished product. Ordinarily, the organizational processes become increasingly complicated. The efficiency of the processes, however, derives more from the concentrated "rationalization" of them through research and scientific studies than it does through competition. More effective processes of extracting raw materials, simplification of design of the product, efficiency in processing, concern for eliminating fatigue in labor, time and motion studies, expedience in transportation—these can profit directly from the rationalization of industry, whether or not there is an added stimulus of competition. The utilization of science in industry is now commonplace and, it appears, there is no large industry today that does not retain its staff of scientists. Even in small industry it is not surprising to find at least a modest staff of research workers. By virtue of the processes of rationalization, we discover the salient facts of industry today to be constant enlargement of size of plants, ever-increasing magnitude of operations, and consequent multiplication of output.

With the growth of physical plants and output, another noteworthy feature of modern industry is the movement toward monopoly or oligopoly. The virtues and dangers of monopoly have been explored for many years, perhaps becoming best known through Brandeis' work on "the curse of bigness." The "curse" has become an accepted fact of industrial life. The attempts to break up trusts, holding companies, and cartels, mostly rather feeble, have been upon business organization rather than on industry. Working arrangements in industry from raw materials to finished product are too well knit to permit of being atomized. Judging from the lack of effective anti-trust legislation, one may question the extent to which it is feasible to atomize the business operations which are superimposed upon industry. Monopolies do have a way of perpetuating themselves. Is this perpetuation due to some indispensable service which they perform and which would not equally well be performed by some other business arrangement?

The virtues of monopoly are said to be increased production, greater efficiency, and reduction of costs to the consumer. The claims to these virtues may be largely, and possibly even wholly, correct—although they concern empirical matters and cannot be settled by theory alone. Even if they are granted as correct, the student of social theory is forced to observe, however, that with the advent of monopoly, felicific freedom is eliminated from the realities of economic life. This is so because the individual *qua* individual is powerless to compete or bargain with the corporate collosus. Freedom can signify only his sitting it out, which in this case can be only another name for attrition. To the extent to which the individual exists in a world of monopolistic economy, his freedom is limited to resigned acceptance or to self-denying refusal. Except for his inner privacies, he has virtually no power for making over the world to fit his heart's desires, and consequently no very real choice. Freedom can come to him only as he can have a voice in the decisions of the corporate enterprises. Before pursuing this, however, we may better observe a middle ground, not far removed from monopoly, which is said to guarantee freedom of choice, that is, through oligopolistic economy.

Oligopoly, it is sometimes argued, provides an alternative which guarantees choice at the same time it exploits the virtues of large-scale industrial production. Being large scale, it enjoys the efficiencies that are possible where there exists a complete set of industrial operations. In addition, it secures to enterprise the virtues of competition insofar as a corporation cannot far lag behind its competitors without destroying itself. Oligopoly, the conclusion runs, retains the advantages of both quality and quantity without sacrificing either.[16]

The tangled issues involved in the economics of oligopoly are indeed complex. Our purpose is limited, however, to those aspects of oligopoly that bear more or less directly upon the topic of freedom. Freedom has traditionally been associated with competition. But oligopolistic competition such as prevails among industrial giants in the United States today cannot be compared with competition among many small firms each of which is competing for some modest share of the market. As Mr. Berle points out, the hardships suffered when one of these firms goes bankrupt are marginal, and, although not insignificant, they do not nevertheless constitute national disasters. The position of a gigantic corporation stands in a different position, since its bankruptcy and sudden cessation of activities would be nothing less than a national calamity. In reducing hundreds of thousands to a state of unemployment, it would produce social chaos, not marginal hardships. Under the circumstances, it is unthinkable that such an event could occur. Reorganization or nationalization, possibly, but sudden cessation of production, never, except in a conflagration which would destroy modern society itself.

Competition among giants must then mean something quite different from competition among numerous producers, the elimination of some of which would nevertheless leave an economy largely intact. Price wars among the giants are unallowable, for they would produce national calamity. So, the analysis continues, competition must be in quality, in styling, such as to cater to the varying tastes of individuals, without any one oligopolistic corporation reaching the point of ruinous destruction of its competitors, save perhaps as peaceful mergers might occur. The consumer is accordingly able to register his preference in the market by the purchases he makes, and he remains free to choose as he will. His, moreover, is not the only brake placed upon the powers corporations may exercise. Besides the power of consumers upon the policies of corporations, there is also the power of countervailing labor policies, public opinion, and, even more importantly, direct government intervention or the threat of intervention. In the light of these controls, are we not entitled to hold the conclusion that individual freedom is secured under an oligopolistic form of economy?

There is no doubt that a person possessed of an income has a measure of choice in the commodities he purchases in the market. Unfortunately, this option provides no unambiguous conclusion as to man's freedom in the world. If the choice is between x and y and z such that the chrome trim runs horizontally, vertically, or diagonally, or between s and t and u such that the label carries the picture of a man or a woman or a peacock, a person may well wonder whether the choice is not, after all, bootless. Or it may be, as Professor Galbraith has eloquently argued, we are dealing here with a second order of things in which the choices are really trivial. If it is true that in an affluent society basic needs are cared for, then the further choices of goods lack any real vitality and are more likely to confuse man than to aid him in significant decisions.[17] Moreover, if freedom is a matter of making insignificant decisions, it loses all connection with the serious issues of life. Under these circumstances, the advocates of dreadful freedom cannot but gain in numbers to the extent to which thoughtful persons come to regard felicity as depending upon options such as x, y, z or s, t, u, above.

The analysis suggests, however, the desirability of looking more closely into the nature of the economic processes, rather than of flying from them as being alien to man's decisions. Otherwise, there can be only the forceful splitting of man's nature into parts which romanticize one segment of him while making the other neuter and irrelevant. Yet if recent historical inquiry has shown anything, surely it is that the kind of romanticism that prevails in any age is conditioned by the economic system which it accompanies. What is suggested by this connection is that, so far from being neuter and trivial, the economy itself is a potent factor which, whether positive or negative, is nevertheless a substantial ingredient of the kind of life man can lead. This being so, we should expect not that a man's freedom lies in any economy whatsoever, but rather that an economy is but one institution among a number that can either facilitate or hinder his freedom. What then of the potencies of oligopoly for twentieth century freedom?

Freedom under oligopoly is similar to that under monopoly. Consumer choice under the one may be no more effective than under the other. Oligopolistic competitors, it has been suggested, produce goods whose differences are trivial, and that therefore they by no means constitute a basis for man's serious choices. The far-reaching and profound decisions are made at the level of production, not at that of consumption. Moreover, in modern oligopoly the decisions have a stability based, not necessarily on collusion, but on conventional practice.[18]

These practices are such that disaster would result if price competition were in effect. Consequently, oligopolists rarely consider trying to get a corner on the market. Rather, they prefer, according to the theory of games, to try to figure out the decisions their competitors would make under varying conditions in order to maximize their own opportunities.[19] Consequently, the considerations of catering to consumer demand are overshadowed by the considerations of how one's competitors would accordingly counter by catering to his appraisal of consumer demands. The decisions thus have the character of being intercorporate decisions primarily and consumer demand decisions only secondarily. This makes for stability of production, even though its consequences for a viable economy may be less than happy, to the extent even of visiting considerable hardships on vast numbers who are dependent upon the well-being of the economy.

The conclusion is unmistakable. Oligopolistic corporations respond primarily to their oligopolistic counterparts and only secondarily to consumer demand. Thus they employ various devices to induce demand to conform to what is offered to the consumer rather than to accept current demand or to make products conform to a rational demand. This is done under the guise that the consumer is free to choose the commodities he wants under a competitive system, whereas the competition is far more strictly circumscribed than the oligopolistic advocates of "a free economy" are willing to admit. Roughly, it seems, oligopoly partakes of monopoly more than it does of the pure competition. The truth of this is further sustained when we recall that monopoly is never quite absolute. Substitute products are almost invariably available, even though the substitutions may be rather far removed from the commodities which would most appropriately satisfy given demands. The truth of the matter is that there is a scale of systems of economy from pure competition to absolute monopoly, between which lies an infinite variety of mixed economies. In the United States, among the oligopolies that set the policies for basic industries, experience might well prove that they are essentially a variation of monopoly and closer to it than they are to pure competition. If we are correct in regarding oligopolies as variations of monopolies, then the principles that apply to the one apply *mutatis mutandis* to the other. This signifies especially that since the lone individual cannot effectively combat the policies of corporate enterprise, whether monopolistic or oligopolistic, there is need to make those policies responsible ones through the combined strength of individuals in their social capacities, and not just in their personal ones.

To make policies, and the power, of corporations responsible, and not just responsive to oligopolistic forces in the business world, is to arrive at policies that maximize the freedom of the many rather than of the few. This end is achievable if and only if freedom is regarded as objective, corrigible, and rational. Freedom is objective when there are live options which increase men's power to advance the civil state. It is corrigible in that actions which detract from civil life permit nevertheless a return through discussion and criticism to the old option or to a new one which enhances civil life. It is rational in that the aim is constantly to seek new harmonies within institutional life consonant with the urgencies of knowledge, as well as of the practical and fine arts. However much there should be left room for human whimsies, dogged obstinacies, and stubborn regressions, only catastrophe results if these prevail as the guiding policies of a whole society. Education, cultivation of tastes, plus a great tolerance for all kinds of curiosities in the private realm, can promote social freedom where it is most needed—that is, in the public realm of responsible actions. Morality, and therefore moral freedom, may under these circumstances play a role which includes not only the economy but every other major institution within a society. Freedom so conceived will not be tied to the dogmatisms of an economic system, such as felicific freedom historically has been, nor will it invoke the alienation of man from economic life, as dreadful freedom does. Moral freedom is committed to the search for a measure in which man the producer, man the distributor, and man the consumer can express human qualities in these capacities as well as in the more commonly recognized expressional aspects of human life. The conditions of such freedom are those arrangements which permit men to live at peace with themselves and with some dignity in their relations with others.

Social freedom signifies freedom to alter existing social arrangements at any time they become oppressive to large numbers of persons, or even to small numbers when the likelihood is that the new arrangements will not create new oppressions equal to or greater than the old. Almost any change is likely to hurt someone, yet when the net balance appears to be a liberation of the many at the expense of the few, or when the oppressions are traceable to arbitrary and unjustifiable impositions, social wisdom, if not plain decency, calls for appropriate changes. Social freedom is freedom *from* the oppressions of ill-devised or antiquated institutions and it is freedom *for* the creation of those institutions that provide greater liberation for men collectively within the bounds of an authentic culture and distributively so far as it is not destructive of that culture. Any society which consistently silences freedom of discussion and of criticism and prohibits freedom of association thereby removes the conditions for establishing an authentic culture and the kind of power-relations which can sustain it. There is, then, a close connection between freedom and power such that the issues of the one cannot be dissociated from those of the other. Moreover, it becomes increasingly apparent that unless power is exercised for the general welfare freedom is "noble in sound but squalid in result." It behooves us, therefore, to turn our attention to the conditions of power which make it possible for social freedom to be embodied in the very fabric of social life.

Chapter 6

THE POLITICAL DIMENSION

Politics may be defined as the art of the distribution of power. It falls between the appeal to morality and the exercise of force, and partakes of both. It can give concrete expression to profoundly moving human objectives, or it can avoid serious issues and become primarily a theater in which the politician plots to advance himself as far as he can. In rare instances it may combine to a remarkable degree both the serious and the self-interests of politicians. A moral appeal that provides no means for men to carry on with their settled convictions in life is in vain. On the other hand, when the convictions are exploited as a blind for the employment of force to achieve ends that are no part of the convictions, politics dissolves into intrigue at the higher levels and the currying of favor by subordinates at the lower levels. In this case, politics turns into rule by decree, and policy into the organization of forces to execute decrees.

Opposite objections to politics come from the moralist and the activist. The former regards politics as dirty business and politicians as unclean animals motivated by a lust for dealing in self-aggrandizement regardless of the human misery that may result. Cold and calculating, the politician is not supposed to be moved by any appeal to the human sensitivities that will not at the same time promote personal ambition. And even if he were attuned to emotional appeals, the forces of politics would only remove him from the scene in order that less susceptible men may take his place. The activist's objections see the politician, not as a strong, relentless person, but rather as a useless and fumbling character. Immersed as he is in his petty bickerings, he is incapable of taking decisive action. Instead he squanders his substance in endless debate and superficial talk. A people require a sure authority which can exist only as supreme power resides in an official who can take action when he deems it necessary, and without first haggling with those who represent partial and distracting interests. Neither objection is quite irrelevant to social life, but either one pushed to its ultimate conclusion spells the death of politics. The complex question is whether or not and in what sense politics is desirable. A positive answer to the question will necessarily depend upon whether it can satisfactorily combine both power and morality.

No great amount of reflection is required to see the error in the old saw that power corrupts. Taken in its blatant form and unqualified, it connotes the desirability of impotence, and in the context of politics it connotes in a wavering sort of way the need for government without power—or, at a very minimum, a government of checks and balances. The net result is a negativism, if not anarchism, which contains no germs for the growth of public policy. *Laissez-faire* is not so much a policy as it is a skeptical frame of mind for refusing to try to ascertain what is for the general welfare and what, consequently, may legitimately be promoted to enhance the life of a people. Clearly, governments either must have power commensurate with the responsibilities with which they are charged or else they will be composed of functionless supernumeraries who cannot but be the targets of slander and ridicule. Power corrupts only as it exceeds what is required for carrying out the responsibilities of an office. Any less power can only make a mockery of public service, and any more would surely be used for extraneous purposes. An intelligent system of checks and balances is not a substitute for establishing policies for positive action. It is at best a technique for securing those policies by seeing to it, first, that they do not conflict with other policies which are given priority, and secondly, that they are not used as a blind for doing something else than what was intended by the establishing of those policies. How the precise degree of power is to be attained is a matter of good sense, good will, and objective criticism which respects both. To this end, it is more important to keep avenues of criticism open than it is to take a niggardly attitude toward the public use of power. The legitimate end of government is responsible power, not fears about human nature or about threats to personal privilege.

The formal answer to the question of whether politics is

desirable is now in sight. As long as there is a collective good that a people may enjoy, whether in the forming of a more perfect union, in the establishing of justice, insuring domestic tranquility, providing for the common defense, promoting the general welfare, securing the blessings of liberty, or any other end deemed worthy in the collective life of a people, so long is politics desirable. For in ordaining these ends, a people is committed to the appropriate means. The questions of politics, then, are the questions of (1) the redefinitions of the ends in the light of changing circumstances and developing knowledge, (2) the formulations and reformulations of concrete policies which give precision to the ends, and (3) the instrumentalities best adapted to the policies agreed upon. Politics is appropriate to each of these three areas as well as to their intricate interrelations. I proceed to some comments about each.

The proper ends of government, except in academic philosophy, are likely to be the object of concerted, focal attention only at those times in which profound social changes are occurring. The birth of bourgeois democracy was one of those times, and the struggle for a new distribution of power was everywhere evident in the labor pains occasioned by its coming into being. From the period of the establishment of parliamentary governments through the liberal revolutions, the ends of government, at least in the Western World, were not seriously challenged until the advent of the twentieth century revolutions which effected the overthrow of parliamentary rule. Once governments become stabilized, they are likely to enjoy that security which, in the words of Harold Laski, comes from "agreement on fundamentals." There may be some tinkering with governmental forms, but of the sort which signifies the acceptance of its ends, rather than of the sort which is critical of them. Only rarely do there appear attempts to draft new bills of rights which try to come to grips with changing circumstances of social life and the rise of new technologies, which together constitute revolutionary social conditions.[1]

With the phenomenal developments in the sciences, social and biological as well as physical, there are not only the dramatic military challenges of the space age, but there are the equally important challenges which pertain to matters of health and industrial organization, both of which have radically altered our whole concept of the good life. Employment which is both useful and creative has come to take on new meaning. Health and education have come to be seen as national issues and not merely those of parental decisions or of family doctors, supplemented by charitable institutions. Access to proper medical care and to institutions of learning, higher as well as lower, can no longer be regarded as a privilege of the elite, but rather a right for all who are in need of them or capable of significantly profiting from them. Equality has become a realistic goal of positive action. No longer can equality be regarded as a race for success during which we remain neutral to the differences in persons' native constitutions or in their inherited, privileged accesses to the goods of life which provide some of them with a head start. Just as liberty has taken on a new meaning in a political arena which encourages the struggle to achieve the legacy of free men and the pursuit of happiness for the many, so equality too has come to emphasize the access in fact to participate "in an advancing civilization." These are political ends, some of which are still being debated. Many of them, together with allied conclusions, however, are now commonly adopted, so that with respect to them the questions that are being debated are those of how to form realistic policies which make these ends precise, rather than those of whether or not the ends are acceptable.

The genius of contemporary politics consists in the capacity to utilize concerted and directed knowledge in the formation of public policy. Politics today has advanced beyond the stage in which a politician and his cronies can devise a program of action to cope with political needs. To meet the problems of a complex, intertwining, industrial existence, more expert knowledge must be commanded. Hunches, intuitions, and a sensitive feel for the urgencies of contemporary man still have a place, but their place is not the burden of the responsibility for devising intelligent policies for governmental action. Investigative techniques for ascertaining relevant facts, the marshalling of them into a coherent form which defines the needs of social life, and finally proposals for meeting needs—these are indispensable to realistic politics today. Debate has the burden of being informed, and although those who enter it are not required to be experts, they cannot engage effectively without familiarizing themselves with the fundamental relevancies that expertise proffers. Only foolishness comes out of policies grounded in ignorance, and ignorance cannot be made to be the stuff from which political policies are fashioned.

Once political policies are adopted, the need for executing them becomes apparent. This is the managerial function of government which, taking over the plans thus formulated, accommodates itself to translating them into actual practice. At times the blueprints are well enough specified that they can be read off with little difficulty, and the functions of government can proceed according to plan—provided only that sufficient latitude of action is accorded to government in order to give effect to the plans. If, however, funds are insufficient or if restrictions on personnel and organizational requirements are narrowly imposed, or if interference and harrassment from outside sources is countenanced, the policies cannot but be stillborn and the functions of government frustrated. Thus, power being incommensurate with responsibility, government can only creak with a burden too heavy to bear by the vehicles at its command. Action becomes stifled, and policies become mere verbiage.

There is, however, a kind of debate which is not just managerial but which has a legitimate political character—namely, how are novel policies to be instituted? I refer to the kind of debate in which a policy either is not sufficiently precise to be read off as an unambiguous blueprint or is in conflict with some other policy or policies. In case the adjustment of policies is not left to the discretion of an administrator, some other means for adjusting the controversy is required. It may be that the debate is turned back to the public for reconsideration and revision. In this case, it is not different in essence from the processes by which the original policy was formulated, debated, and adopted. It simply requires better and more informed expertise and more precise agreement as to intent and feasibility. Or again, the debate may be shunted into another form for adjudication by another function of government designed precisely for the consideration and resolution of controversy. Such bodies of adjudication are usually constituted as commissions or courts. The debates may be less noisy but they are political all the same, for the assumption is that the advocates of the various interests can be heard and that justice can be meted out on the merits of the case. In the process, the judge necessarily undertakes the part of a legislator.[2] Once the verdict is reached, the revised policy, if anything is left of it, is turned back to administrative officials and the execution of it presumably left to their competence. In case, however, of alleged incompetence of administrative officials, the issue would be turned toward a new kind of debate, pertaining not to policy matters as such but to the nature and function of the offices of government and to the qualifications of persons who occupy office. The shift is thus from substantival policy to procedural form.

The various issues in the actual practice of politics are, of course, all mixed up, sometimes beyond the point of disentanglement. Usually, one can distinguish the elements we have above spoken of as ends, policies, and instrumentalities. Each involves distinctive kinds of questions, even though necessarily interrelated with others. Abstracted from each other, questions of ends and instrumentalities are out of focus and not quite real. The disjunction yields ends sundered from means, making the one sentimentally utopian and the other brashly activistic, even though at times principles do require justification as ends to be desired, and procedures do require appraisal concerning the degree to which they are realistic in practice. What modulates the two is the formation of political policies. These we might call "the middle axioms" of politics. In them we find the genius of imagination which translates ends into working principles of political action. With respect to ends, they contain a precision which, "hung with weights," keeps the understanding "from leaping and flying," and with respect to the concrete particulars of practice, allow a "just scale of ascent" in which they are constituted as "the true and solid and living axioms, on which depend the affairs and fortunes of men."[3] Less like truisms, they give direction to ends, even as scientific laws make possible the prediction of future eventualities. Yet rising above the particulars of experience, they reveal generalities by which the continuities of life may be preserved. They are, in short, the principles of immanent criticism, which in their perfection, negatively, reveal spurious inadequacies of social life, and positively, guide action to the paths of a genuine culture. They can do this because they combine expertise with democratic practice. Born of natural knowledge and imagination, they are tested in the crucible of public discussion and debate and thus meet the double challenge of overcoming ignorance as well as of dissent. Both public opinion and expertise are amalgamated into a coherent whole which provides policy with all but the agents whose competence is the final test of the success of policy.

I do not mean to suggest that officials of government may not themselves serve both as the experts who propose policy and the agents who execute it, but I do wish to point out the need for distinguishing the two functions. Regardless of where the experts turn up, inside or outside government, policies which are not open to full and complete public debate will inevitably incur flaws when they are put into practice. Flaws will be incurred just because public policies impinge upon interests of the people, and only public debate and discussion can reveal how impingements will be regarded by those affected by them. Nothing discloses so quickly the shortcomings of expertise as the attempt to dictate the needs of people when they are not ascertained by methods of consultation and authentic communication. Isolated as the expert is, he is doubly isolated when he is the dictator of policy. As an expert, he is not supposed to share the common prejudices of people. He must therefore hold himself aloof in order to be neutral. But when in addition he possesses the power to make practical decisions, he cannot but surround himself with the fawning who adulate him or with the intelligent who manage to hedge their criticisms or cynically to repress them. Dictators cannot but remove themselves to a dream world, and they thus eventually become in their oneiric retreat the butt of ridicule, if not the object of a conspiratorial overthrow. However benevolent a despot would be, his role as despot silences opposition and transforms his benevolence into a disposition to satisfy needs which are made unknowable by the very silence he unwittingly provokes.

The employment of expertise in the formation of public policy in a complex industrial society constitutes one of the truly agonizing problems for modern politics. There is no simple solution of it. The nearest approach to a simple solution appears to be contained in the aphorism of one wit that the expert should be on tap, not on top. The real complexity, which makes the aphorism only partly useful, is that the expert is himself a part of a culture and consequently his expertise is most apt to reflect precisely those prejudices that most need to be combatted— namely, those which reflect the cultural focus of a society. The expert who would dissociate himself from the focal emphases of a society would for that reason render himself suspect, and however fruitful that dissociation might be from the point of view of culling significantly new facts, he becomes even in his role of expert one who is forced *hors de combat* and thus one who is ineffectual as an agent of reform. Nor can he effectively seek support by enlisting the aid of converts, for he would then place himself within the political arena, and thus assuming the role of a protagonist, he becomes a partisan instead of an expert. Thorstein Veblen's argument that the engineer should become policy maker leads to a similar predicament, for as soon as the engineer becomes responsible for political decisions, he is transformed from an engineer into a politician.[4] There appears to be no practical way of escaping the fact that as soon as the expert is catapulted into the position of making policy, instead of remaining on the plane of providing information for policy consideration, he is metamorphosed into a new kind of being who, by virtue of his position, can occupy it in the only way possible, that is, by becoming an autocrat.

Autocracy, to be sure, is not entirely out of fashion today. On the one hand, it has its supporters from those who would rationalize the industrial system and make technocracy into a rule by those who are capable of organizing and governing society according to principles derived from efficiency in production. On the other, it is supported by those who, primarily alert to the incredibly complex problems involved in international affairs, would seek for both the formation of policies as well as their execution by officials qualified by virtue of reliable information, study, experience, and capacity to make responsible decisions. Both cases are imposing ones, and each deserves special consideration. For reasons of continuity of discussion, I shall treat them in reverse order.

On the American scene, no one I know of has made a more searching analysis or a more provocative case for expertise in public policy, and especially as related to international affairs, than Mr. Walter Lippmann.[5] In his recent statement he has argued that we are today suffering from a malady, and the essence of it is that private interests, partial and ill-conceived, contravene the necessity for formulating with clarity and decisiveness policies which will benefits the public and not just factions who wish for, and may be capable of pressing for, special consideration and privileged treatment. The malady is, in his words, "a derangement in the relation between the mass of the people and the government." It has made for a "devitalization of the governing power. . . . of democratic states." And he makes it quite clear that the governing power is the "executive power" as opposed to "the elected assembly and the voters in the constituencies."[6] By virtue of this derangement, one may expect the further decline of Western liberal democracies, unless, of course, there comes to be a radical revision in accord with the principles of the public philosophy. He argues eloquently that public policy must take precedence over private interest, that responsibility belongs to the *office* which is the organ of the public philosophy, and that those qualified for office must be given latitude to exercise their capacities in the fulfilment of their charges. Popular opinion, it turns out, is no substitute for formation of policy, and the general electorate has neither the intelligence nor the competence to formulate policy. The function of elections is not to decide policy but, at best, to decide who shall be responsible for deciding policy.

Mr. Lippmann, certainly one of the most incisive and best informed critics of foreign policy, speaks with authority and with more than ordinary knowledge. In contrast, how can Mr. John Q. from Chillicothe speak but nonsensically on matters so varied as the Suez, the unification of Germany, aid to non-industrialized countries, trade with Red China, revolutions in Bolivia, the defense of Alaska, race relations in South Africa, together with thousands of other equally important and equally perplexing questions arising in every part of the world, and even beyond? The amateur who has opinions on every one of these questions cannot but make a fool of himself in the eyes of those who have knowledge. But is the amateur to be counted out in the process of formulating public policy? A more profound search may reveal that he can play a significant role.

Essential to the democratic process, I assume, are debate, the enhancement of public opinion, responsibility, and at least a minimal agreement on ends. How and whether these elements support democratic practice are questions of context and fullness of interconnections, not of disclaimers against anti-democratic commitments. It is crucial to observe how an author treats them rather than to admit that any scheme which somehow includes them is therefore democratic. Our question is, how does the "public philosophy" fare in the interpretation of these elements?

The "public philosophy" is not against debate; on the contrary, it welcomes it, but it is *for* a separation of functions which makes for strong executives sheltered from the clamor of divergent interests. In effect, therefore, it confines debate to an area which is isolated from the seat of decision. Instead of being the antecedent which leads up to and induces decision, debate is only casually related to decision, more akin to dispensation than to democratic process. The public philosophy would strengthen the power of the executive. This can be accomplished only by robbing it from deliberative bodies. The net result is the coalescing of the function of effective deliberation with that of execution. The combination of the two within a single office clearly signifies that deliberation is limited to whatever the executive chooses it to be. The burden of carrying in the same office the responsibility both for policy formation and execution has historically belonged to autocrats, not democrats, or in utopian schemes to philosopher-kings, if not only to God. The alternative is not to suggest that executives are not to deliberate, but rather that they need not, even in the interests of effective government, be made to bear the whole brunt of the burden of policy formation.

When the responsibility of deliberation falls so completely upon the executive branch of government, it invariably limits the pool of intelligence to a small handful of men plus the advisers whom they must themselves pick. This being the functional agency, extra-cameral discussion can be only incidentally useful, and then only as the governing agency chooses to listen to suggestions from outside. For the most part, it is reasonable to believe that general discussion and debate would fall on deaf ears of persons already overworked in their exhausting capacities of governing. So far from being enhanced, public opinion need not even be a reality in the sense that it is formed or shared by the public or even made known to it. Policies are enunciated by governing bodies only as they are required to by law or are believed to be expedient for the purposes of governing. The first cannot be applicable to executives who are themselves the judges of policy, and the second is not to any great degree necessary for bodies who, harrassed by the functions of government, cannot be made accountable to the governed, for in the "public philosophy" the people cannot even be constituted as a public. Without the existence of a public (and surely it cannot exist when its functions are absorbed into official bodies) there can be, moreover, no public opinion. At best, there can be only private opinions and debates, which, in the absence of vigorous political give-and-take, can have no stimulus to maintain themselves. Once more, one may say, the alternative is not that legitimate executive functions may not be undertaken—and undertaken with authority—nor that they may not include state secrets as well as the conduct of diplomacy screened from the purview of fluoroscopic publicity. Rather, the point is that when a government exceeds legitimate and occasional secrecy and transforms it into basic policy, it thereby deprives a people of the knowledge and information which is necessary to support and to enhance public opinion. Such a government does this because it has, in truth, destroyed the possibility of the formation of public opinion. And with it, it has destroyed democracy itself.

The advocates of the public philosophy would no doubt repudiate this conclusion, once more disclaiming anti-democratic commitments. Their disclaimer inevitably is accompanied by an insistence upon the need for responsible judgments. Responsible judgments are, in the public philosophy, judgments formed in a disinterested and benevolent atmosphere of clear and informed rational thought, deaf to the stridency of private and special interests.[7] Mr. Lippmann argues, and no doubt with justification, that public philosophy is concerned not only with the present generation but with the next generations as well. He insists, therefore, that no plebiscite can be of use in formulating judgments of what the public interest entails. The wisdom which he would call upon in order to establish sound principles of government is awesome —so awesome, in fact, that we may question whether or not it could possibly have worth in the affairs of men.

Must the alternative to an unattainable awesome knowledge be a pragmatism so narrowly conceived that it can only drift with the immediate prevailing temper which can muster sufficient force to evoke a favorable decision from a weak government functionary? Neither alternative is a happy one for meeting the standards of political life. The one is as dreamy as the other is debasing. If there is a realistic escape from this dilemma, it can be only one stated in terms which regard a people as capable of achieving a degree of good sense and good will commensurate with the challenge of the approaching catastrophes they must in the contemporary world constantly face. As H. G. Wells long ago pointed out, the burden this places on education is immense. But in all soberness, this appears to be the only alternative to an insufferable autocracy or an equally insufferable chaos, or what might today paradoxically be both. However, we may conceive the precise function of education, the principle involved is unmistakable: the great majority must be capable of education to the point where they are sound judges of a policy, whether or not they are capable of formulating policy. Either this, or democracy is doomed.

The empirical arguments opposing this view are not as convincing as their advocates might have them appear. First of all, the results of opinion polls, including the colossal ignorance they seemingly reveal, are inconclusive, partly because of the unreliability of the polls themselves, including the way in which questions are posed, and partly because of the unreality of the questions posed—both by virtue of the nature of the questions and by virtue of the possible reforms in education which would show up the shallowness of the pollsters' results. So far from being shattering criticisms of the possibility of achieving democratic practice, the results of opinion polling can be employed as aids to the diagnosis of the ills of a society which would become more democratic.[8] Secondly, there are those arguments against the feasibility of the democratic processes which monotonously cite evidence of men's apathy in taking part in politics. Judging from the fact of increasing participation in our own recent elections, one may regard the charge as not entirely true. Moreover, what truth it does possess may be traced back in part to the kinds of practices which have increasingly prevailed, especially since World War II. Administrative expertise, the committee and bureaucracy procedures which have been devised and which kill creativity, and finally a stuffy view in prevailing politics, safe and secure from charges of innovation, bold decision, and plain, humane considerations—these are unquestionably aspects of the eclipse of virile politics today[9] This conclusion points not to the need for insulating policymakers from the public. On the contrary, it points to the need for reducing the distance and for making them more responsive to it.

Responsibility in politics, we may conclude, is more a matter of accountability to the public than it is of formulating clear and benevolent judgments in a haven protected from public criticism. He who would serve democratic ends would better seek ways of perfecting accountability than of blocking it by advocating that policymakers become immune to criticism. Immunity, it seems, makes for irresponsibility, not responsibility. The public philosophy apparently contains a serious error. Perhaps it is not ungenerous to suggest that the root of the error lies in a confusion of the attainment of knowledge with the process of administration. Where immunity is called for is in research and the furthering of knowledge of our world—that is, in the work of the expert. His responsibility is in the gathering of pertinent information, of checking and evaluating its truth with absolute honesty and integrity, whatever its bearing may be on policy. The expert cannot do this—certainly he cannot do it well—if he is harried with preoccupations and responsibilities that are no part of his expertise. His work is that of a scientist, and as scientist he deserves that immunity necessary to the advancement of science. The administrator *qua* administrator, on the contrary, is not a scientist. His concern is with practice—the practice of bringing together knowledge, things, and persons to effect the proper ends of policies. His ways are ones that must be perfected in practice, in adjustments, in a sensitivity to what is going on in the making of history, and in how policies must be fashioned to the realities of the state of knowledge, changing circumstances, and the states of men's minds. His task is to be alert to criticism and to learn from it, not to be immune to it. Not his benevolence, but his appreciation of criticisms and his sympathetic appraisals of the aspirations and convictions they contain are the marks of the competent administrator. To be such a one, he may be expected to be close to and accountable to the public, not removed and alienated from it.

If all is discordant, it is true the administrator must turn deaf ears on the clamor. But if all is discordant, we might as well recognize that democracy is an idle hope. Then not persuasion and sweet reason but the mailed fist and authority will rule. Where there is no "agreement on fundamentals," catastrophe and authority or both are men's lot. The magnitude of the democratic task is doubly compounded. Fundamentals change, and with them men's minds must change too. There is no science of discerning fundamentals, although human sensitivity may be adequate to observe symptoms of the necessity for radical changes in human attitudes. Immanent criticism can reveal paradoxes and spuriousness caused by cultural lag. But to overcome lag is a matter for contagious genius. Administrators traditionally have not been outstanding in their capacities to point the ways to needed reforms, and although there is no reason to count them out, certainly there is reason to seek out political genius in whatever quarter it may be available. The ends of governments, new bills of rights, new liberties to overcome oppressions, reinterpretations of the necessities of brotherhood and equality—this is the stuff of political debate which when clarified, made into policies, and unflinchingly agreed to, constitutes the essence of democratic practice. Unless, however, we are careful to distinguish end, policies, and administrative processes, and to ascertain the kind of criticism appropriate to each, we shall certainly diagnose badly the ills of democratic government. When, for example, it is asserted that its malady lies in the derangement in relation of government and the masses, we may find that this is merely symptomatic of a deeper malady which lies within the world itself. By criticizing the practical relations within government, we may thus be concealing the true sickness, which consists in the failure to cope with the problem of vital ends rather than with that of administrative techniques. To delegate power is essential to all administration, but just to relinquish it in the absence of agreement on ends and of consideration of public policies is to escape politics in the death-wish for democratic practice. If the sickness is really this deep seated, the cure is no longer in ourselves but in our stars.

Chapter 7

THE CULTURAL CONTEXT

THE RECURRENT NEED FOR REDEFINING AGREEMENTS upon social life is dramatically testified to by the adoption of new bills of rights. A measure of democratic practice finds expression in them to the extent to which they embody a consensus of more than passing moment and to which they embody guides for redirecting social action to conform to the urgencies of humane existence. Bills of rights induce consent, not by their solemnities, but by their respect for common humanity. And they achieve a degree of permanence by virtue of their capacity to engender vitalities essential to the general welfare. Neither consent nor vitality can indefinitely be taken for granted in ends or processes of government once asserted; nor can they be once and for all guaranteed by some automatic formula or built-in mechanical device. The democratic faith requires renewal and reassertion as the conditions of life change and as the older expressions of belief become transformed into oppressions of practice. Bills of rights are just such renewals of faith as well as statements of new necessities grown out of the cumulative experience of a people.

To adopt a bill of rights is to acknowledge legitimate claims that a person may make upon certain kinds of social relations, whether they are constituted as immunities to be protected by the collective power of the state through its agents, or as services similarly to be rendered by it. Whether the rights are the protection of life and property, the regulation of monopolies or unions, the eradication of spyings by secret police, the promotion of education, health, housing, or employment—despite the vast differences of the kinds of action implicated—rights are the legitimation of personal claims and the obligation of a state to render the acknowledgment of them into realities of social life. Traditional democracy has regarded the substantive rights of persons as being primarily immunities from interference by either persons or governments. Historically, the "escape clause" was, of course, that of "due process." By virtue of it, points of view more sensitive to collective needs, rather than that which was wedded to rights regarded as indefeasible, were capable of being adopted. A more social version of rights arises with the recognition of the pressing problems created by highly industrialized processes. Programs of "social legislation" deemed necessary to meet the plight of the workingman and his family responsibilities are in essence determined efforts to secure rights which originate in the industrial processes. A state which wishes to secure these rights empowers its agents actually to promote interests themselves, and not just to protect interests already created by private persons. This shift is recognized in the well-defined movement from the old conception of the police state to the newer positive state. Although the change in conception of the state is momentous, the fundamental principles pertaining to the nature of rights remain much the same. Basically, their functions are to form a more perfect union through the consent of the governed, establish justice, and promote the general welfare. In the absence of any of these elements, democratic government is imbalanced.

No principle of democratic government is more difficult of application in a mass society than that of government by consent. In some sense, consent is inapplicable to government—so much so that there are those who simply repudiate it. When, for example, governmental agents exercise authority, they do so because it is, or is regarded as, law, not the consent of those affected. And even when law is made by the representatives of the people, there are the old standby-arguments that representative government can surely not be considered to constitute consent, since anything less than direct voice vote on all matters affecting a people falls short of it. The arguments appear to be unanswerable. Yet he who would in a democratic form of society repudiate the element of consent is due for a shock. Statements and adoptions of new bills of rights seem to reflect an urgency to re-establish a consensus. They are not adopted casually or mechanically. On the contrary, they are given fullest publicity, and only after ample opportunity for discussion and debate and consideration of objections are they made into law. Moreover, by virtue of their concern for vast

179

numbers of individuals as well as growing inequities, they embody popular appeal and invite widespread acceptance. Consent may in fact manifest itself as general acclaim, regardless of the fewness of persons who may be directly responsible for transforming it into law.

Traditionally, bills of rights represent reforms long overdue. The popularity they enjoy is in a large measure a function of the inherent justice they contain. Inequities which grow out of established institutions can be corrected only as law-givers invent new institutions to accord more adequately with what is morally justifiable. Irrelevant and arbitrary privileges give way to rights which belong to those who have been improperly discriminated against or who by virtue of their common humanity possess a claim for humane and respectful consideration. When social organization brings about a clear imbalance between what the differences among men warrant, when the maintenance of status for the few is preserved at the expense of the many, when nationalistic, racial, or cultural dominances destroy the chances of whole populations to achieve an existence meaningful to themselves—then the time has inevitably come to propound popular measures for reform.

Under the circumstances, justice would seem to demand an overriding of the refusal of the holders of privilege to consent to the necessary changes. The adoption of proposals for social reform, it may be assumed, will always prejudice some interests. When, however, the interests are constituted as unjust privileges at the expense of legitimate rights capable of becoming cultural realities, there is no doubt concerning which interests deserve to be forsaken and which to be fostered. Popular consent is not likely to be supported by the holders or privilege. Whether, however, the latter agree or not is less important than whether a society is capable of discerning privilege at the expense of rights and outlawing it in favor of a larger measure of justice. The very meaning of a bill of rights is to exorcise interests which conflict with civil purposes. If, therefore, consent is construed so broadly as to make exorcism impossible, it becomes an idle plaything of speculative thought, not a principle applicable to government. Since, under the circumstances, universal consent is not possible, justice can at least lend its weight to the already tipped scales of popular reform. Perhaps it is in this sense that we are entitled to read the principle that governments derive their *just* powers from the consent of the people.

The conclusive factor that makes the scale quite incapable of tipping back to the side of privilege is the general welfare which is served by a bill of rights. Whether it is the maintenance of private property, religious freedom, educational opportunities, unemployment insurance, or what-not, the crowning justification of a bill of rights nourished and protected by a society is the well-being of that society which it in turn broadly serves. The virtues, even when minor injustices are incurred, are so compelling that they are thought to be worthy of extraordinary inviolateness. Prohibitions against wire-tapping and against unlawful searches, respect for rights against self-incrimination, and the like, are thought to be of importance superior even to that of law-enforcement agencies. Speaking of freedom in the community of American universities and the vital role played by those responsible for guiding and training our youth, Chief Justice Warren wrote:

> To impose any strait jacket upon the intellectual leaders in our colleges and universities would imperil the future of our nation. No field of education is so thoroughly comprehended by man that new discoveries cannot be made. Particularly is that true in the social sciences, where few, if any, principles are accepted as absolutes. Scholarship cannot flourish in an atmosphere of suspicion and distrust. Teachers and students must always remain free to inquire, to study, to evaluate, to gain new maturity and understanding; otherwise our civilization will stagnate and die.[1]

Decisions like this judiciously point the way to the nature of democratic consent as well as to what is required for a people to get on with their business. Consent, Chief Justice Warren indicates, is antagonistic to "an atmosphere of suspicion and distrust." Could it be, then, that consent is itself the conditions of open and frank discussion with one's fellow men? Could it be that the only unity that counts in a democracy is the community of interests arrived at by encouragement of talents which contribute to civic life, and not in attempts to coerce men through fear, threats, and loyalty oaths to conform to standards alien to their wills?

181

Should we not find consent in the spirit which Thucydides long ago expressed in saying that Athenians are not exclusive in public life nor suspicious of one another nor do they cast sour looks at their neighbors?[2]

The democratic attitude of mind, it appears, is genuinely encouraged by focussing attention on the problems of men. For example, in education we do better to recognize our ignorance and shortcomings in order that study and learning and a sense of challenge may belong to our schools. Chief Justice Warren calls attention to the need for advancing our civilization, for in this way we can better serve "the future of our nation." No cheap nationalism can take the place of authentic civilization. The promotion of human welfare requires a knowledge of the human condition. When this is combined with a belief that human beings are bearers of civilization through the multitude, and not just through an elite, then civilization is properly regarded as democratic. Consent is implicit in their actions, which support a community of interests. This community, moreover, is authenticated in "an advancing civilization"—that is, in a genuine culture.

Modern industrial societies that would be democratic are plagued by two not always reconciled beliefs. There is, first, the belief that an effective society must constantly increase its supply of material goods. There is, secondly, the belief that all able-bodied persons should share in the burden of production and that there should be some equitable distribution of the goods produced. The former is now quite generally regarded as that which makes possible a large measure of equality in the industrial world, for with the plenitude of goods which modern man is capable of producing, the ostensible differences between the wealthy and the vast majority become increasingly insignificant. There is little doubt that in contemporary industrial societies with expanding production the spread between the two has diminished greatly. In an interesting passage in *Technics and Civilization* Lewis Mumford effectively illustrates the diminishing spread in regard to the use of artificial light. In the eotechnic age, conspicuous consumption is noteworthy in the multitude of candles the wealthy can burn in comparison with the poor. Under neotechnics, however, the use of the incandescent lamp virtually obliterates any significant class distinction marked by the availability and use of artificial light. Other examples readily come to mind pertaining to the tendency to obliterate the distinction between classes by virtue of the levelling process made irresistible by the machine. Mass production goes a long ways toward eradicating inequalities, and those that remain can render comparisons increasingly less invidious. The argument that an opulent society makes for a greater equality among men is an entrancingly new version of the classical theory that "private vices are public virtues," that the greater the degree of business activity, the more the multitude enjoys a status of diminishing inequality with their benefactors.

A conclusion as optimistic as this somehow seems to belie a pervading temper of uneasiness with which modern man surveys his future. An optimism of automatic progress is not the outlook of industrial man in mid-twentieth century. Even in the nation in which men are largely surfeited with material goods, there is detectable a pessimism which augurs an uncertainty. The shift from "the Puritan" to "the social ethic" is not an entirely happy one. It smacks more of the organization man than it does of a world of confident, challenging, and buoyant relations. Its extroverted standards are a little too strident and a little too gregarious to satisfy deeper urgencies of mature emotions. The chrome splendor of modern life cries out for some aging that belongs to a world of rot and rust. The novelties arising from planned obsolescence cause breaks with the past instead of an accumulation of experience. Even the recurrently heard plea for a return to the Protestant ethic is not exactly heartening, for besides being mostly irrelevant, it harks back to the same split between the inner and outer world upon which the social ethic is predicated—only it represents the other face of the split. The malaise is one which may well cause us to look more deeply to the proposals that we cure our social ills by maximizing economic production.

Whether or not maximization of output leads to a greater degree of equality in the world, there is a real question whether it can be regarded as an intelligible economic goal. Put in its simplest terms, we may suggest a critical attitude toward such a goal by calling attention to the classical formula of economics that supply and demand are a functional relation and that to alter supply is senseless apart from considerations of demand. (Or shouldn't we even say "effective" demand?) In most cases we can assume that there will be some takers of almost anything produced. Classical economics ennobled the phenomenon by calling it a utility, and the verification of it is the price it is able to command in the market. But "utility" is a euphemism, or at best a statistical datum, certainly not a precise fact. The scandal of utility comes into the open when one recognizes that "utilities" may be prohibited from the market in the name of the public welfare. The production of some things which nevertheless may command a price have to be regarded as lying contrary to public policy. The contradiction is that "utilities" may be constituted as "disutilities" and can be banned from legal operations.

Present-day optimism is not necessarily shattered by the discovery that considerations of legality are superior to economic productivity, and that the economic realm is not autonomous. After all, even Adam Smith recognized instances in which the wealth of nations required control over "private" economic affairs. Yet whether we adopt Smith's point of view or a more modern one, reflection shows that the economic cannot really be autonomous and that in principle it is rightly subordinated to a higher law, whether we call it the wealth of nations, the public welfare, or just plain justice. The awkward instances that don't permit us to accept the autonomy of economic activity suggest the need for a more mature point of view: economic activity requires a directive principle which it itself is incapable of supplying. Otherwise, it may lead to senseless things, even if by doing so it brings about a kind of equality—for that equality may be of a senseless kind too. Professor Stigler observes this when he writes: "Maximum output and greater equality are on an equal footing as proximate goals, and neither has content except as part of a philosophical system."[3] The burning question thus comes to be, is there not a grounded evaluative principle by virtue of which we can determine the worth of economic activities themselves?

Our previous discussion of values would suggest that there is such a principle—a moral principle—however difficult of application it may be at a particular time.

The moral principle—that is, the positive social relation that enlists the whole man in a whole society—is not capable of being made concrete except in a genuine culture. Short of this, economic activity may be the mark of the spurious rather than the authentic, for it has no proper ends by which it can certify itself. There is no need to belabor the criticism that production for production's sake is self-stultifying. There are so many other things that are better than work and its products regarded as an end. Even John Ruskin, although he was sometimes overenthusiastic about the need for regarding work (especially of happy workmen) as an end, is incisive in his conception of economics when he writes in *Munera Pulveris,* "The object of Political Economy is not to buy, nor to sell labour, but to spare it." Just because modern economic theory finds that production stimulates more production and in return provides more goods for all is no satisfactory reason why men should devote themselves to more rather than to less work. Such paradoxes suggest that we search for a principle which will define what we mean by need.

Only in a very simple and not very satisfactory way can needs be defined by biological and psychological urgencies. There is general agreement among men that biological needs must be cared for in order that life itself may be sustained. Nor in this age is it difficult to set forth with precision the minimum standards required for nourishment, protection, and health. One of the great scandals of the time is, of course, that modern man fails to do what he can to attain the degree of health and nourishment within his power. Only a moral perversity can explain the shortcoming, for the question is not really moot. Rather, it pertains to knowledge and expertise available and willing. More difficult by far is the problem of assessing psychological urgencies where we possess no clear line of demarcation between wishes, needs, and perversions, and consequently are not clear as to whether the principles that apply are those of felicity or morality. Even to try to measure the urgencies in relation to total personality falls short of the moral requirement, for morality is not definable apart from a culture—

185

and, in fact, a genuine culture. Short of this, man may agonize in his total aloneness; he cannot come to terms with a world from which he is estranged.[4] Economic theories, therefore, which regard psychological urgencies manifested in price as ultimate fail to recognize the necessities—and realities—of public policies which are an attempt to mold urgencies and definitely to prohibit those which fail to take account of other persons who exist in a common world. Only as this molding process has already gone into the make-up of human personality does the "law of supply and demand" have moral standing. Supply and demand are recognized to be not autonomous economic relations but cultural facets of a life conditioned by historical antecedents and justified by wider cultural ends to which an economy may contribute. Hence, the range of variation of production has limits imposed by a culture, and schedules of production are not quite intelligible except as extrapolations from what a people are already accustomed to, and the "utilities" at work are already defined by tradition rather than as representing ultimate, atomic facts of economic life.[5] The practical problem then is to be able to define utilities in the context of public policy, where policy itself is an expression of morality.

The definition of public policy, it turns out, is one of the most decisive tasks to be undertaken in a culture. How a people regards itself—and others—becomes clear from the policies it acts upon. Whether it is an elite society or a democratic one, whether it encourages human life or merely dissipates it, whether it achieves a viable culture or only one of enforced conformity and injustice—these are what can be read from its operative policies. What distinguishes the democratic from the non-democratic society is, in the final analysis, the derivation of policy from bills of rights that have a deep concern for all human beings of a society who are capable of participating in a life of dignity. If it is private property or the safeguarding of contracts that defines dignity in a given period, an authentic culture will not wince at mustering its energies to protect these rights. If again it is education or development of natural and human resources or cultural achievements, it will likewise not wince at throwing its effective weight on the side of these activities. How and where these rights are to be located is a matter we have already discussed. That bills of rights are

186

necessary to channel economic activity, or political, or religious, or any other, is the crux of democratic policy, for they are realistic measures designed to cope with the moral problems that each age must face in its own way, either to resolve them in equity or else to postpone them in disingenuity.

The deeper significance of bills of rights now becomes apparent. On the one hand they are meant to cope with the realities of the social order—the limited potentialities of actual life. On the other, they are meant to cope with the "infinite potentialties" of human existence. The expressions are awkward and sound contradictory. This confusion needs to be cleared up. Social life does have limited potencies—this is the fundamental fact of culture. Culture, we have seen, is binding on man; it is the mold through which he must come to express his personal urgencies, and without which he could not be human at all. The personal urgencies are a range of indefinable urgencies, expressed or thwarted, within a culture. A bill of rights is a recognition of the range within which the urgencies may be sanctioned by a society and, by virtue of being rights, are, except as they are necessarily defeasible, sanctioned for all. Since both the conditions of defeasibility as well as those of expression are universal, a bill of rights is the most profound expression by which a society can realistically assert the equality of men.

The doctrine of equality can be stultified in either of two ways: by being defined too broadly or by being defined too narrowly. Too broadly defined, equality is a function of the genus, man, a sentient being who in his universality belongs to no culture whatsoever. He is not even a being capable of entering into communication for, as cultureless, he has no language nor habits nor character by virtue of which he could communicate anything to anyone. As a universal being, he can have no human qualities and cannot in truth even act as a moral agent. The abstraction that results in this conception makes equality into a principle incapable of fruition. Too narrowly defined, equality creates sanctions for actions which reduce some to a position in which they are subject to the power of others, and consequently to a position diametrically opposed to equality in fact. Rights, once distributed equally to all, become, by reason of changed circumstances, oppressions of some over others—ordinarily the few over the many. Both the too broad and the too narrow definitions fail because they fail to come to grips with the cultural realities.

The equality that counts is that which gives realistic consideration to all persons, even though it cannot guarantee that the outcome will be equally happy for all concerned, or that some will not retain advantages over others. Even Kant never said that persons may not be used as means, but rather that they may not be used as means *merely*. Between the ultimacy of ends, which by themselves are sterile, and the indignity of degrading persons into mere means, there is what Tawney suggestively speaks of as "equality of consideration." This is not an equality which encourages the most fleet to win the race. In fact, the whole conception of winning is foreign to equality of respect and consideration. As he puts it:

> So to criticize inequality and to desire equality is not, as is sometimes suggested, to cherish the romantic illusion that men are equal in character or intelligence. It is to hold that, while their natural endowments differ profoundly, it is the mark of a civilized society to aim at eliminating such inequalities as have their source, not in individual differences, but in its own organization, and that individual differences, which are a source of social energy, are more likely to ripen and find expression if social inequalities are as far as practicable, diminished.[6]

The challenging problem of equality is, we may repeat, that by which men create for themselves public policies which provide the maximum latitude for the expression of differences within a genuine culture. A genuine culture encourages the fruitful commerce among men; it stimulates their faculties, facilitates communication, favors the creation of artifacts necessary, desirable, and beautiful, and maximizes the sense of wholeness and integrity. A society which displays a concern for such equality cannot but work for a balance between the personal and the public. An equality which makes dignity so subjective it can never be expressed in a common world is one which suffocates personality in agonizing frustration. An equality which smothers the personal in a robotonous conformity to the public order is not fit for men. Because equality is essentially a cultural affair, it cannot but ultimately be an expression of fraternal life.

The tough problems of social life are set by the necessity of having to reconcile power with legitimacy. No society can exist without institutions of power. But we may also ask whether it can exist *with* institutions of power—that is, assuming that existence is not just a form of tyranny in which the few control the institutions of power and the many suffer them. The history of internecine warfare is too well documented to try to shut our eyes to it. The state, the market, the law, have been machines of oppression too often for anyone to accredit them automatically with being instruments of civilization. Yet to deprive them of their power is no more an answer to man's liberation than to try magically to make him immune to the force of gravity. Our discussion, I fear now somewhat over-prolonged, has had as its aim an answer to how power can be legitimated. If liberty is power and power is good, then plainly, it is good for all. If, however, liberty is good for all, then all should have access to it—that is, equal access. Yet may it not be that equality cancels out power, thereby destroying liberty that might otherwise be a reality for some—and thereby destroying what might have redounded to the greatest possible benefit for all, even though not equally? Classical capitalistic theory argued in some such way as this and even arrived at the most astounding conclusion that by allowing power to be expressed primarily by the few, the many would benefit, the wealth of nations would be increased, and fraternity would come to its highest realization. Today men generally view skeptically the correctness of this conclusion. This skepticism is reason enough for us to raise one last question about the institutions of power, and to ask how fraternity can both express power and legitimize it.[7]

If liberty is the release of power and equality the division of it, then fraternity would seem to be the harmonization of power. Traditionally, this harmonization has been a function of the state insofar as it has been responsible for composing differences which would otherwise rend the community into warring factions. Regarded as the supreme umpire or sovereign in matters to which there can be no other effective appeal, the state has for the most part elicited the highest loyalties of man on earth. A structure capable of maintaining itself so well intact for centuries must have some secure foundation in the realities of modern social existence. Superior to the liberties of men, it has been charged with the responsibilities for protecting them. Impartial to the private interests of men, it has been the source of adjudicating conflicts not otherwise resoluble. And, especially more recently, capable of performing public services, it has initiated actions, established authorities, and made possible goods not feasible for lesser organizations. Is this imposing structure alone capable of harmonizing power and legitimizing it? We can properly answer this question only as we can come to understand the connection between the fraternal ideal and the genuine culture.

To arrive at any adequate version of fraternity for the modern world, we need to borrow from conceptions as disparate as that of the tribal society and that of the universal brotherhood of man. From the tribal conception comes the suggestion of kinsmanship in the small community in which personal relations possess both a happy conjunction of intimacy and formality. Tribal relations, being first-person relations, necessarily call upon human ingenuity in the give-and-take that is inevitable when persons are directly confronted by other persons in their attempts to cope with the urgencies of life. Insignificant as the issues raised may appear to an external observer, the satisfactory resolution of them is of first importance to those whose very outlets of expression depend upon them. In fact, the kinds of issues that arise and the manners in which they are allayed themselves determine a way of life. They are constituted as the substance of a culture itself, for at its heart are found the common elements—the dispositions, attitudes, emotional expressions, and implicit assumptions—by which a people is assured of a continuity, which together with its engagement and absorption of constantly fresh ingredients makes life meaningful. The formalities of social life are needed to sustain its continuity. They provide the texture in which may be woven the intimacies of personal life. The resultant designs are capable of great variation according as human ingenuity is capable of employing the interstices of formalities to support a more personal dimension of novelties, climactic discoveries, and resolutions. The joys and sorrows which result, the compassions and hatreds which are engendered, the conquests and defeats which are experienced —these are the threads of personal life. As the more rewarding or the less rewarding becomes the rule, so there is the more or less justification of a culture being perpetuated. The fact that many different designs of an essentially rewarding nature are possible constitutes the basis for a multitude of cultures. What raises for us the painful question today is whether the loss of the tribal element, which makes possible the ease and intimacies of cultural life and gives assurance to personal endeavor—whether it is not just this loss that has made contemporary life poverty stricken, artificially segmented, and personally sterile?

The common complaint of the industrial world is that these intimacies have been engulfed in the impersonalities of machine-enforced behavior of men. Abstract cerebration has too much been substituted for emotional at-homeness, and shadowy counters have taken the place of human substantives. Even the family, which was regarded as the great stronghold of emotional stability and the haven of sustaining intimacy, has been dismembered in the concatenated institutions of the school, from nursery to the university, the playground, from sandlot to sports arena, the clinic, the automobile, the club, the church, as well as a host of others catering more to the obsessions of busyness than to the need for gratifying fulfilments. Proposals to remedy the need have been as divergent as those of the arcadian flight from the city, the husbanding of the small community, and the enhancement of the region.[8] That a sense of the re-establishment of the community is needed and that neither megalopolis nor suburbia provides reasonable answers become increasingly apparent. The city responds to some of the necessities of industrial organization along with closely related business, financial, and governmental operations. Suburbia responds to the more bucolic longings of man, together with his desire to escape to a haven of quiet and repose from the noisiness and tempo of the industrial world. The former loses all sense of the fraternal by reason of the callous demands of the necessarily bureaucratic operations of industry, business, and government. Fulfilment is alienated by the requirements of the job. The latter dissipates the fraternal in the overly subjective cuddling of the passions to oneself. Epicurean-like, it demands a walled garden from which prying eyes can be shut out. Neither the civic nor the suburban is quite capable of cultivating a morality which sustains fruitful social relations in institutions that can be admired and wholeheartedly nourished. In both, the sense of the tribal is destroyed either in institutions in which man can take little pride because of the empty objectivity which alienates him from his fellow men or in the meaningless subjectivities of life which can have no proper outward expression.[9] For similar but opposite reasons, both are spurious and both negate the conditions of authenticity demanded by a genuine culture.

To reinfuse something of the tribal spirit into modern industrial life without succumbing to hopeless romanticism becomes one of the most pressing problems of contemporary social theory. Various solutions of the problem have been proposed, none of them quite insignificant, yet none of them quite adequate to the proportions of the problem. Regionalism, various attempts at communal living, decentralization, group psychotherapy, industrial reorganization emphasizing human relations, the fostering of the social ethic, urban renewal, and a multitude of other social devices, suggest a growing awareness of the need to come to terms with ways in which fraternity can once more be made germane to life in an industrial world. I do not regard it as appropriate here to canvass the multitudinous suggestions or to try to evaluate them, for such a task as this should be undertaken only on a cooperative basis, involving, as it must, detailed knowledge and expertise far beyond the competence of a single individual. Nevertheless, I cannot resist the temptation to make a few observations on one proposal, simply because of its extraordinary relevance to the terms in which the problems of an industrial society are set, and, judging on the basis of already achieved performance, the promise it holds for the future. This proposal is a form of regionalism.

Perhaps the most impressive aspect of regionalism is its generosity of scope in viewing the varied expressions of human life. Sensitive to the need for conceiving life which is both vivid and intense and also prolonged and rewarding, it attempts to cope with the need for productive relations between men, and it has regard for the natural setting in which human relations are mediated and sustained by man's intimate connections with nature. In other words, it attempts to cope with the continuities of social life by enlarging man's capacity to appreciate and more fully to exploit nature. Natural resources are thought of as bearing some rational connection with a rooted, cultural existence—one in which man is committed to living with nature indefinitely, and not just one by which he can gain some temporary advantage. David Lilienthal recognized this in what he thoughtfully spoke of as "nature's remorseless arithmetic."[10] The context of regionalism, then, is nature and human nature, and the myriads of relations which obtain within each as well as between each.

In the contemporary mode, the relations of man to nature are increasingly mediated through machine-technology, involving as it does the most taxing of human knowledge, from theoretical physics to practical chemistry and applied biology. Folk knowledge and superstition come to be replaced by accumulated information, tested laws, and experiments devised in the meaningful context of human urgencies. The laboratory, the field, and men's hopes jointly enhance and support one another by virtue of destroying the barriers between research and intellectual activities as well as between men's emotions and practical life. Regionalism is a way of providing man with a moral equivalent of tribal life. It is an attempt to encourage social intercourse which, using the hidden resources of a geographical region and establishing a sense of a community of interests, will not be overwhelmed by outside influences, whether economic, political, artistic, religious, or by any other that is incapable becoming authenticated in a community's life. Externalities there will always be, and they will have to be coped with. But as soon as alien ownership, whether of property or of mentality, dominates a region, it becomes lost in the cosmopolitanism of arid conformity. A new tribalism would exploit its own resources to the full. It would not neglect the outside, but it would reject externalities which it could not introduce into the mold of its own genuine attainments.

Regionalism looks to an enrichment of the community in ways that people have ever sought it. In a literal sense, it looks to the enrichment of the soil, and of ways of making it most fertile with the least expenditure of effort. It looks to enrichment of human intercourse, first, just in making it possible for neighbor to come to know neighbor. This it attempts to achieve by laying bare the common ground on which they can creatively enmesh self-interest with common need. By making possible new inter-relations between the personal and the impersonal, regionalism can liberate persons from their stuffy, self-imposed limitations and give them opportunities for creating a more generous life. Thus, secondly, it looks to the further enrichment of human intercourse by exploiting the folklore which gives them a common point of view for a literature continuous with the past yet struggling to interpret the quandaries of their own day. In this sense, folklore is regarded not as an end in itself but rather as myths that cry out for the genius of reinterpretation so that the writer may contribute his insight to the requirements of the cultural processes. Such a regionalism engages not just practical ends but the intellectual and the emotional as well. It engages them all in the charged atmos-phere of the demands upon men to be full participants in a genuine culture.

A culture so conceived is one committed to the peaceful arts, for these are the expression of men's social needs, however much they may at times be obscured by disrupting biological factors and superimposed ideological dogmas. When human life can exist, it is supported by the industrial arts, improved by the fine arts, and bound together by the philosophical arts. The special locus of our perplexities today, as we have already amply seen, is in science and the use made of it in the power institutions of the industrial peoples of the world. The uses to which science has recently been put render questionable the extent to which regions can become the loci of genuine cultures. Whether a river valley development, such as the Tennessee Valley Authority in our country, or a region, say, such as the Middle East, is capable of developing into genuine cultural units depends in the last analysis upon equitable solutions of outstanding differences between the power blocs of the world. As long as these differences plague the world, contemporary man is compelled to concentrate his attention upon responses to threats of his extinction rather than upon the means of his only legitimate destiny—the advancement of the peaceful arts.

War can be legitimated only by peace. For this reason, world war is now obsolete, and lesser wars are so close to the edge of catastrophe that statesmen cannot but bend every effort to outlaw them. The pressure is for them to seek the only final solution possible in the contemporary world: the destruction of the institution of scientific warfare. Anything less than this is a stop-gap and an indication that the will to scourge the supreme threat to man has faltered. Expediency may dictate all kinds of dodges from the bold policy required, but as long as expediency makes use of the very kind of power which it is its intent to obliterate, its dishonesty is obvious wherever there is still left a conscience in the world of nations. Proposals for peace can be only radical or worthless, for as long as scientific warfare remains possible so does total extinction of mankind, and with him the extinction of the peaceful arts. Limited warfare, however enticing for advancing the immediate prospects of peaceful aims, appears also to be ruled out as a way of attaining peace, for it, too, can only perpetuate that which it is meant to efface. Nothing short of a ruthless, concerted will to expunge the means of warfare can make it an unreality for man.

Modern warfare is the supreme instrument of power in the life of man. It is commonly recognized as requiring the total resources of a people and of obliterating the distinction between military and civilian. Virtually no one is excused from contributing to its services, and virtually no one is free from the power of retaliation. Total, efficient, and hierarchial, it lacks all democratic accountability. Once undertaken, it is increasingly incapable of being legitimated and in truth is unmistakable evidence of the abdication of men from devotion to life, whether for themselves or for others. Unable to devise Truces of God or Peaces of the Church, and the like, modern warfare knows no limitation of power other than that imposed by the logistics of itself. Remaining ever an invitation to the arbitrary employment of power, it contravenes all the principles of genuine culture and provides no ends for the direction of life. Since as a power institution it is incapable of being justified by any contribution to a peaceful world, the only pertinent question is how to blot it out.

There is only one way of blotting it out, and that is to blot out the institution of warfare. When men are serious about having a peaceful world, they will do this. Otherwise, they will not. For only as they are willing to destroy the means by which alone warfare is possible are they in the final analysis willing to obliterate war.[11] The institutions of power accomplish their ends only as appropriate tools are devised for them. Economic life requires goods, the market, and, in a complex industrial society, the written instruments of contracts, together with means for enforcing them. Political life requires information-gatherers, policy-makers, administrators, law-enforcement officers, etc. Warfare requires armaments, a military caste, and a reserve of men who can be drawn upon. To destroy these institutions is to destroy their instruments—only in the last case the destruction can go too far, for it may also destroy those who must be saved for other kinds of pursuits. Fortunately, men are not potential armies unless they have armaments. Even more fortunately, when armaments are destroyed, so is the military caste, which can then become only a functionless decoration. The underlying question, accordingly, turns out to be whether it is really possible to destroy the armaments of war.

The question is fairly complex in industrial societies today, because the line between peaceful goods and armaments is sometimes shadowy, and, some insist, may be undetectably crossed. Nucleonics, aeronautics, radar, sputniks, and the like, in themselves neutral, may be put to either peaceful or war-like uses, even though the development of either contributes knowledge valuable for the other. Are we not then actually being unrealistic and naive in believing that anything short of the total destruction of industrial power institutions of the world can prevent the threat of world war? In part, the answer is highly technical, since it may be that even with the dissolution of all that we today regard as contributing to warfare—armaments, military and naval academies, officers, uniforms, insignia, war departments, armies, etc.— some neurotic civilian may still be capable of setting off a world conflagration by means of some "gadget" which was actually intended for peaceful purposes or which could be created by some slight modification of a device so intended. Dogmatism will not do for an answer to this question. Yet it is only reasonable to point out that if our industrial world has arrived at such a state, the elaborate organization of institutions of war with their incredible costs in human and natural resources surely could not be an answer to such a threat. Any reasonable response to the likelihood of such a fiend's ambitions would have to be sought in a kind of police power the civilized world has always legitimately recognized, and this power is not to be confused with organized military might.

Assuming, then, that the institution of warfare requires organized military force, we may still insist that only the dismantling of the military organization provides a real prospect for outlawing war, first because there would be then no instrumentalities to carry on warfare, and secondly because there would be no mentality for it. The result would be to channel social mentality to occupations devoted to the peaceful arts. This would truly be a revolution for man: the revolution of beating swords into ploughshares. Come this revolution, modern man would be forced to express his aggressiveness in forms less lethal to the peoples of the world. What particular forms this aggressiveness might take is no longer our question since it could not under the circumstances contribute to organized world annihilation. What may be regarded as our question, however, is, what kind of mentality need we seek to replace that of the military?

In the final analysis, there is only one mentality that can properly replace the military, and that is the philosophic. Traditionally, this is a mentality committed only to the love of wisdom, not to sectarianism, partisanism, or activism. It favors a method of the dialectic of questioning and answering, but seeks truth wherever it may lie—in young or old, in persons, books, or nature. It refuses to believe in creeds, dogmas, or superstitions. Yet it is humble before irreducible facts and flawless demonstrations. It prizes imaginative insight, clarity, and synthesis. And most especially, it aims to orient man in his world through an understanding of his nature, his institutions, and the world in which they have their being. Human experience, whether common or whether refined in the crucible of social, artistic, scientific, and religious thought, is the material philosophy evaluates and purifies in the processes of analysis, synthesis, and orientation.[12] The creative genius of philosophy has historically been to provide men with "a sense of direction" gained from the interpretation and evaluation of human experience and the forces at work in the world by which this experience can be made more meaningful.

Religion and science, the two dominant forces in the occidental world which have at different times been intimately related to the power institutions of politics, both have occupied central positions in philosophical thought. And both have evolved and been defended on universalist grounds. The philosophic justifications of each have necessarily been trans-nationalistic. Experience has suffered, and philosophy has degenerated into mere polemics, under attempts to confine justification of these subjects within nationalistic or provincial outlooks. Clearly, the reason is that philosophic justification, even when it appreciates particularities, is cognizant of the universals which render justification of the particulars. Save when philosophy is confused by an inadequate realization of its own stated principles—such as happened in both Hegel's and Spencer's dicta on politics—its orientation is toward man and the world in which he lives. However difficult actual philosophical communication may be today, it aims nevertheless to be rational and trans-national. It shares a mentality with science in both these regards, and with religion in the latter regard.

The philosophic mentality can flourish only as communication and the discourse of men in society are furthered. The military mentality can flourish only as communication and discourse among men are severed. The former entails a will which can be only partly known and which comes to ever new concreteness as communication advances. The latter entails a will that knows itself, without doubts and questionings, and seeks to express itself by eliminating obstacles. The former seeks continuities of growing experience, the latter the discontinuities that leave experience complacent by shutting out disturbances that would otherwise challenge pre-commitments. The former is tentative, reaching, and open; the latter dogmatic, grasping, and tidy. The mentality of philosophy is international and, more and more, seeks international congresses to further its ends. The military mentality is national and seeks blocs to bolster its position. There can be no doubt which of the two fosters international co-operation and which tries to prevent it.

The mentality of philosophy is by nature favorable to, as well as favored by, a peaceful world. By effecting syntheses, philosophy makes for the maximum of continuities in human experience and a minimum of segmentation, alienations, and frustrations. The impetus of discourse is to penetrate the obscurities of life. Poetry and art enlighten the dark emotions and dumb feelings of man and turn them into shapes become intelligible in expression and capable of being shared in vivid and intense communication. Giving experience words and rhythm and colors, they transmute it into a form the human spirit can savor and in which it can deepen its insights. Science, too, penetrates life's obscurities, but in a rather different way. It dissolves the pictorial shapes of things into refined structures, adequately grasped only when they are stated in the language of mathematics. Art in its particularity and science in its universality constitute two poles of communication that challenge philosophy to seek paradoxically the universal in art and the particular in science. The full realization of the task of philosophy is so to enlighten an age that morality can be supported by science and humanized by art. This has been, at least in the Western world, the historic function of philosophy—the drive to interpret the good, the true, and the beautiful in a way that reasonably permits man to be at home in the world.

"To be at home in the world"—this is at bottom to adopt the fraternal ideal. A philosophical outlook which rejects it is overly prone to the immediacies of the institutions of power and obtuse to the realities of human existence. By inverting the part which power rightly plays in supporting brotherhood, the narrow outlook comes to regard power in some chauvinistic terms that can serve only to debase brotherhood. Narrowly conceived, brotherhood inevitably leads to senseless clashes among men. It stems from an invidious insistence upon establishing and maintaining relations of prestige. And it finds its supreme justification in death where death can mean at best only sentimental martyrdom and at worst violent extinction of life.

The broader philosophic mentality aiming at the maximization of communication requires as conditions of its practice peace and co-operation. A philosopher's credentials consist not in prestige, not in age or popularity, but only in the quality of his ideas and his willingness to subject them to criticism, which alone can validate them. The learning it requires is that which can be brought to the level of discussion as relevant to the argument. But it requires, in addition, the community of interest which can make it profitable. The conditions and practice of philosophy are democratic. Any of the experience of mankind is relevant to its scope. No one is excluded from advancing his arguments. Every claim must be justified. Criticism is undertaken by the community of minds, speaking, listening, challenging, and agreeing as far as the validation of the argument demands. The unity is only the community of those who feel impelled to give expression to their deepest insights and who are willing to share them even at the risk of having them turn out to be "wind eggs." The community of the spirit, universal, peaceful, and democratic is the condition of the philosophic enterprise. Anything short of this is a hindrance to philosophy and represents a bondage of the power institutions over the human spirit.

From the universality of the spirit of philosophy, I wish briefly to draw a few major implications for nationalism and world government. I shall not try to spell them out in detail.

Nationalism is cultural or imperial or, usually, a mixture of the two. Imperial nationalism is no longer justifiable. In its imperialistic phase, it is brute industrial power exercised over a militarily weaker people. The patently hypocritical slogans of bringing civilization to the uncivilized no longer fool anyone, East or West, industrial or non-industrial. Whether the power is exerted as a direct military power or threat of it or of any indirect economic hegemony with all its political consequences, the exercise of that power of one nation over another, unilaterally conceived, is beyond the pale of justification, despite the fact that it has been the fundamental premise of international relations from the first beginnings of the nation-state to the League of Nations. Such power is unjustifiable because, first, it is wantonly destructive and therefore improves neither the wielders of power nor those against whom it is wielded. Secondly, it is partial in that the interests it furthers are rarely representative of the interests of the nation and are therefore biased and involve invidious comparisons. Thirdly, they are costly and inequitable in that those who are required to bear most heavily the financial and human burdens of imperial power are those who least benefit from them. Fourthly, imperialism is immoral, for it destroys the human spirit both of those who as colonials are enslaved by a power which must remain alien to them, and of those who exercise a power which alienates them from the subjects on whom it is imposed.

Of the various political forms of imperial nationalism, fascism, in the generic sense, is the worst. It is the worst simply because it is an intensification of the most inhuman aspects of national life. It predicates its nationalism on the most arbitrary of grounds: those which are intended, as for example in race, absolutely to alienate all but an elite group. And even within the elite, communication is a one-way affair—from the leader to the led, with an insistence upon absolute discipline of the led. Still more important, however, is the insistence that the elite be maintained by its combined military power to be exercised over the rest of the world. By its intrinsic nature, and not by accident, fascism is a menace to world peace, the worst possible, and the least excusable, form of nationalism.

Cultural nationalism, on the contrary, is a determined attempt to achieve more intense and rewarding forms of communication among those who can share a common language, common folkways, and other historical roots on which may be grafted a lively play of the human spirit. It is exclusive only in the sense that it excludes all who are unwilling to become converts by the exacting business of learning the language, customs, and history of the people and of engaging in the give-and-take which perpetuates national life. Cultural nationalism requires institutions of power for supporting itself, but, as with cultural regions, the use of the institutions of power aims to make the external internal, rather than the internal external. Their relations to the rest of the world are viewed through the potentialities for co-operation rather than through those of dominance and conflict.

The most serious and effective criticism of imperial nationalisms lies in their disrespect for international relations. The most serious and effective criticism of cultural nationalisms lies in their disrespect for regional integrities. Further discussion of the coercive and unwanted effects of imperialism on other peoples is in this day unnecessary. But a word about the discontinuities caused by cultural nationalism is called for. National boundaries are likely to be insufferably bad from the point of view of cultural separations of peoples geographically juxtaposed. Nature's seamless web is violated by historical accident which, by being rigidly perpetuated, destroys opportunities of peoples to come together in ways mutually stimulating and functional. Cultural nationalisms can become—and increasingly are becoming—obsolete, either because they are too big or too small. A nationalism proves to be too big when it imposes a cultural uniformity which robs a region of the functional diversities which would otherwise be sustained. Overwhelmed by traditions remote from, or only casually related to, a people's lives, the diversities succumb to a conformity incapable of supporting vital beliefs and consequently incapable of providing functional orientation for their actions. On the other hand, a cultural nationalism is too limited when it divides regions by, say, river banks, where fruitful commerce and harmonious development of life in the valley is thereby impeded by divisions abhorrent to the natural impulsions to social intercourse.

The complement to regional development turns out to be more and more the need for a sane world of international relations. Economic life demands it, industry favors it, politics increasingly acquiesces to it, and the threats of modern warfare make it indispensable. Trade barriers among nations become ever less reasonable. The sharing of industrial wisdom approximates a moral obligation. Insistence upon the sovereignty of nations can only make a mockery of civic life, forever precluding the only power that can reasonably sustain it. The dialectic of fraternity cannot be satisfied today with any embodiment short of a world power sufficient to prevent military encroachments and therefore sufficient to adjudicate conflicts in the collective lives of the peoples of the world. Short of this fraternity, no culture is safe from violence. Beyond it, new social realities are capable of arising in a variety of institutions devoted to the expression of the peaceful arts.

PART IV

The Institutions of Expression

" . . . amenability to diffusion is an essential determinant of true excellence. Things which can be 'appreciated' only by the few are not excellent; they are taboo. The supposition that only the elite can appreciate true excellence is not merely snobbery; it is ceremonialism, pure and simple."—C. E. AYRES, *Southwest Review,* Spring 1959, p. 144.

Chapter 8
CREATIVITY IN THE ARTS

THE INSTITUTIONS OF POWER NEED A PRINCIPLE OF legitimation which can provide direction and purpose. The institutions of expression need a principle of criticism which can provide a heightening of human sensibilities. When government, law, and the organization of economies are not confined to their rightful provinces, they stultify the arts and disturb the artist's mind. When the arts are not permitted to filter into and temper the mentality of the public, its policies cannot but lose some of their potential vitality. The creative vitalities of the arts cannot be realized unless there is a wide, literate public which is sensitive to expression and which encourages its further liberation. The life-blood of the process is criticism, for criticism is the way open to the public to take the arts seriously. Whereas censorship aims to stifle the arts, criticism aims to free them from their arbitrariness and littleness in order to make them important in the life of a people.

Only once in history, it seems, has anything like an extended liberation and criticism of the arts prevailed in the life of a people. In classical Greece we witness the remains of arts which looked to symmetry and proportion as guiding ideals. In sculpturing the aim was to give substance to the virtues of the body, perfected, and expressive of human qualities. In architecture it was to enclose finite space with elegance. In tragic poetry it was not only to spell out the crushing consequences that result from excesses or deficiencies of character, but also to do it in a way which, as Aristotle dryly observed, has a beginning, a middle, and an end. And in every phase of life, private and public, the immediate demands of elegance were such as to caution against an ugly separation of means and ends. Accordingly, beauty became an operative ideal in every aspect of human action. I call attention to classical Greece, not from any desire to urge that we emulate it, but merely to illustrate an engaging instance of social institutions that systematically care for and support human expression. The illustration suggests that it simply is not true that there is any necessary conflict between the creativities of individuals and the institutions (especially those of power) which constitute the rigidities within which the creative life must flow. Yet many persons, especially among those who regard art as a kind of inner expression, are unalterably opposed to this suggestion.

By concentrating primarily upon the inner aspects of expression, one in effect makes it precious. It becomes an affair of the subterranean workings of the emotions, and the more refined the emotions are supposed to be, the more occult they are. Yet, surely it is true that there is no expression without some internal turmoil. And the art which results from such turmoil is certain to mirror the anguish out of which it came to be created. Moreover, the creator of such art inevitably breaks through the habitual perceptions and standardized conceptions of things, whose primary virtues are customary and utilitarian rather than aesthetic. The demands for freshness, for breaking through encrusted tradition, for forging a new language appropriate to new insights—these demands are to be met if there is to be any creativity at all. There is no doubt that the arts stand as indisputable testimony to the creative processes wrought through the emotional life of man.

The questions which these introductory remarks raise begin to carry us beyond the platitude that somehow the arts of expression and the institutions of power are reconcilable. We want to know in a more precise way what is involved in expression and what connections it has with the kind of life a people may lead. We want to know what is the nature of the hidden subjectivities and how they can possibly come to be the source of those objectivities we call works of art and which others besides the creator may enjoy. We want to know how creativity bridges the gap between the inner and the outer, and how, once this gap is bridged, creativity, which has the stamp of individuality on it, can possibly possess significance for other individuals, each with his own unique outlook. We want to know what the common ground is by which individuals can share their insights and thus contribute to a life greater than that of a single person or of any esoteric group of persons. We want to know why some kinds of creativity may be called great while others are trivial and inconsequential. We want to know what those who do not create art can significantly say about it and why, in fact, they should be able to say anything about it that the artist hasn't already said better in the work itself. Again, we want to know why there are various forms of expression making for different kinds of arts, and whether there may not be new forms that we have not anticipated. These are some of an indefinite number of questions to which we want answers. In order to come to grips with them in a more systematic way, I propose to consider them under the large topics of: (1) what expression is in the arts, (2) the function of criticism, and (3) the kinds of arts and their role in culture, especially in a genuine culture for today. I shall break each of these topics into what I regard as their significant elements and try to determine the relations they bear to one another.

"Expression" is one of those terms which is so abused that it has become almost meaningless. In itself it is much too broad, if not ambiguous, to denote anything precise. As a blanket term it may become useful only as it is defined in relation to its ingredients. There may be some advantage in first applying it to the fine arts in connection with (a) the nature of creativity, (b) aesthetic form, (c) aesthetic meaning, (d) the function of art, and (e) greatness in art. Each of these deserves to be amplified.

Creativity has two major aspects, depending upon whether we regard it as an end or as a process. As an end it denotes synthesis, a kind of wholeness in which the parts are held together by meaningful tensions. By virtue of the dynamics involved, mind can run through the elements in a way which causes them to merge into an organic relationship. In its simplest form, the creative synthesis is exemplified in perception. The essence of perception is an experience, a unification of qualities, which if taken separately are abstract and therefore not quite perceivable, but which taken in their relations one to another make sense as an aesthetic whole. Thus when I perceive this old shoe or that locust tree or the distant snowy mountain range, I perceive the elements subordinated to a unity in a way such as a painter might want to "catch" it in his painting. Perception is the simplest form of effecting a synthesis, which, however humble, is the prototype of man's creative activity. It contains the basic ingredients of the higher forms of the creative imagination, and, despite its apparent simplicity, it is a complex, and in many ways a baffling, order of experience. Its apparent simplicity is, I suspect, a somewhat paradoxical consequence of the fact that the complexities are concealed by the thoroughgoing unity of the experience itself.

When creativity is regarded as a process rather than as an end, one begins to appreciate something more of the intricacies of the amalgam which the experience contains. The tensions it involves, the emotional elements, pleasures as well as agonies, memory together with its further associations, the intellect and its transformations in being recast into the immediacies of experience— these appear to be aspects which enter into the synthesis which we call perception. The joy of perception possibly hides them from consciousness. Depth psychology, however, has made us more alert to layers of meaning within experience contained in processes that rarely rise to the level of consciousness. There is a literal sense in which we may say of the artist that he knows not what he does. We need not repeat the allusion to "the poet, the lover, and the madman of imagination compact," but the integral connection between the irrational and the rational can hardly escape us once we come to penetrate more deeply what is involved in the creative act. It is not difficult to understand why so many who attempt to analyze the processes of creativity finally surrender and declare them to be a matter of "genius" or "inspiration," which is said to be basically incapable of being analyzed. Surely anyone who seriously tries to penetrate the cavernous sources of the creative spirit cannot but wonder whether the mysteries and paradoxes are ultimately capable of being explained. Yet to capitulate to the belief of their being inexplicable brings no real solace, nor does it necessarily make for more sensitive appreciation of the actual creativities to be found in our world.

The challenge is to discover a point of attack which will disclose the secrets that underlie creativity. Such a point of attack ought to be functional and it ought to avoid stringing out of verbal synonyms which add nothing to our comprehension of the creative process, such as either identifying it with the fresh or the novel, and the like, or of opposing it to the imitative, the mechanical, the contrived, and so on. What, then, would constitute a functional attack? The first and probably most obvious suggestion that comes to mind is that it should be one which aims to analyze the whole into its elements. No great amount of experience is required, however, to see that this suggestion will not do. It will not do simply because the whole becomes dissipated into its elements, and although we may have a firm grasp of them, the very thing we have been looking for escapes us while we clutch other things that do not add up to the aesthetic whole. To avoid this there appears to be no alternative but to try to penetrate the nature of the synthetic process itself. But to do so means, paradoxically, to discover continuities in what appears to be discontinuous. Such an attempt may well be doomed to failure. Yet even though it may not yield the solutions we want, a strategy calculated to disclose the nature of the creative process may at least be expected to reveal more accurately the kinds of problems that are involved in an understanding of it. Bearing in mind these various injunctions, I can think of no better strategy than to engage in an analysis which regards the process as having a beginning, a middle, and an end. This kind of genetic approach is least likely to distort the nature of the process. It is best suited to permit observation of both the continuities and the discontinuities that it contains. It is designed to avoid useless verbalisms, and it is calculated to exclude an appeal to some human faculty whether it is called an aesthetic or a creative faculty, or what-not, which could only beg the question at hand.

The art-process begins in tension, which is at first an inchoate restlessness, scarcely better characterizable than a mood, whether forbidding or sanguine or any of an indefinite range between the two. It may be the "Ides of March" that suggests the tragedy to follow, or it may be the birth of a child whose history the writer is to unfold. It may be a room in some disarray and a color-scheme that sets the mood for an anticipated sequence. For example, Dostoyevsky gives us a foretaste of *Crime and Punishment* in these opening words:

"On an exceptionally hot evening early in July a young man came out of the garret in which he lodged in S. Place and walked slowly, as though in hesitation, towards K. bridge." We are further told, "He had successfully avoided meeting his landlady on the staircase. His garret was under the roof of a high, five-storied house and was more like a cupboard than a room." He wished to avoid his landlady who lived below, and whose kitchen he must pass, where the door invariably stood open. "And each time he passed, the young man had a sick, frightened feeling, which made him scowl and feel ashamed. He was hopelessly in debt to his landlady, and was afraid of meeting her. This was not because he was cowardly and abject, quite the contrary; but for some time past he had been in an overstrained irritable condition, verging on hypochondria . . . he dreaded meeting . . . any one at all. He was crushed by poverty, but the anxieties of his position had of late ceased to weigh upon him." Creeping down the stairs, he thinks, "I want to attempt a thing like that and am frightened by these trifles." Exactly seven hundred and thirty steps from the gates of his lodging, he goes up to a huge house on the canal. Ascending the stairs, he goes to the old woman's apartment.

> The old woman stood facing him in silence and looking inquiringly at him. She was a diminutive, withered up old woman of sixty, with sharp malignant eyes and a sharp little nose. . . . Round her thin long neck, which looked like a hen's leg, was knotted some sort of flannel rag, and, in spite of the heat, there hung flapping on her shoulders, a mangy fur cape, yellow with age.

Then the room into which he passes is described as one "with yellow paper on the walls, geraniums and muslin curtains in the windows." Scanning it, he finds

> nothing special in the room. The furniture, all very old and of yellow wood, consisted of a sofa with a huge bent wooden back, an oval table in front of the sofa, a dressing-table with a looking-glass fixed on it between the windows, chairs along the walls and two or three halfpenny prints in yellow frames, representing German damsels with birds in their hands—that was all.

This description has style. Out of a highly impersonal, almost reportorial account of a man in cramped quarters, unwilling to face his landlady because of the trivialities inevitable in his meeting with the old woman, practically yellow with age, like the setting of her apartment, Dostoyevsky gives us to know that crime must be committed. We perceive that this is a deranged mind, but with superior qualities, not ordinary ones, even if they are not superior enough to transcend the quality of crime. This is the beginning big with a future and crying for an explanation of what the forces might be to bring a man to such a state. We cannot but identify ourselves with a character who, although somewhat mad, has the engrossing madness of a person we must come to know and for whom we must have a sympathy. In Raskolnikov, Dostoyevsky makes, even in the first impression he gives of him, a creature through whom we come to discern a quality in life. In the matter of a few paragraphs so much is said, if only we are capable of penetrating its meaning.

"So much is said" but so little is heard—this is the reason why we must go on to attune our ears to the theme and to hear eventually in the reverberating echoes the qualities desiderated by the writer. Perhaps a creator of art doesn't quite know in the beginning what its qualities are, and probably it is necessary even for him to write the novel, or paint the picture, or compose and orchestrate the symphony, before he knows precisely what its distinctive nature is. Whether or not he knows it in advance of creation, the master somehow intuits it even in the beginning. The appreciator, more vaguely and less surely, may sense it through the movement by which it is delineated and through which alone he can come to share with the creator the perception of it. Can one account more accurately for the intuiting or sensing of what is to come in the unfolding of the work of art? I am not sure that I can, or that in this context it is appropriate, to ferret out the intricacies of what in the process arrests the attention and yet creates a dynamic of movement. Yet some comments on the topic may be useful.

The fact of the matter is contained in the glaring paradox just suggested. Attention must be arrested and yet carried on in a moving way. This double aspect of attention is indispensable to art if, one, it is to be interesting, and, two, it is to be moving. Frankly, a person would find it awkward to believe a thing to possess the qualities of art if it were not engaging in both senses.

To become the object of engaging attention and to be engaged in a movement towards fulfilment—these seem to be conditions essential to any noteworthy judgments pertinent to the qualities of anything we may reasonably a work of art.

To be engaging in the first sense is to be an object of perception. Some would regard perception as a kind of original fact of experience, not capable of being analyzed into simpler components without destroying the character of this particular form of experience. To analyze percepts into sensations and then to find some intelligible way of making them again cohere into the kind of whole that perception is hasn't proved to be a very happy procedure, as William James in his objections to the analysis of lemonade into its component qualities effectively argued long ago. But whether perception has some relation to the emotional and volitional life is a different matter. Such a suggestion may help to indicate why there can be a sustained interest in perceiving, an interest which gives roots to what is otherwise an inexplicable datum of consciousness. By relating perception to the conative phases of human life, we can better understand how a person comes to focus upon some things rather than upon others and to find in what he perceives a relevancy to life which would otherwise escape him. Since there are so many things to perceive, we need a theory of why a person is receptive only to some things, and especially why, in view of the vast number of things capable of being perceived, he is able to exclude the vast majority of them. Because consciousness is drastically limited in what it can take in, it is saved from the shambles of reeling confusion. This limitation is a condition of the ordering of experience. Accordingly, only by insisting upon a principle of relevancy of percepts to emotional and volitional life, as well as to the intellectual, can we hope to derive an explanation of what is involved in aesthetic meaning.

We are often reminded that the understanding of a work of art should not go beyond its frame, or as Archibald MacLeish has expressed it, "A poem should not mean, but be." Surely there is some sense in which this is so, even though the beginnings of the processes of both appreciation and creation cry out for connecting links which can provide a work of art with stuff that comes from the rougher texture of crude experience.[1] There is reason to enjoin our not going beyond the frame of a work of art, but there is even more reason in observing that the frame is fixed to the work after it is completed, not before. The painter begins with a blank canvas. When he paints, he often slips off the canvas and at times must even contrive to keep the painting on it. The success he has comes when he can drain his meaning into the pigments which are only later marked off as an independent artifact, a thing which comes to have a life of its own separate from that of the creator. To refer again to Mr. MacLeish's "Ars Poetica," we note that he doesn't begin by telling us that a poem should be and not mean. He begins by invoking images of globed fruit, motionless climbing moons, and memories of the mind, together with other reinforcing similes. In a sense, we may conclude in more philosophical language that existence precedes essence, where essences are to be understood only as they come about through the prior existences which intrude into them and give them substance. Otherwise essences are pale logical subsistences, too universal to contain sensuous, aesthetic embodiment.

Because of the connecting links due to pigments or words or the other media of the various arts, we are not only justified in seeking the beginnings of aesthetic meaning in the non-aesthetic, but we seem compelled to do so. The very fact that, for example, a poem is given a title is a recognition by the author that it is legitimate to suggest something of the nature of the link between the aesthetic and the non-aesthetic. The serious difficulty which this point of view involves is, of course, that of explaining how the non-aesthetic can enter into the aesthetic, for is there not a fundamental breach between the two? The question is fairly raised and deserves an appropriate answer.

Actually, the question refers once again to what was earlier said to be the paradox of aesthetic meaning. Aesthetic meaning involves both discontinuities and continuities of experience. How then can things which are only externally related become internally related in a flow which makes them confluent in the art-process? What is the means by which the extra-aesthetic is transmuted into the aesthetic? The explanation appears to reside in the fact that perception is doubly oriented. It pertains not merely to the immediate content of experience but also to the fact that experience is moving—it carries on, or, according to the irresistible metaphor, it is a stream. Essentially, the aesthetic is perceptual and selective and involves tensions, not just a dislodgement of an external force against which one responds. The kind of dislodgement which may be regarded as aesthetic is perception which seeks fulfilment in its intrinsic movement. Words, sounds, colors connote. Even as with lines, they are dynamic. They set up thrusts which require counter-thrusts and resolutions. When the poet wants us to perceive yellow, and not just watch it, he contrasts it with another. Thus, against yellow is placed black, and against black is pale. Opposed to pale is bright red. But the genius of the poet is to sense that bright red is hectic (consumptive) red. This is aesthetic engagement as a moving experience. From

> Yellow and black and pale and hectic red
> Pestilence-stricken multitudes

follows as inevitably as fever from dis-ease. The lyrical and the rhythmic exist not just on their own account, musical as they may be. They complete the meaning; they bear its implications, as the flower is born by the bud, different yet continuous with it as it opens to the sunlight. Perception is not bare like a sensum. It is clothed like a body which is nevertheless revealed in the directions of the folds of the drapes. This it is which makes perception both arresting and engaging.

From the beginnings of the art-process, there are the shadings that imperceptibly lead to the middle. The difference is more one of emphasis than of kind. So subtly do the tensions carry us on, we are scarcely aware of the movement, say, from the wind to the "leaves dead from an enchanter fleeing." The fact of the matter is that perception takes time. It is not so much a "given" as it is something lived through, an *Erlebnis*. In many ways, the experience of art makes a stronger claim for capturing the essence of the life-processes than does so-called practical experience. The dynamics of the art-process set in motion a genetic development in which the connective tissues cannot be ruptured without ruining its very character. Very often practical experience is divisive and its economy reductive. By reducing consciousness to data having only partly intelligible references to other data, it rends consciousness into elements which lose their intrinsic value in favor of extrinsic meanings. The aesthetic, on the contrary, is marked by the cumulative movement from beginning to end. To borrow from T. S. Eliot with an intent, of course, quite different from his, we may say, "In my beginning is my end," as well as "In my end is my beginning." The middle is just that which mediates between beginning and end.

Since the middle mediates beginning and end, it partakes of both. As regards its likeness to the end, it is fundamentally cumulative and resolutive. The earlier is borne over into the later in clarifying and explicating the tensions, not just in adding to them. At the same time, the process is one of climaxes and partial resolutions, constantly gaining power and certitude for reaching the supreme climax which the energies involved are capable of expressing. In order to achieve such a resolution aesthetically, there must be, however, the "perches" which permit the gathering of new energies in the savoring of the immediate meanings before their power stimulates renewed flight. The perch represents the end conceived as a culmination of what has gone before. It also represents a beginning in respect to further development. It is like the beginning of a new stanza of a poem in which the poet, say, having developed his theme in reference to things on dry land, begins a new episode by diving into the sea and allows the theme further to evolve through watery things. By seizing upon contrasts and similarities, the poet need not confront the awful breach between poetry and dumb feeling, even though something of the same breach is present in the radical period that ends a stanza. Although his momentum is not completely lost in the period, the rhythmic cadences are not enough to produce the novelty that can come only from extra-rhythmic sources. In other words, the creative spirit requires an endless store of materials which can be molded into form consonant with the demands of the tensions to be resolved.

The middle, then, requires whole sequences of new starts. But they are sequences and therefore not so arbitrary as the start which we have called the beginning. In fact, the genius of the creator is found largely in the sequence of starts. Whereas the less gifted will often drain the quality from a start until it becomes dull rather than expressive, the genius will hit upon new turns and juxtapose materials that provide a seemingly inexhaustible richness of aesthetic meaning. No tawdry imitator, he infuses personal insights into a logic of artistic development that combines uniqueness with universality. The starts provide contact with the arbitrary world of existences, unexpressed impulses, and ununderstood feelings. The creative process is one through which existences come to be transformed into essences, impulses come to be expressed, and feelings come to be understood. The processes culminate in the quiescence of tensions, the expression, which is the end of the art-process.

The end of the art-process is the decisive testimony of whether the artist has succeeded in turning his materials into a veritable work of art. In it one confirms whether cumulation upon cumulation finally issues into that synthesis of expressive elements which in truth constitutes expression. Expression is the more complete realization of the less complete expressions characteristic of the middle. It is the more solid perch from which can be surveyed the totality of beginning-middle-end, so integrated that a person may be said to have gained insight from it. In it the various themes have come to their conclusion so that if it is, for example, of the leaves dead, of the dirge of a dying year, or of the sapless foliage of the ocean, they all bear upon the trumpet of a prophecy that "If Winter comes, can Spring be far behind?" Whether it is the regeneration of life, the assurance that good fences makes good neighbors, or whatever naturally brings to a conclusion the varieties of impressions the poet selects for bearing the process of poetic movement, the movement comes to be stilled in the exploitation of their expressive potencies. Having made the impressions say what they have to say, the poet can say no more.

The magic of art lies in its finalities, or at least in the feeling of them as finalities. The lesser finalities are those perfect phrases or lines which, inevitable once they are created, cannot quite be anticipated in advance of creation. When Shelley speaks of "the steep sky's commotion" or of the closing night which will be the dome of a vast sepulchre, "Vaulted with thy congregated might," one cannot but acquiesce to a power of expression that outdistances that of ordinary mortals, yet which once spoken is intelligible to all who will hear. The fuller expression of a complete poem is but the magnification and intensification of this kind of experience to an overwhelming degree. Writing in a somewhat similar vein about creativity, J. Middleton Murry interestingly observes,

> Of the last act of poetic creation there is nothing to say. We cannot explain it; but it is no longer utterly miraculous. We have seen how the main materials lay ready prepared for the final harmonious ordering; part, and not the least part, of the final harmony had already been achieved; we may fairly say that the actual composition of this great poem ("On First Looking into Chapman's Homer") was but the conscious last of a whole series of unconscious acts of poetic creation.[2]

The sense of ineffability would seem to result from the conclusiveness of a work of art. It is worth reminding ourselves, however, that the conclusiveness is conclusive only because it is the conclusion of a cumulative process, the course of which can be pointed out and recognized. From the various confluences entering into the stream of a work of art, we can see that the artist is not shutting himself out of the world but rather that he is filling himself from the world in order to bring those aspects of it to which he is especially sensitive to fulfilment. The fulfilment may be experienced as the ineffable, a characteristic which Kurt Lewin once described as the "Aha experience," yet the ineffability may be regarded as just the final phase of expression. If this observation is in essence correct, we can see now why the frame comes at the end of the experience, not at the beginning. It is we who need to frame the art, that is, to focus it and bring it to its climactic involvement, which is, if not the physical, at least the aesthetic frame. The process of purifying experience, which is the process of expression, is the genius of the artist who is capable of coming to an understanding of the stuff of the world and of giving form to it. Expression is accordingly best defined as the genetic process by which the expressive materials selected by the artist reinforce one another to effect a totally integrated experience. The complexities involved in the resultant experience are many. To explain them further, I wish to consider them first in respect to aesthetic form and secondly in respect to aesthetic meaning.

Aesthetic form is that form which is consequent upon the expressive elements which are brought to expression in a work of art. It is not an essence which can exist independently of a sensuous embodiment. On the contrary, being embodied in a sense-medium, it comes into being through the medium. It is a result of the *work* of art, and has the stamp of the creator on it. Molding his materials, the artist creates aesthetic form in the very process by which he produces the work of art. This being so, the form is not separate, or even separable, from the materials through which it comes to be. It would be absurd to suppose that the artist has a supply of forms which, given appropriate subject-matter, he could impose one of their number upon a subject. A still-life painter will want to arrange on a table his apples and gourds and carafes and napkins in a special way, but the order in which he places them is an order of nature, not of art. Aesthetic form is the transmutation he brings about on the canvas, and however isomorphic it may be with the subject he paints, the difference is that the one possesses aesthetic form and the other does not. Should there be any doubt about this, all we need do is to observe two artists painting the same subjects and then compare their work. Assuming that each is an artist and produces a work of art, we can, by appreciating the different canvases, appreciate the aesthetic forms which differentiate them. The remarkable differences are just the differences of aesthetic form.

To analyze aesthetic form is not simple. Each authentic work has its own form and consequently deserves analysis peculiar to its own expression. Otherwise, art is created by formula and is more of a potboiler than a work of art. If, as it is commonly thought, a work of art is an organic whole such that every element modifies every other, then the difficulty of art is essentially that of arranging every element to enhance every other. A portrait-painter, for example, will seldom be successful if he paints his subject first and then adds a background to fill in the rest of his canvas. On the contrary, he will need to conceive foreground and background together as being integral to each other. Generalizing, we may say that form is the result of mutually enforcing relations, such as contrast, antagonism, modulated repetition, support, balance, tension, supplementation, and transitions, which conspire to achieve a singleness of purpose. Vividness and intensification of experience which the artist achieves is a result of his deftly handling materials to make them express his purpose. No part of an authentic work of art will fail to add to the expression, even though the importance of some parts will be vastly less significant than others.

When an artist calls too much attention to subordinate parts of a work, he is guilty of mannerisms, which can only detract from aesthetic form. Too much woodsie horns in Wagner, too much noisy blasts in Sibelius, too much instrumental color of individual parts, magnificant as it can be, in Debussy—these are tell-tale clues as to who the composer is, yet they appear to be marks of mannerisms instead of expressive elements patterned into a meaningful composition. Idioms in music or in any other art are necessary, and help to create style. Too much repetition of an idiom, however, is a substitute for thoughtlessness, an adumbration of creativity, no more fresh than proving again a theorem one has already learned. When, however, idioms are transcended, they are no longer just mannerisms of a not-too-creative artist, but are the essence of style—a completely expressive work in which the artist delineates his intent, his reflection on the world, and expresses it in the only way it can be expressed: that is, through his work. In this sense, style is one with aesthetic form. It is the best of thoroughgoing creativity.

We may delight in lesser aspects of artistic creativity, but it is important to recognize that, like desserts, they are not the substantial fare which constitutes the more serious, and ultimately the more satisfying, kind of expression. The lyrical, the musical, the rhythmic in art are indispensable, but it is an error to assume that they are the substance of art or that they are sufficient to make what is otherwise ugly or unacceptable into what is beautiful or acceptable. The form which makes something aesthetic is that which flows from it, not that which is superadded because of the intrinsic delight a person may take in it. The lyrical is aesthetic form only in an incomplete way. It is a form of easy art appropriate to a *divertimento,* not to serious art, which requires a ground bass strong enough to support an expression of a reality singled out by the artist. The lyrical is too pure to support more than sheer delight. It cannot maintain its independence in the presence of the heavier insights of intense experience.

Rhythm is essential to any art, for there is no art without the lyrical. But rhythm cannot be the whole of art. Whether jingoistic, frothy, or even complex, rhythm becomes tiresome before long. For this reason, Mr. Sigmund Spaeth is quite correct in calling attention to the shortcomings of "the foot-listener." In his *First Symphony,* Brahms can make the opening drum beat out an exciting introduction to his first theme, but it is an introduction to it, not the development of it. For all its nice qualities, the unaided drum is not supple enough to express more than the simplest forms of drama. It cries out for an implementation, either in the form of the dance or of the symphony. Otherwise, it requires mystical incantations for the sake more of ritual than of art. To make of that which was ritualistic rhythm a pure form of art is to achieve a sophistication that is anaemic as an art and ridiculous as a ceremony, even though a person who cannot appreciate the beauty of the rhythmic is lacking in his sensitivities. Aesthetic form is incompletely present in partial expressiveness; it is completely present only in expressiveness brought to expression.

Aesthetic form is not capable of being defined by straight lines, circles made by a lathe, serpentine curves, the golden section, or even Mr. Birkhoff's "aesthetic measure," as being a ratio of complexity and order.[3] Repudiating the mathematical ideal of defining aesthetic form, others assert the existence of a special faculty, an aesthetic sense, for the perception of beauty. The crucial objection to such a faculty is, of course, that it explains nothing and merely compounds the mystery of the beautiful by supplying an *ad hoc* sense for its apprehension. A more reasonable assumption is one which asserts that all our faculties are implicitly aesthetic, since expressiveness seems to be a characteristic grasped, not just by some extra-sensory intuition, but by all the receptors as well as by memory and the intellect. This assumption at least has the virtue of permitting us to garner all aspects of human experience as the stuff which goes to make up aesthetic form. It permits us to relate what we earlier spoke of as the various "starts" which seem to enter into the creative processes, legitimately, if not necessarily. Looking to all life as expressive, we emphasize the richness of the arts and not just their purity. True it is that there is a distillation of experience in the creative processes, but should we not remember that it is a distillation and not an alienation? The purification is not so much an artist's escape from reality as it is his coping with it in order to bring home more vividly what he regards its import to be. His task is to filter out the irrelevant and thus to show more clearly and intensely what reality is, whether as an ellipsoidal orange, an heroic spirit, a dope-addict compassionately understood, the dance caught in bronze, or any other subject-matter capable of vividly communicating in its local habitation an interpretation of reality.

In order to make his interpretation concrete—to give it a life contained in its own ambit—the artist chooses his medium through which he can most adequately express his intent. He must dwell on his sensuous materials. He lives his pigments. He must be playful with his metaphors in order to feel their potencies as well as their limitations. Gertrude Stein learned the magic of making us feel that the world is round. Hers may be a lesser art in her pluralistic, playful world. Her forms may be little forms, but they are forms nonetheless, totally exploited for what they are worth. The more cosmic outlooks require an architecture which leads progressively from the expressive to the expressive to expression, so that much of the intensity of the expression is traceable to the architectonic of detail upon detail until finally a vision breaks through of some *Weltanschauung* which it is the artist's intent to create. This is aesthetic form in its most taxing and splendid expression—that is, philosophical art.

Aesthetic form, our discussion has assumed, varies from one work of art to another. This form, which comes about through the unique expressive qualities as they relate to one another in a total structure, is traceable to the artist's outlook as concretely expressed in art. The artist as creator is confronted, then, with the double and simultaneous task of creating his language as well as his outlook, and neither is intelligible without the other. Serious art is difficult just because it is necessary to learn the language of each work of art. As innovator, the creative writer adds to the richness of a language, but his innovations are for the critic or the appreciator, not for another generation of creative writers, who are themselves burdened with making their own innovations. The old metaphors, however elegant, can express only the old ideas, old attitudes, and old responses. The vitality of aesthetic form is that it conveys aesthetic meaning. These meanings are as rich as the history of art plus the unborn works which are a challenge to the human spirit wherever it contains life. Anticipating that, like aesthetic form, aesthetic meaning, too, is necessarily unique in each work of art, we may nevertheless observe the bridges between it and the cruder stuff of life which gives it a relevance to human existence.

Art is a vivification and intensification of experience. No wonder it has been sought after and cultivated from the dawn of man, even though it is only the few who can make aesthetically meaningful scratches on the wall of a cave or tell an intrinsically exciting story or sing a lilting song. Those who can, convey not just information, but something else, hauntingly difficult to characterize. Their secret is that of creating art, and although they conceal nothing in its expression, to say what it is that makes art meaningful is to broach the most difficult subject of all.

It appears relatively certain that art-activity, which appears in all but the crudest or most vicious societies, is not to be regarded as meaningless. Surely people would not accord it the respect they do unless they found in it the answer to some hunger in the human soul. But the question remains, how may we characterize the kind of satisfaction that art appears to provide? One extreme of meaning is the pure delight a person takes in what he directly apprehends by his senses. Dazzling bright colors, and the kaleidoscopic forms they may assume, are a joy not just to children but to adults as well. Musical tones, fragrances of pines newly glistening with rain drops, the velvety feel of rose petals—in short, sensuous materials given freshly in any perception which we are free to savor arouse delight in us. Experiences of this kind are commonly enjoyed by all. But are they experiences we usually call meaningful? If they are, what can they mean except the sensuousness which they just are? If this is all, we may well doubt the propriety of speaking of them as meaningful, and simply remain content with the delight as a fortuitous gift to our perceptual faculties.

On the other hand, we may embroider our delight of immediate sensuous perception with associations and rangings of the imagination far beyond anything given to the senses. When these further references are external and habitual, we are more likely to speak of the one as a sign of the other. Road signs, for example, are essentially arbitrary and conventional ways of giving directions, and even if one is made in the form of a finger pointing out a direction, we still need to interpret it as signifying in an external way the direction to which it is believed it points. Or again, casual connections are "conjoined" in a way which we learn more by habit than by any intrinsic connections which we can perceive, as when the litmus paper signifies the presence of an acid. Even symbols, though we are more likely to dwell on their intrinsic properties, such as those of the flag or the cross, are likely to refer us beyond, rather than to fix our attention on the immediate presentation as the locus of meaning. It is probably an exaggeration to exclude on principle all symbols from having a legitimate part in works of art. No doubt the kind of treatment they are given is more important than their mere presence or absence. The cross may be an effective form of the cathedral; halos may be used indiscriminately or they may be used artistically. Flags, newspaper print, and what-not may be exactly what are required to complete a collage. Probably no material is intrinsically incapable of figuring in a work of art.

Conceptual elements, too, may enter into works of art. In fact, it would appear that, except in pure designs, no work of art is entirely devoid of conceptual material. The reason that this may be hidden to casual observation consists in the fact that the conceptual aspects of art are clothed in the sense-medium. A dead tree, an eagle, the wind are painted to give the sense of aridity, desolateness, and poverty-strickenness, but the artist can say this only in his individualized expression of it. Concepts are defined or uttered, conceptual ideas in art are expressed—so transformed that their universality can be perceived in the treatment the artist has accorded it. Icons can be abstracted from art, and iconography can go far in systematizing and classifying the kinds of conceptual elements painters have exploited. Dürer, however, as painter and creator of woodcuts, makes use of icons and symbols in an aristic medium and in a way which de-emphasizes the conceptual in the perceptual. The question we need so urgently to answer is, what are the circumstances under which the foreign, the external, the conceptual, becomes integral to a work of art instead of defeating it?

If our analysis of creativity is in essence correct, we need to look to the way these apparently external things can figure in the creative process. Our question is directed primarily to meaning *in* art, not the meaning *of* art. Central to the creative process is the way in which the artist molds his materials in order to make each aspect contribute to the consummatory effect which he intends. This is "engagement" in the double sense of the focussing of attention upon the expressive elements and of being moved by them to achieve the sense of fulfilment which, taken together, they intrinsically contain. This two-fold aspect permits one to dwell upon the expressive, to delight in it, and also to find a deeper satisfaction in the fulfilment which its immanent movement provides. The loss of either ruins the art-process. Delight without consummation is sickly aestheticism, the titillation of the senses, what Ruskin called the "tickling and fanning of the soul's sleep." Consummation without delight is grim utilitarianism, means sacrificed to an end, an overpowering activism destructive of the rhythmic and the lyrical in experience. In the one case, the aesthetic is foreshortened and without consummation. In the other, it is crushing and degrading because it fails to respect the material and to make for a rapport between man and nature. In either event, man is deprived of a kind of realization and vitality which gives him a positive bearing in his world.

A balance between the static and dynamic elements of the art-process depends upon the potencies of the subject-matter to express aesthetic intent. In the drama, this has classically been the problem of realizing a balance between character and plot. If the playwright dwells almost exclusively on character, he deprives the drama of the conflict which is indispensable to it. On the other hand, if he subordinates all to the plot, he forces it into a mold that can make only a deadening form, not worth the bother. There simply is no substitute for exploiting the themes which interest him and which flow by their own logic through their consummatory patterns. If this is broken into by propaganda or preachment from an external point of view or by employing a patent device, such as putting a speech in the mouth of the district attorney to the jury, the resultant jar is the mark of an obvious shortcoming in the work. A play within a play is a device too. Yet when handled by a consummate writer, it can catch the conscience of the king and reveal exactly his character at the precise time which, since Hamlet's character has already been established, makes the rest of the plot more or less inevitable. By combining spectacle with character and movement, coupled with language totally expressive, Shakespeare reveals the quintessence of aesthetic meaning.

Art has a kind of life of its own, or it is not art. The view I have here adopted and which seems to render most adequate how that life is constituted is one which regards art as developing in an immanent, engaging process consummated in the expressive brought to full expression. This view seems to do justice to both the aspects of the delight we take in art and the kind of fulfilment it contains. Yet, philosophically speaking, there appears to be another aspect of art which, paradoxically, denies that art can be totally self-contained and have a complete life of its own. Apparently, there are connections between art and gross experience. The question is how to conceive of such connections.

In Western thought, possibly the oldest statement of the connection is that in which art is regarded as a kind of deception. Gorgias seems to have suggested that the masques in tragedy are conscious attempts at deceptions which we may as well enjoy for their own sake. Plato, surer about the realities, deprecated the deception as being thrice removed from the real, catering to the baser elements in man, and, more often than not, containing blasphemy. Metaphysically speaking, the serious criticism is that art is a copy of a copy and so distorted that it leads men away from realities instead of towards them. At least in its bald statement, this theory of imitation certainly appears naive and not quite worthy of Plato's more mature insights. And even though painters like Zeuxis and Parrhasius played tricks on each other by seizing upon techniques of foreshortening, the kind of verisimilitude Plato speaks of, say in Book X of the *Republic,* is unquestionably a burlesque of what the artist's intent is. Commentators on the history of the subject seem to be relieved when Aristotle speaks of imitation as of a universal instead of a particular, and hence avoided the naïveté of art's being a kind of photographic copy of nature. Can this emendation, however, really dissolve the difficulties? Are we much better off with a copy twice removed instead of three times? Moreover, are not all qualities in a sense universal, and if so, have we gained anything by an appeal to universals? Cezanne's rocks, Shostakovitch's syncopations, even Carl Sandburg's slaughter-houses are all universals. Is it for this reason that they are constituted as art? An affirmative answer is not reasonable.

The question of universals in art may more properly be conceived of as to whether art deceives us or whether it actually reveals something to us we would not otherwise understand. When van Gogh paints a bed in all its garish colors, not even children or the simple-minded are deceived by it. Or again, the story-teller as artist must be amusing. Once he confuses art with reality, he is no longer a story-teller, but a gossiper or preacher or something else. The shift in attitude from story-telling marks a refusal to let the story tell itself and permits the alien to enter and to destroy its intrinsically expressive qualities. What the artist must reveal, if he is to be an artist at all, is precisely those qualities which are the further expressive qualities sustained by the dynamics of the subject-matter. Van Gogh's bed is more diamond-shaped than rectangular. Does this signify that he couldn't draw very well? Or rather, does it signify that the composition calls for a scrunched shape determined by the linear problems and not by those of verisimilitude? If van Gogh's "slice of reality" calls for distortion, it does so, one may argue, because of the perspective from which it is seen, not from the importation of something alien to it. May we not reasonably assert, then, that a universal perspective actually provides the key to the meaning of a work of art? A satisfactory answer to this question is apparently more complicated than is at first apparent.

One kind of meaning, which I assume we have for our purposes sufficiently analyzed, is the immanent meaning that is intrinsic to the unfolding process. This we noted to be both arresting and culminating. Surely some version of immanent meaning is indispensable to the understanding of art. The other kind of meaning is what we have spoken of as the connections between art and the gross experience from which art takes its rise and which it somehow illuminates. There must surely be some appropriate way of bringing together both kinds of aesthetic meaning in a general theory of art. A theory which regards art as so pure that it can only be contaminated by intimate connections with anything else is romantic beyond any reasonable aspiration. It can reflect only the attitude of an aesthete unwilling to come to terms with the serious issues of living. Is the only alternative, then, a theory which drains from art its distinctive value and makes it a stimulus to action and thought which are themselves, if not anti-aesthetic, at least non-aesthetic? This latter view appears to denigrate the emotional life, to subordinate it to the practical or the intellectual, and consequently to deny it the autonomy it deserves. Clearly, we need a theory of aesthetic meaning lively enough in its grasp of the vitalities of art and sympathetic enough to the divergencies of human action to make clear both the distinctiveness of art as well as its capacities to relate itself to the serious concerns of living. No doubt the classical theories of imitation, deception, reflection, expression, communication—all contain some aspects of the relation of art to the real world. Yet, because of the confusions of interpretation, a fresh approach may be welcome. I think this may best be done by asking ourselves a somewhat different question—namely, what is the function of art, or better, what are the legitimate functions of art?

To try to force art into a single pattern with a single objective will not do. The spirit of man, and consequently of artists, is too diverse to confine man's works within a single kind of objective. Even to speak of art as vivification and intensification of experience, although I believe this to be essentially correct, nevertheless covers a territory ranging from irresponsible joy to purposes of high seriousness. Some art, we have observed, is scarcely more than amusing; other art is moral or philosophical in outlook. And the subdivisions of each are no doubt legion. To classify purposes possibly least calculated to promote dissent, we may regard art as ranging from that which at one extreme primarily gives delight or is amusing to that which at the other aims to make man at home in his world by helping to bring him to terms with life and nature, if not with ultimate reality. Between these two there is art which in varying degrees interprets, celebrates, and humanizes experience.

Those who seek absolute purity in art find its significance in the uncontaminated joy of apprehending the form which the artist creates from his plastic materials. This they deem to be distinctive of art, and this and this alone they regard as the appropriate aim of the artist. For example, Roger Fry, a critic of great sensitivity, asserts:

> I have admitted that there is beauty in Nature, that is to say, that certain objects constantly do, and perhaps any object may, compel us to regard it with that intense disinterested contemplation that belongs to the imaginative life, and which is impossible to the actual life of necessity and action; but that in objects created to arouse the aesthetic feeling we have an added consciousness of purpose on the part of the creator, that he made it on purpose not to be used but to be regarded and enjoyed; and that this feeling is characteristic of the aesthetic judgment proper.[4]

The undeniable challenge of the purists resides in the fact that there is no art without form. The formless is either non-aesthetic or it is aesthetically ugly. Speaking of Matisse, Herbert Read insists that "The theorist of modern art . . . must claim that no definition of painting which does not include in some way the concept of FORM can survive application for long."[5] He further insists that the same is true in all branches of art, including literature. Our only quarrel with those who seize upon form as the definitory characteristic of art is that they leave the concept in limbo. Clive Bell, for example, who has attempted as diligently as anyone to define it, is in all honesty compelled to employ the qualifying adjective "significant" in connection with it. This qualification clearly begs the question at issue, since precisely this term is the one the analysis of which we are asking for. There is no doubt that the purists in art reject amusement as an appropriate end of art. Theirs is a serious concern and they are searching for the painterly qualities that make a painting a painting, or, generalizing, the artistic qualities that make a work of art a work of art. Their severe formalism is a determined attempt to cope with the problem of art, and not to confuse it with the problems of man. In relation to this ideal, the amusing is a holiday objective, not to be spurned as a kind of relief in our lighter moments, but also not to be pedestaled as the kind of art for which a man should sacrifice his talents. If a Turner, a Cezanne, a Picasso, is achieving something significant, the purist regards it as a way of putting paint on a canvas which is independent of politics, love, or religion and which is a way of capturing experience in a purity of vision for all to see who can see. And the significance is to be found in this vision itself, not in something else.

The more intimate one's acquaintance with art, it seems, the more one becomes engrossed in the means by which the artist fulfils his intent. A misplaced line, a false harmonic progression, an ill-drawn character, an inappropriate word—these are the telltale marks by which the hack is separated from the artist, and not by the nobility of his sentiments or the currency of his politics. Yet the haunting question remains that although form is indispensable to art and although form must be pleasing to man, does not art, however objective or non-objective it may be, fail to attain its greater fulfilment if it fails to interpret the world about us?

We may acknowledge, for example, that Cezanne was a master technician. We may acknowledge the perfection he achieved between color and form. We may acknowledge his ability to translate his meticulous studies of natural forms into paint. Yet none of these acknowledgments is quite enough to account for the greatness of Cezanne. There is a painterly meaning in his rocks or trees or apples, but there is more than a painterly meaning of form. There is a compassion he has for the things he studies, a compassion which runs throughout, a similarity of quality whether he paints rocks or trees or apples or houses or gamblers. Cezanne finds a continuity in all things, an underlying reality in nature, in artifacts, and in man. A failure to sense this continuity reduces one to talk about composition, repeated rhythms, balancing colors, and the like. The reduction misses the one quality that makes his techniques worthwhile. It misses the connections between the transmuted forms and the things from which they were transmuted. When Cezanne says that he does not "reproduce" nature but that he "represents" it,[6] he is telling us in the language of analysis that art has a significance in the way in which it *re-presents* nature. Only by bowdlerizing the term can we call this imitation. The painting which re-presents is a new experience; it has a freshness of its own. We not only see apples; we feel them in paint. Similarly, we feel a depth, a solidity, against which a two-dimensional, surface phenomenon, or even a three-dimensional cube, pales into insignificance. Sense-data are, we must after all remember, data. Cezanne transcends the discreteness of data to make us feel a continuity—one may even say, a community—of all things. And what he gives us is not, as some would say, a reading into his painting; on the contrary, it is a reading *out* of it. Otherwise, there simply is no understanding of his art.

Our conclusion suggests that the present-day movement called "non-objective" art is a misnomer. In fact, many of the artists who call themselves non-objectivists do themselves less than justice. If we could re-baptize them, only slightly changing their name, we might better call them trans-objectivists, or perhaps better "quintessential objectivists." The name applies to, say, the painting of Ben Shahn (in his late phases) or of a Jimmy Ernst. Also it does suggest the legitimacy of ignoring the minute, reproductive detail Ruskin was so insistent upon, and of following rather his ideal of Turner, who by means of a few lines, a calculated smudge, and a spot of color could make a simple sketch of the Estuary of the River Dee into a little masterpiece. Like Cezanne and Turner, the best of the so-called non-objectivists do not ignore nature but rather guide one into it in transmuted form, which is the essence of artistic signification. They guide one into nature in such a way that smoke or rain or steam or children at play or apples can never again be seen in the naive way we saw them before seeing them through the eyes of the painter. Art and nature are different, but related.

Whether in the musical arts, the literary arts, or the plastic arts, significance is a transmutation of one world into another. The lyrical or rhythmical may be used to express earthly love or reach for the empyrean or run a gamut between them. In words they may express experiences in their inexhaustible range from objects to thoughts, from emotions to actions, from fancies to metaphysical beliefs. The composer or the writer may appeal to such aspects of our world as the above in order to make meaningful the creative process. Like the painter or the sculptor, they too always transform the world into realities which can be expressed only in the medium of their art. The composer does this not merely in the more or less obvious, and usually not very satisfactory, language of the tone-poem, but even through the more abstract forms of the rondo or fugue or sonata. In them he can create realities of tenderness, brittleness, conflict, courage, triumph, and the like, that give man new insight into his world. The range of instruments and the range of their colors are a challenge to expressions from the shrill to the reverberating, from the singing to the blasting, from the plunking to the banging. The composer is no more limited in the range of his tonal effects than is the painter in the effects he can make his pigments express. A Prokofief, a Bartok, a Webern, proves that he can invent new idioms to express new ideas quite comparable to a Picasso, a Kandinsky, a Beckmann. The outlook is as modern in the one as in the other. Both are related to men's collective experience in a world altered by science and technology, by the cadences of the motor, the tempo of industry, and the modulations of institutional development. There is a sense in which music relates more nearly to the inner experience of emotional life than to the outer experience of nature, and consequently a sense in which its significance relates the transmuted forms more to psychological processes than to things we can more directly point to, like mountain peaks or persons or bar rooms. For this reason, it may be thought that music is a purely formal art, signifying nothing but itself. There is some evidence to lead us to believe, however, that music gains meaning, not just from its own internal harmonies, but also from the harmonies that relate it to the spirit of man.

In the literary arts, as in the plastic arts, referential meanings are easy to find, even if at times deceptively easy. Words usually stand for things. Essentially they denote. The poet, however, employs terms which denote and through his genius makes them connote. Consider these few lines from MacNeice:

231

> World is crazier and more of it than we think,
> Incorrigibly plural. I peel and portion
> A tangerine and spit the pips and feel
> The drunkenness of things being various.[7]

The connotative meaning of a tangerine, pungent, warm-colored, full of rounded smooth pips made for spitting and for making one gloriously feel "The drunkenness of things being various" is curiously suggested mostly through denotative terms. The poet achieves his intent more by his juxtaposing words with the creation of an effective syntax than by inventing new terms, although he is bound to do both. The need for expressing new meanings forces him to exploit new means for making a poem. The freshness of the poem is primarily a function of meaning, and only secondarily a function of other qualities of words. MacNeice makes us know this, as all true poets make us know this. Clearly, rhythm and song are important in his poem, but mostly in order to make us see that things are "incorrigibly plural," not in order to bring about action or some particular set of practical attitudes. Rather, realization is in our senses, in our insouciance of spitting pips, in our feelings cut loose from habit. Poetry and literature can do many things because their materials—words—can sing, move, create, express, and communicate, always in a personal way, but a way which is nevertheless continuous with the impersonal. For this reason, the personal has leverage in a world made public.

I see no need to belabor the point that the literary arts—especially the drama and the novel—seek to delineate some quality of life that the writer regards as important in the human outlook. His art is an interpretation of life, and whether he celebrates it or criticizes it, he humanizes it. A Willy Loman may express all the tawdry values a salesman can embody—all the cheap virtues of the athletic fan, promiscuous sex, ill-conceived fame, ill-gotten wealth, together with their assorted connections—but Arthur Miller still makes Mamma say to her boys that they must pay attention to him. The sordid is not all. Along with it is a human being. All the effective staging of the play has point because it contributes to the humanizing of a modern character, one who in many ways epitomizes the weaknesses of modern man. The spirit is still the spirit of tragedy, but tragedy written with a view not to princely characters but to the heroic which wants expression in all men, despite the limitations of what may be a stifling culture. Serious literature is constrained to humanize life, whatever the form it might take. The novel may prove the happiest form for twentieth-century man. It has the advantage of informality and the kind of dissemination that can appeal to a vast reading public. Yet whether in the novel, in drama, or in poetry, the humanizing of life is but trash if the canons of art are forsaken. The novel can easily degenerate into the reportorial, the propagandizing, or cheap moralizing. Any of these can make the writer become dull, turgid, and irrelevant.

The intensity and vivification that constitutes art in its singular fulfilment is that which rediscovers man in a world no longer alien to him. To interpret experience as the artist does is to humanize it. His power is one of bringing us to see ourselves and our world differently from what we ever saw before, for he is capable of turning means into media fraught with meaning—that is, meanings caught in the idiom of his language. This is why we quote phrases from poetry or drama, or why we see clouds heavy and mordant as El Greco saw them, or feel joy as Beethoven sings it in the *Ninth*. Our capacities often too obtuse for discovering unaided our world for ourselves, we lean upon others with greater talents in order to see nature, to revivify life, and to probe human character. Creation is mostly a struggle, a strain, and is properly spoken of as a *work* of art. But it is an *art* too. It has realization in it at every step. This is a mastery that men may share with the creator, and in realizing it, we come to terms with our world—by making it come to terms with us. There is an employment of the medium to make it reveal secrets that are otherwise hidden in mere means which, taken to signify something else, can never disclose them. The artist reveals continuities between the psyche and society and nature. Otherwise, there are only privacies, gasping in their muteness, or mores, thwarting the human spirit, or material forces indifferent to the life of man. The magnitude of the problem of interpretation permits little insights by little creators, and greater insights by greater creators. To note the difference is worth our attention; we may well pause to ask, what is meant by greatness in art?

Ruskin, I believe, makes a good start when he says that the artist of first rank is one who sees clearly and thinks clearly even though he feels deeply. We recall that he regards the second order of artist as he who can see clearly because he doesn't feel, and the lowest order as he who feels strongly but sees obscurely and thinks badly. Ruskin's statement may commend itself to us primarily because of the way in which he insists on making feeling, vision, and thought coalesce. This three-fold conception of mental processes is in the tradition of classical psychology, which as interpretive psychology may still have significance for us today. Let us start with feeling.

Many writers today seem to think that a human being can be adequately characterized by the fact that he is sentient. As long as a person feels, it makes little difference whether he is a dope addict, a lazy son of wealth, a nymphette, or what-not. Degradation of character is no bar to one's being the object of artistic portraiture. In at least two senses the artist is quite correct: first inasmuch as anything can legitimately be the subject-matter of art, and secondly, inasmuch as nobility is rightly regarded with suspicion in the twentieth century, belonging as it does to the hankering after a feudal order. But whatever kind of character the artist may feel impelled to portray, we have some right in preferring an imagination with scope to that of the morbid. The so-called dregs of humanity are dregs, I suppose, because there are human impulses to which they cannot quite respond. The groans, the hysterical laughters, the calloused indignities—these we can understand and appreciate on a scale of values. We may even want them to be expressed with all the power a talented writer can muster. But does elegance of expression raise them to a level consistent with the talent through which they come to life again? It is as if the writer were blind to dimensions of experience which supply meaning and not just oppressiveness to a mind made morbid.

I have already referred to Miller's *Death of a Salesman*. There it was noted that morbidity is not for its own sake. Without preaching, Miller is able to contrast the morbid with the healthy, and to point to those confusions which prevent us from disentangling them. Even the effectiveness of the stagecraft in the play derives from the expression of this intent. Dream life and real life, at first carefully divided, become obscured. In the consequent illusion, inner and outer become indistinguishable. Then in the utter delusion of the backyard, life is snuffed out, first in the form of a plant, then in the form of a man. This is a struggle to cope with the meaning of death that is more than the loss of sentiency, although the loss of it is the final stage. The pathological and eventually death come to be understood through life. The poet connotes the celebration of man in life by denoting his death. This double range of vision reflects the morbid as a distortion of the sane, and by virtue of this the poet is revealed also as critic. Through his capacity to express the human condition, he at the same time judges it. The greater art is, we may say, the more the spotlight broadens into the floodlight.

A fallacy which, I think, still has common currency is that feeling is understood by the sheer fact of its being felt. To know love or shame or anguish one must feel love or shame or anguish, however inarticulate one may be in trying to convey these feelings to another. Feelings are like sensations, it would seem. In having them, a person knows them, and an inability to have them forever shuts him off from those facets of experience. The negative part of the statement is no doubt true; the positive part contains an egregious error. In themselves, feelings are dumb, inchoate, indeterminate, and therefore never quite capable of being grasped. If the study of aesthetics shows anything, surely it is that feeling becomes articulate and definite only as it is expressed. But to express, we have seen, means to create a language which can make feeling precise. Otherwise, we are left with the "oh gee whizz," or the "how wonderful," or the "most awful," as vain attempts to communicate something unique. The artist knows that feeling is not an answer but a challenge. It is the beginning and not the end of a struggle to make clear to oneself, let alone to another, what he feels. He seeks to discover the nature (we might say "the aesthetic form") of the feeling, and its nature is a determinate kind, which can exist only in an expressive medium which has come to expression. Feeling is not great, it is not profound, it is not intelligible, until it is expressed—that is, converted into a form which can be grasped. In itself it is shocking or overwhelming

235

or, as the Existentialist would say, vertiginous, but, as the adjective clearly suggests, it is more of a response to something foreign than it is an understanding apprehension of something prized.

The artist turns feelings into shapes; he embodies them as art-objects and, through their embodiment, expresses them. Feelings are morbid when they are not adequately expressed. Instead of contributing to clarity of vision, they obscure it. They make for a subjective life from which all objectivity is severed. This is why they are morbid, and this is why Ruskin spoke of them as implicating the pathetic fallacy.[8] As long as feeling distorts vision, it is pathetic, because it cuts a person off from the public world and consequently immures him within a confine, suffocating and debilitating. The personal becomes private—a mere stream of consciousness—which tries vainly to give significance to a world, but which, like Proust's jealousies, can only gnaw at one's inner vitals.

In the twentieth century no artist can ignore the inner. The Freudian point of view, the need for understanding inner impressions, the need for exploring the stream of consciousness—these are all too thoroughly imbedded in our folklore to permit being neglected. O'Neill and Tennessee Williams, Picasso, Dali, and Chagall, Joyce and Stein, in various ways stand as reminders that the inner life is to be taken seriously. These are not necessarily great artists, although O'Neill and Picasso from here look like giants; yet they are all important enough to make us realize that idyllic nature lovers have little to say to a world engrossed in controlling nature on the one hand and coping with our inner anguish on the other. The scope which greatness requires, one might suggest, is one which can come to a clear realization of the double aspect of man's condition and realistically come to terms with it. When the artist senses what neither the humanities nor the sciences have quite sensed, he may turn us toward sciences more humanistically oriented as well as to humanities more scientifically oriented, to the mutual reward of both.

If feeling may be pathetic, suffocating and morbid, may we not find the antidote in thought? Thought is objective, full of endless implications, and capable of superb elegance. The classical philosophers have generally placed it at the top of the virtues, made it into the supreme distinction between man and animal, and some of them even discovered in it the means to absolute perfection. The question is the extent to which we may rely upon thought as correcting feeling, keeping it within bounds, and directing it to consummatory and approved ends. But once the question is posed in this way, we are confronted with numberless mysteries as to how thought can perform this function. It looks as though it is so powerless to combat the mighty forces of feeling that we frequently believe a person overcome by them may be excused even from the penalties of the law. The great Plato himself found it necessary to invoke a third faculty to co-operate with reason in order to subdue feeling. In his famous analogy, the charioteer could subdue it only as spirited animal assisted in checking the appetitive one. Thus, at least as far as the world of practical action is concerned, he was forced to conclude that reason could not alone control feeling.

In the modern context, despite its waves of anti-intellectualism, we have certainly committed ourselves to rationality to the extent to which we rely upon the sciences. Prejudice, bias, emotional conviction—these we regard as subject to correction through the methods of science. Progressively, we give up old beliefs in favor of new ones supported by evidence and reason. The age of science has, it seems, displaced the emotions as the guide to living in favor of deliberation and calculation ranging from maternity and infant welfare to old-age pensions and burial expenses. We prize the scientific attitude of mind, and we devote sizable proportions of our resources to the development of the sciences, both basic and applied. The recognition of the import of science—the recognition of its potentialities for human life in a secular scheme of things—has taken centuries. But to recognize and to prize the sheer magnitude of a Kepler, a Boyle, a Lavoissier, a Darwin, a Faraday—this could, and did, come with their contemporaries who were willing to apply themselves to the studies in question.

The cultivation of the intellect and the advancement of it has been the task of a minority. Lesser minds learn from the greater, not as innovators but as imitators. Their function is one not of originality but of support, a function not to be belittled, however. On a scale of greatness, surely thought has to be placed

237

high above feeling. Everyone can feel; thought is much rarer. And although everyone above the level of a moron can think, the extent to which persons do think, and their ability not to let their emotions confuse thought, is strictly limited. Yet in all seriousness and without any intent of derogating thought, we may still ask what is the extent to which it is creative. Classical philosophers as divergent as Bacon, Descartes, and Kant have asked in their own ways whether thought is capable of creating something new, or whether its task is essentially that of formalizing something already known. This criticism regards thought in a narrow and precise sense, and probably this is just what is required if we are to be clear about it, for only in this way can we come to detect another element which seems to be responsible for what we are looking for—namely, the originality which thought can have. Formal thought is a fine instrument, but it is an instrument. What gives it substance is the kind of imagination which underlies it, for then the beauty of system is impregnated with a vision which gives it substance, and possibly even greatness. It was Ruskin who said: " . . . the greatest thing a human soul ever does in this world is to *see* something and tell what he *saw* in a plain way. Hundreds of people can talk for one who can think, but thousands can think for one who can see."[9] Abstract thought is important, but is it important enough to be placed at the top of the scale of greatness?

The question may appear to be unreal, since in a world dominated by technical processes and experts, people may be concerned primarily with the prosaic in life, together with the small comforts it affords. The heroic, except for a few who seek a strenuous life at odds with the provisions society has made for human welfare, seems to have been relegated mostly to the past, while the present appears to be an age of practical action rather than of ideals, or even of important ideologies. The truth is surely not easy to get at, with a beatnik cynicism and a naturalistic disillusionment expressing one extreme and a Hollywood romanticism and a transcendental idealism quite an opposite. Whatever the popular attitudes may be toward the future of man, the central problem of the arts is to make attitudes meaningful, regardless of their magnitude or degree of originality. If it actually is vision which we find to be central to art, and not just some therapeutic treatment, then we should point out that it is capable of being broader or narrower, more or less penetrating, and more or less relevant to the human condition, and that these are aspects by which we judge works to be of greater or lesser import.

Some art is trivial, some is timely, some is timely and also hauntingly persistent. It seems as if the last combines in intricate ways extremes which the genius of the artist is able to keep together. It is an art which is deeply personal and yet goes beyond personality, an art which is timely and yet which is capable of speaking to other ages, an art which is socially embedded and yet frees us from social involvement—these are some of the paradoxes the more inspired artists seem to resolve. Tolstoy or Sholokhov are able to write about war, intrigue, drunken wedding celebrations and make them intense and vivid experiences for non-Russians as well as Russians. Tschaikowsky, at least in his more sophisticated moods, and Stravinsky can do much the same in music. So with the other arts as well. Repetition can make us tire of any artist, Shakespeare included; for even if there exist those who are nearly inexhaustible in content and suggestibility, our imaginations are limited both in what they can bring to and extract from works of art. Regardless of the greatness of the classics, men will always want fresh art cast in an idiom which contains an imprint of contemporary conditions of life. The fresh art, like the best seller, may soon go stale, but some of it may have a depth and cogency which places it in a class with the greats. The question is, what are the standards to which art must measure up if it is to be in this class?

Without intending to be dogmatic about an answer to a question to which men will constantly propose a variety of answers, I would suggest that our preceding analysis presupposes one which may as well be made explicit. Without feeling, art is empty and awkward; without thought, it is limited and evanescent; without vision, it is trivial, absurd, and probably escapist. Can we fairly conclude, then, that great art combines feeling, thought, and vision? This is precisely the conclusion that needs to be made explicit. The principal reason that supports it is found in the life of man—the engagement of all his faculties in his relations to other men and to nature. Good art, let alone great art, must be engrossing. An art which cannot command the attention of one's whole being is deficient. But to do so, it must enlighten as well as command, and enlightenment is an affair of perceiving relations, those of the self to other persons as well as those which support and make possible our ambience. In short, great art reveals continuities in life—those which are man-made and those which are natural, together with their interrelations. So conceived, art is indispensable to an authentic culture. It challenges man to become conscious of his predicament; it interprets life, and in interpreting, it celebrates the human contribution. The function that art serves makes understandable the tendency of some persons to identify art with culture. By virtue of the heightened sensitivity which art calls for as well as its capacity to mirror life, one can understand why it should occupy a position of pre-eminence in the mind of man. When the connection between art and culture is regarded as reciprocal functions of each other, we can see why, for example, Periclean Greece or Renaissance Italy or Elizabethan England are frequently taken to be models of greatness in human culture. In these epochs art illuminates and expresses culture in a way that easily makes other epochs by contrast look dreary.

The test of great art may, by way of conclusion, be said to be the degree to which art as an activity engrosses man as fashioning and as fashioned by a genuine culture. This test contains two principal corollaries. First, man so regarded is the whole man. Secondly, great art is an exponent of a genuine culture. The first corollary follows by virtue of the fact that in a genuine society, man is respected as man, and not by virtue of some distinguishing faculties that belong to the mystique of a one-sided ideology. Militarism, industrialism, asceticism, as well as other forms of societies that starve human cravings, the satisfaction of which is essential to his well-being, single out some faculties for expression at the price of fatal repression of others. As a consequence, men seek freedom from repression without being sustained in a freedom for expression, save in the limited and insufficiently rewarding actions sanctioned by a spurious culture. The complexity of man's predicament is thus revealed in the fact that wholeness is achievable only in a culture which co-operates to bring to expression the inner forces of man as well as the objective necessities of social existence. No individual act of will is by itself capable of achieving the end.[10] A person's will cannot achieve wholeness because the will is not the whole man. Nor is it even possible adequately to conceive of the whole man except as his nature is sustained and furthered by a society which has a care for individual well-being. Recognizing this as in indispensable condition of the good life, we can understand why naturalists otherwise as disparate as Samuel Alexander and John Dewey insist upon individuality and sociality being opposite sides of the same fact. The first corollary underscores the assertion that morality is a function of the kind of life men lead and the denial that it is an affair of the will.

The second corollary reinforces the first by asserting the indissoluble link between greatness in art and genuineness in culture. We need not cavil at the proposition that artists are born and that talent is an endowment, rather than a matter of inculcation through teaching. But having conceded this, we need only observe that what is born can become ill-formed through improper nurture and the endowments may be abused or rot through carelessness. More specifically, an artist can no more create a culture than can a philosopher, a moralist, a scientist, a statesman, or any other single person. Cultures are institutional and have a life of their own. Innovators can propose fresh patterns of thinking, of creating, of living, but they can catch on only as they are conceived as outgrowths of what has preceded them and as possessing a relevance which makes them appropriate extensions to human life. Artists who are not publicly sustained die, of course in oblivion. A writer whose works are not published, a playwright whose plays are not produced, a composer whose music is not performed, in short, an artist whose work is not known and appreciated almost certainly withers in his seclusion.[11] The reason is not hard to decipher. Genius in one of the arts needs company in that art, in other arts, and in other aspects of culture.[12] If, as we have contended, greatness in art requires a perception of reality, especially social reality, which goes beyond technique in that particular art, artists will inevitably need support from quarters other than those of their technical fraternity.

In order to gain a point of vantage to elaborate this conclusion, I believe it advisable first to consider the theory of criticism. Following this, we may return to the major question of how the arts significantly relate to culture, especially to contemporary culture.

Chapter 9

THE ART OF CRITICISM

PATENTLY, NOT ALL ART IS GREAT, BUT IT IS ADVAN-
tageous to have before us a concept of great art that we may better
understand the not so great. In any event, criticism can be at its
best when the critic is capable of singling out a standard of greatness which provides a working basis for his criticism of art, great
or trivial, good or bad, relevant or irrelevant, with all the intermediary degrees and mixtures of each. Something like this appears
necessary if the critic is to have any useful function. He cannot
compete with the artist. There is no useful purpose of his trying
to say what the artist can and does say only in the idiom of his
work. The eloquence of the artist is the eloquence of his work.
The critic's eloquence can be neither that of the work nor of a
translation of it. Hence, his eloquence, if he has it, must be of a
different sort and have a purpose different from, even though
related to, that of the artist.

"The function of the critic"—the phrase conceals a multitude
of theories and controversies concerning various ways in which
art may be interpreted and discussed. The minimum we expect
from the critic is that he show us something significant that we
would not see otherwise or would see less perfectly in the absence
of criticism. How he does this depends on his own sensitivities
and intelligence, his philosophic outlook, and his powers of communication. There is no substitute for sensitivity and intelligence.
If a critic lacks these, he is not worth listening to, no matter what
other virtues he may have. Having them, however, he cannot
perform very valuable service unless he can communicate consonant with his insights. He must, in other words, possess a style
appropriate to his intent. These are elementary qualifications of
anyone who would be a critic. Having them, critics are further
divided into schools according to their philosophic outlooks. Of
these I wish to consider three, which although not exhaustive,

do embody major alternatives. I shall consider them from the following points of view: (1) the transcendental, (2) the subjective, and (3) the social points of view, respectively.

The transcendental point of view[1] is at least as old as Plato, and transcendentalists, old and new, find their rallying point in regarding art as an image of God or, in Plato's version, the Idea of the Good. At the outset, this suggests a schizophrenic attitude as to whether art is idolatrous and blasphemous or whether at its best it serves a function of leading men to a recognition of the good life by pointing to an ideal of perfection, which they may imitate, and through imitation hope to achieve a state of grace otherwise denied them. The task of setting about to achieve this state is awesome and to be undertaken only after rigorous preparation of one's inner being. Plato's elaborate educational scheme, carrying one into later life, and the Christian preparation (*imitatio*) for cleansing oneself through a life of devotion suggest something of the extent to which one must discipline oneself in order to be readied even for a possibility of receiving grace. The ascetic element makes it clear that a person needs to avoid the "honeyed muse, whether in epic or in lyric verse," that he must beware of the "charming or alluring" and that the true artist is one whose "mind has been taken away by the gods" and that he is "inspired" or "possessed."

The prospect of enjoying the *aesthetic,* the sensuous, is not altogether promising. At first sight, it looks as if the aesthetic were unalterably opposed to perfection, which is necessarily timeless, unchanging, eternal. Surely, under the circumstances, the arts cannot be allowed an autonomy, for this could mean only unbridled discipline for a lawless creature. The sensuous is a constant source of embarrassment to the transcendentalist. On the one hand, there is no art which is not sensuous, music included. On the other, the purpose of art is to conduct the soul to a state of perfection, of which the sensuous is by its intrinsic nature an insurmountable obstacle.[2] The troublesome question is whether anything sensuous is capable of perfection. The theory of Forms would seem to imply a negative answer. Yet at least in the *Philebus,* Plato finds that lathes and rulers and squares can produce straight lines and curves and surfaces which are beautiful eternally and absolutely. I think we are compelled to take issue with this statement both on empirical and on theoretical grounds. Empirically, it just doesn't seem to be so. (Ruskin, it may be recalled, went to the extreme of denying that any but a curved line could be beautiful.) Theoretically, these are not illustrations of perfect forms, but at best imperfect approximations to them.

The objection on theoretical grounds is supported by later transcendental critics who try to save the theory by an appeal to art as itself containing the universal. Thus, Aristotle's revision is frequently believed to be an emendation which rehabilitates the transcendental point of view. Art is then said to be the universal history of the particular. As applied to drama, it is said of tragedy that it should conform to the probable, even though the probable may be contrary to fact; it should never conform to the improbable, even if the latter actually happened. If the answer to Plato is in essence an appeal to the universal in the sense of its being constituted as a logic or system in a work of art, this appears both reasonable and necessary. Surely every artist must believe that his work contains an intrinsic order, otherwise there could be no such thing as success or failure in it. But order in this sense is not two things, a universal and a particular (plus, perhaps, a relation between them); it is one thing, the work of art in its concreteness. The universality of art is not so much illustrative as it is experiential and consummatory. Its perfection is internal rather than paradigmatic. It is transcendental in that it carries over to other embodied meanings, that is, sensuously expressed, not in that it refers to a world of disembodied Essences or Universal Forms. The idioms of an artist do carry over from one work to another, and, at its worst, we say that an artist really created only one work, which he repeated on other occasions. In this sense (of repetition) the idiom is a universal, but to interpret it as a universal in a disembodied sense emasculates it by thought, and transforms it into a ghost of sensuous reality, incapable of producing anything like the luminous experience from which it was born.

Although the opposite of the universalism is particularism or nominalism, in rejecting the one we need not adopt the other. We may suggest a third alternative in which universals as abstractions have only a semi-autonomous life of their own. Inevitable and indispensable as they are, they do have a logic of their own, which is daily coming to be better understood. The kind of perfection they possess is the sort which permits of rigorously deduced implications, not that of expressively enhanced satisfactions. At best they lead to contrivances, not to creation of worlds or of works of art. Metaphysically, the nice questions raised are whether there are two independent realms or one, and whether, if two, one can plausibly serve as the standard of perfection for the other. Although we cannot quite avoid both these questions, it is the second which is especially important for a theory of criticism. Our purposes are better satisfied by concentrating upon it.

As far as criticism is concerned, Emerson vividly kept alive the transcendental ideal in an American version. He writes in his essay on "The Poet" that "Art is the path of the creator to his work. The paths or methods are ideal and eternal, though few men ever see them." Or again in his essay on "Art," he urges that "so much as we can shove aside our egotism, our prejudice and will, and bring the omniscience of reason upon the subject before us, so perfect is the work." These words stand in stark contradiction to our insistence that reason is not a creator, that art as belonging to the institutions of expression has a relevance to the lives of persons rather than to ideal and eternal paths, and that perfection is a matter internal to a work of art and is not an adumbration of a universal spirit. Perhaps our insistence is born of the general blindness which Emerson finds to be so prevalent. In any event, one cannot but admire both the buoyancy of his outlook and what for him appears to be no real discrepancy between two worlds. Less of a Platonist, he nevertheless in the realm of art seeks for a significance that leads him to a realm which must by its nature be radically disparate from the world of sense experience. Perhaps his optimistic beliefs, invigorated by the fresh enthusiasms of a new country, concealed something of the extreme opposition between the two worlds.

In a more tired age, the starkness of the opposition becomes clearly revealed in the words of one of the most sensitive of the poet-critics the contemporary world knows. T. S. Eliot makes the opposition a tenet pertaining to the whole range of his conception of culture, including art, philosophy, religion, manners, and even extending beyond into the realm of politics.[3] In art, he seeks for a purification which goes far beyond that which Emerson insisted upon. Emerson wrote that "As in useful art . . . the work must be strictly subordinated to the laws of Nature . . . so in art that aims at beauty must the parts be subordinated to Ideal Nature, and everything individual abstracted, so that it shall be the production of the universal soul."[4] Eliot, in a more frankly escapist attitude of mind, extends the point of view even further by contending that "Poetry is not a turning loose of emotion, but an escape from emotion; it is not the expression of personality, but an escape from personality." And ironically he adds, "But, of course, only those who have personality and emotions know what it means to escape from these things."[5] In context, this quotation becomes a key to Eliot's transcendentalism in his theory of criticism as well as in his poetry and drama. Whether in *The Wasteland* or in *The Cocktail Party,* unmistakably he makes clear that man can find only hopelessness and delusion in the things of the world.[6] He would have us turn rather to "pure contemplation from which the accidents of personal emotion are removed," and through a labor largely of intelligence have us seek "that stage of vision *amor intellectualis Dei.*" In this kind of intellectual love we are supposed at last to be able to recognize clearly the illusory character of the world of flux.

Sometimes obscurely, sometimes with luminous clarity, Eliot pursues his theme of man's struggle to gain enlightenment. He is a serious critic and a serious poet whom we must respect even if he does not convince us of the correctness of his point of view. The point of view, however, is difficult, if not impossible, to sustain. For example, the making of a saint out of the Archbishop in *Murder in the Cathedral* topples of its own weight. The process implicates an assertion of the ego which can itself only contradict the end to be portrayed. Saints are not made by intent, whether theirs or that of the poet. The humility which Thomas à Becket is finally supposed to manifest is destroyed in the certainty of his own righteousness. Nor is this an isolated instance in Eliot's work. *The Cocktail Party* displays the same sort of weakness. Reilly, the psychoanalyst playing God, can no more maintain his role than can the Archbishop in *Murder*. The earthly embodiment of the divine makes for interminable contradictions and horrors, such as Celia Coplestone's going to Kinkanja to fulfil God's will, but crucified near an ant-hill by the natives. The death of three sisters in a Christian village becomes melodrama that even a theology surpassing human understanding cannot quite resolve. Logic is thrown to the winds, and dogma destroys the truly poetic elements which are unable to come to fulfilment. When Eliot has Reilly say of Celia that "She paid the highest price / In suffering. That is part of the design," one cannot but wonder about a design which entails inane horror such as that with which *The Cocktail Party* confronts us.

Yet Eliot is perhaps the most interesting of the contemporary English-writing transcendentalists because of the intensity with which he holds to the point of view as well as his superb talent. His fearlessness, his uncompromising respect for the division of the two worlds, make him a formidable critic. There is a form of transcendentalism that is much more colorless because it looks simply to perfection in a classical sense, rather than in a militant theological one. For example, Phidias' idealization of the human body may be taken as representing a kind of universal in art. Or in less obvious sorts of idealization, universality of what is said to be excellent art may always be attributed to a *class* of things, even if it is necessary to create a new class which is "the finest of its kind."[7] The universal or the typical may lead us back to Greek art as the standard which we are asked to ape, or it may signify little more than a new kind of expression which is recognized as important and because of its importance we are asked to generalize it and fit it into a newly created class or kind. Clearly, the virtue of it will not be because it is fitted into a fine kind, but, on the contrary, because it has fineness we may project it into a class of a fine kind.

Transcendental art, so-called, inevitably makes a claim to being sublime. Classification by itself will not aid us much in discovering the essence of the sublime. Perhaps this is the reason that transcendentalists usually hark back to something like Plato's account of love, and find in it, as he did, a love of beauty, which is also a love of perfection and, being perfect, is eternal and immutable.

However much this love may be qualified, as for example by being called "intellectual," still it transcends the intellect, as Plato realized when he spoke of it as being divine. Those unsympathetic to this approach are likely to criticize it from two points of view. First, the end is not really intelligible because it carries one beyond art to a contemplation which not only is ineffable but which in its purity must repudiate as spurious the space-time world, including that of concrete works of art. Secondly, even if the end were intelligible, it would not supply us with a knowledge of the processes which underlie the sublime—that is, the processes by which sublimation occurs. Since, in other words, the functional processes are unknown, we are left with a sense of the mystery of love but with no understanding of how love explains the actions of men, including their production of art. The questions arise then, may we not investigate the subjective springs of human actions and in this way understand art as a part of the human enterprise instead of standing in awe of it by virtue of contemplating it only in its sublimated form? To regard art in these terms is to take towards it a radically different point of view.

The old sophist, Gorgias, also regarded art as a kind of deception, but one to be enjoyed in a make-believe world. Although the origins of Greek tragedy are certainly obscure, there seems little doubt that they were connected with the wild Dionysiac festivals, and that something of the orgiastic outbursts may even be detectable in the sophisticated make-believe that is called tragedy and to which men accord a new kind of reality of its own. Various forms of subjectivism have from time to time been preferred as more or less complete accounts of the interpretation of art together with the kind of criticism which is appropriate to it. But there is one in recent times which has indelibly placed its stamp upon the modern mentality and which deserves serious attention. I refer, of course, to the Freudian or psychoanalytic interpretation of art. In some quarters, the contributions of Freud to our understanding of art have even been compared with those of Aristotle.[8] Whatever the verdict we may finally be able to arrive at, there can be no doubt that the psychoanalytic theory is at least engrossing. Certainly, it increasingly calls forth the nod and many are heard to say the "I think there is something to this."[9]

The danger of a layman's plunging into psychoanalytic theory is grave, for there is no orthodox interpretation of the theory. (Psychoanalysts and historians of the movement constantly repeat the old saw that Freud could never have been a Freudian.) And, above all, we are constantly reminded of the variety of springs of action which Freud and the psychoanalysts have invoked in their attempts to arrive at satisfactory interpretations of the enjoyment of the arts and of the kind of criticism that is appropriate to them. Certainly no dogmatic appeal to the libido or to some generalized sex urge will adequately characterize the theory. Sex motivation cannot be omitted, but unless the conception of it is enlightened by clinical practice, it apparently will not serve as a satisfactory principle of interpretation. Perhaps the whole matter should be left to the professionals? But this won't do either, because we are addressing ourselves ultimately to questions which are philosophical, not clinical. We may as well enter boldly into the fray, even if the professionals disallow the interpretation.

If there is anything like bedrock doctrine in psychoanalytic theory which is at the same time distinctive of it and virtually new in the history of ideas, that doctrine seems unmistakably to be an interpretation of behavior which asserts the existence of unconscious motives, unacknowledged and unacknowledgible. Frustration, although an element of the theory, is not distinctive of it, since men have no doubt recognized without the aid of psychoanalytic theory the existence of frustration from the dawn of human life. The frustration in psychoanalytic theory is of a special sort. Nor is this sort adequately defined by relating it to love as the motive power, for theories as divergent as those of Empedocles, Plato, the Stoics, Christianity, and Buddhism have proposed this. Surely the distinctive element can be nothing other than an attempt to explain certain forms of human responses (or the lack of them) as determined by forces over which the individual has no control because he cannot consciously recognize them. By virtue of this disability he is powerless to act boldly, intelligently—and (may we add?) normally. The kind of conflict which prohibits free flowing action is not just that of incompatible ends. Everyone suffers from this kind of disability, and most persons come to terms with it in one of a variety of possible ways. The disability to which psychoanalysts point is much more serious, for by being located in the unconscious, it leads to a range of "abnormal" behavior extending from the mildly neurotic to the bizarrely psychotic. Such actions are not just stupid. In fact, they curiously mark a way of a person for coping with his problems, even though he does not cope very well with his environment. The radical disjuncture between the social and the non-social signifies the degree to which one's problems may be regarded as normal or abnormal, however imprecise the distinction may be in borderline cases. Taking as our standard, then, the need for depth analysis as the distinguishing characteristic of psychoanalytic theory, our problem is at first sight two-fold: How does depth analysis account for the birth of art and how, having accounted for this, does it provide a basis for a theory of art-criticism? Interestingly enough, it may turn out that the questions are not really two but one.

The first question evolves into something immediately baffling—at least in Freudian terms. From the point of view of creation, we would expect that the subjective spring of creation is at least a mild form of neurosis, which allows the artist to sublimate his conflict by giving expression to it in that realm of fancy called art-production. Freud actually gives us some solace in the correctness of this interpretation when he writes:

> The artist is originally a man who turns from reality because he cannot come to terms with the demand for renunciation of instinctual satisfaction as it is first made, and who then in fantasy-life allows full play to his erotic and ambitious wishes. But he finds a way of return from this world of fantasy back to reality; with his special gifts he molds his fantasies into a new kind of reality, and men concede them a justification as valuable reflections of actual life.[10]

Art would thus seem to be a kind of therapy through which the artist achieves a degree of normality, not just in the creation of art, but in the fact that it is accorded a place in society and *for this reason* satisfies the requirements of normality. There are two obvious objections to this interpretation. First, must an artist be at least mildly neurotic in order to create? And secondly, if he does suffer from some neurosis, is this evident in the work that he produces; and does he become conscious of the hidden forces which originally plagued him in their unconscious workings but are no longer plaguing because he is now capable of coping with them on the level of consciousness? I turn to the two in order.

In principle, it appears that satisfied people do not create. The principle, however, is next to worthless, inasmuch as probably no person is satisfied. But is he dissatisfied because he wants money, or because he hates exploitation, or because he wants fame, or because he must solve some puzzle? Any of these may lead—and probably have led—to the production of art. But if so, no profound psychoanalytic theory is required to explain its origins. The dissatisfactions which the psychoanalyst seeks are deeper-laid in the personality of the creator, and on his theory do not involve such ordinary motives. At a very minimum, it appears, the springs to action must be irrepressible as well as not quite capable of being understood—certainly not in advance of creation. Finally, we may say, the psychoanalytic understanding of art demands a way of connecting art (the fantasy?) with the concealed impulses (the reality?) which gave rise to it. Whether this account of art-production signifies that the producer suffers from neurosis is in part a matter of definition. That the artist creates fantasies is beyond question; whether or not these fantasies make his life difficult, even agonizing, is also not really questionable, for to write, to compose, to paint, is hard, often unbearable. But most important of all, the artist does not adopt standards of approved conduct, but on the contrary his conduct comes to be approved by virtue of the quality of the fantasies he creates and to which society later attributes a respectability.

Whether or not the artist suffers neuroses, those who offer a "soft" interpretation of the process find the origins in play, which by being repeated, lose their painful characteristics; or again, those who connect beauty with sexual attraction[11] may be true to the letter of Freud, but they lose track of the distinctive contribution to aesthetic theory. Karl Groos, Schiller, and others have called attention to the connection between play and art, and at least from the beginnings of Dionysiac art, man has been conscious of the connection between art and sex. But none of them pointed to the horrors of the repressed instincts which made for the tragedies of the infant's mind. "Before humour and other aids to mental digestion make their appearance," writes Ernest Jones, "these aspects [the jealousies, hatreds, and murderous impulses] of the infant's mind are entirely tragic, and all the tragedies of poets are ultimately derived from them."[12] This suggestion is something new in aesthetic theory and, if correct, signifies the need for depth analysis through which alone we may come to a more complete understanding of art.

Mr. Jones's analysis of *Hamlet* may turn out to be "persuasive" because he makes a case for (1) the statement of "the problem of Hamlet"—his vacillation and incapacity to act, not adequately accounted for in the play, (2) the similarity of personality traits of Hamlet and of Shakespeare, (3) a correlation of the dramatic and tragic elements in *Hamlet* with corresponding "facts" in Shakespeare's life, and finally (4) a plausible resolution of "the problem of Hamlet." According to this reading, *Hamlet* comes to be something different for the reader who has come under the spell of Freud from anything possible for one who has not. By virtue of this kind of analysis, we begin to appreciate the "hard," not the "soft," interpretation of Freudian criticism. The neurosis is not just Shakespeare's; it is also Hamlet's. Were it not, the interpretation would turn out to be not just useless but a postive hindrance, for it could only engender further mysteries without providing any enlightenment we could not get simply from a careful reading of the play itself. In this case, we would be better off in adopting the theory of art for art's sake, better off in believing that "the play is the thing," without trying to catch any further conscience.

The value of Freudian theory resides in its repudiation of art for its own sake and in its insistence upon the continuity of art with the life of man, involving as it does a kind of universality. The universality is not to be achieved by the placing of a work of art in a class, "the finest of its kind." Since the ends of art are as multitudinous as the possibilities entertainable by the creative genius of man, they might better, at least from the Freudian point of view, be recognized as unique rather than universal, just because a work of art is a unique way of resolving a unique problem. The universal is the driving force, which in truth unites the artist with the lover and the madman—or, to assert the proposition with the complete generality of which it is capable—with all men. This is so because the drives are regarded as instinctual. The madman and the lover resemble the artist in that they live in the world of imagination in a more intense degree than do the others. All are neurotic because all men are neurotic—unless, perhaps, they pass beyond neurosis to absolute madness. All men have fixations; no one achieves a state of maturity, however mature some, or even most, of his actions may be. But to say this is not to say that the artist is the lover or the madman. They share a kind of imagination that "cool reason" can never comprehend. But if the madman cannot contain his devils in vast hell and if the lover fixes on Helen's beauty in whatever he sees, the poet nevertheless is free to move unhampered until he turns things into shapes and conquers his world by giving it a local habitation and a name. No more demons, no more frantic visions, his is a world within bonds, a world of names, which is once more ordered so that cool reason can again find its way about. The artist has transformed a chaotic world into one of nicest discriminations and so has humanized it.

Shakespeare's vision and Freud's vision of the artist both still him in a gratification by giving the neuroses a local habitation and a name. Once they become the object of gratifying contemplation, their power is spent, and whether or not they are turned into things of beauty forever, they can never dictate to man as they had before. But the question remains of how the neurosis is stilled. May it not be just a dream from which the artist can awake only to be troubled again by the demon he thought he had destroyed but which rises again to plague him further? The most adequate answer lies, not just in the artist's gratification, important as that may be, but in the acceptance of his work in a culture that gives it a place in the lives of a people. The test of the bounding, the containment, the giving of a name to a thing, is whether it is called by that name—in short, whether it becomes part of the folklore of a people. And this it can become only as it answers some need for them—insofar as it gives them an image of themselves and helps to make them at home in a world of vicissitudes and uncertainties.

Implicitly, this answers our second question. Criticism is in Freudian terms an extension of creation. It looks for the hidden meanings in art in order that gratification may be more complete. Gratification is possible only as art is seen to be part of the human enterprise—insofar as appreciation of it discloses the continuity between man and his creations. If art extends back into life, it does so because the artist is a bone-and-flesh being whose neuroses are in some degree everyone's neuroses and whose reflection on life in his art is a reflection which orients us anew to life. Neither his nor our neuroses are necessarily done with, but by virtue of those neuroses with which we have come to terms in art, we gain perspective and are better prepared to face new ones from the vantage point of greater maturity, and not just innocence. In the words of a contemporary poet, " . . . to try / To backtrack to simplicity / Is fatal. Every Walden fails." Interpreting this in psychoanalytic theory, we may say that the conversion of neuroses into acceptable art-forms is the humanizing of the mind through cumulative experience—that is, through a maturing mind. The more mature mind does not destroy evil, but it finds to that degree a more human way of coping with it. In its dramatic form, evil is coped with by coming to an understanding of the sources of its inevitability, even if it physically leads the hero to death or madness or blindness. Humanly, the classic poets display it as the tragic sense of life. Their wisdom may be regarded as a maturing of "the strong imagination" which "grows to something of great constancy."

On this view, art is not just libidinous. Indeed, the better case is to be found in the continuity the Freudian observes between the libido and eros. The advantage of this interpretation over Plato's consists in the fact that while recognizing the hierarchy of forms of love, Freud is capable of indicating the lower in the higher without bowdlerizing it and without detaching from it one iota of the imaginative content the artist has embodied in his work. Freud differs from Plato in recognizing that there is a continuity between sickness and health, between the child and the man (or innocence and maturity), between the irrational and the rational, between fantasy and reason, between nature and

255

human nature. In place of Plato's asceticism, he looks for reason in nature, where the sublime is not projected into a realm separate from the processes of sublimation.

Freud has looked deeply into the processes of human nature and seems to have found levels of meaning in human life which have escaped all but the poetic imagination—especially that of the tragic poet. His humanism does not deny rationality; on the contrary, it ferrets out the irrational in order that the rational may come to its just fulfilment, not dominated by sickness. The sickness of the human soul is precisely that which is divisive, the most extreme form being psychosis. Health is a matter of uncovering the hidden aversions of man, examining their sources, and of seeking satisfactory outlets in harmony with men's reasonable aspirations. Some degree of complacency and gratification is a requisite to the good life. A person who cannot believe in himself cannot believe in others. Human intercourse evolves effectively and richly only as mutual respect is sustained by self-respect. Communication which does not originate in the depths of one's being is trivial, stilted, and unworthy of man. Freud has in his way reiterated the tenet of Socrates, "the unexamined life is not worth living." May we not also say that an art which does not originate in the depths of one's being is not worth creating? However the question is answered, we perceive that such an art is a form of aestheticism, and that as an ornament of life it is pleasant or perhaps even alluring, but possibly not worth the bother. This appears to be an inevitable consequence of Freudian theory. Only that which contributes to the sense of wholeness possesses vitality.

The conclusion is at least as old as Greek culture, and it is no sheer coincidence that the key terms of Freudian psychology are borrowed from it. But with a difference. Freud's interpretation of man's agonies moves less on a cultural plane than it does on an individual one. His concern implicates more the intimacies of the inner spirit than the prevailing tribal customs, which some regard as giving support to and providing direction for the life of the spirit. The question is then whether there is not another whole dimension—a distinctly social dimension—which is relevant to the wholeness of life, and which an expanded Freudian view would be compelled to explore. There appears to be good reason to consider the social dimension.

As in the Freudian point of view, so in the social point of view, art may be regarded as an extension, a complement, of human life, rather than an escape from or an impediment to it. The function of art from this latter point of view is to communicate through works, individual and personal, realities which embody the ambience of human life. The most abstract art attempts to do this by expressing the most general features of ambience—space and time. It is true, of course, that there is no art which does not explore one or the other or both. The ingenuity of the painter, for example, is endless in the treatment of these features, separately and in combination, varying all the way from poised action of animals inscribed on the walls of primitive caves to the sophisticated sense of simultaneity that Picasso and the abstractionists represent in exhibiting at the same time different perspectives of the same subject. Sometimes there is an attempt to eliminate one or the other of these features, by idealizing time-lessness as in the *Madonna of the Rose Garden,* or, paradoxically, to transform space into time as Italian Futurists attempted. Movement and rest, combining as they do infinite varieties of spatial and temporal features, can be shown to exist, I think, in all the arts. But the question is whether these features are not by themselves so abstract as to constitute caricatures, and whether as realities they do not engender other features that give them living qualities. This question deserves more than a dogmatic answer, even though we may not be quite able to answer it with certitude.

Space and time are abstractions of an order so high that they call for intermediates to relate them to human life. Some connective tissue, or better, some operational force, appears necessary to convert the abstractions of space and time into concretely expressed features of works of art. No longer can we naively believe that "real" space is a three-dimensional receptacle in which motion occurs in an irreversible and equable flow. Foreshortened representations in three-dimensional space were devices nicely calculated to undermine earlier religious art that de-emphasized space, because it de-emphasized the importance of material things.

But once "the natural world" was divided into nature and human nature, it became inevitable (even though it took centuries to bring it about) that artists would have to explore inner impressions and find new ways of expressing them in new intuitions of space and time.

It is not well known what the precise forces are that account for changing intuitions of space and time. From one point of view, their discovery calls for limitless knowledge, not just of art itself but also of all the elements of human culture and experience that are or may become ingredients of art. Perhaps it was the nomadic and hunting experiences that carried over into the spatio-temporal aspects of primitive wall painting. Surely religious beliefs enter into a vast range of art works that try to give man an image of himself. The advent of the Copernican Revolution, and especially of the Newtonian world view, unquestionably led artists to attach new meaning to Euclidean space and to make it central in their conception of experience. And it may not be too wild a guess to suggest that modern abstractionism borrowed heavily from Einstein's concept of relativity, especially that part which pertained to simultaneity. Perhaps more from the point of view of art than from that of science, we are forced to recognize a thoroughgoing plurality of ways of expressing notions of space and time, each of which has its own validity, just because it does make an aspect of experience more luminous. The tough question may then be rephrased: Is there some underlying force which relates the artistic representations of space and time to the luminosity of experience?

In answering this question, it is well to bear in mind that art is not just some subjective experience or inner intuition. It is an expressed or communicated experience. Or to borrow out of context from Mr. Allen Tate an idea already suggested, it is, at least for the man of letters, to "recreate for his age the image of man."[13] The "image of man" which is appropriate for his age is, we may say, the translation of the cultural focus into aesthetic terms. It is to bend the cultural rays upon a work of art and to transfix them in a way which gives man a new understanding of himself in his society. The ambience of space and time will be a wasteland, an open road, a Chicago-land, a me-for-the-hills, or an indefinite number of other notions, depending upon the metaphor by which the poet transmutes experience into the image he is convinced is the most valid for his time. Although the poet seeks to embody in his poetry what he believes should be the cultural focus, there can be no orthodoxy in such matters. Each embodiment is personal; otherwise it is not poetry. Each is novel; otherwise it is not made by a poet. Each is relevant; otherwise he does not communicate to his reader. Because of the need for relevance, criticism may come into play and hold before man a standard of criticism, which implies also a standard of art. But who is to enunciate this standard? This appears to be the fatal question.

Is the question, however, really fatal? Who is to decide what the good life shall be, or the ideal of the family, or of the law, or of the school, or of the church, or of fine manners? In a sense, the answers to all these questions fall into the same predicament. There is a standard, but no judge. Any self-appointed judge may be ignored, defied, or even rudely overthrown. Any person may choose to ignore a standard, even though not without a reckoning. A whole people may defy a norm, but, if it is a valid one, only at the expense of disillusionment, frustration, and even extinction. The timely makes its own demands, and the collective intelligence and wisdom recognize these demands, or else a people flounder in chaos, waste, and desperation. The people of an age make their own decisions, collectively and individually—collectively in the institutions they support and individually in the critical judgments they frame and adopt as guides to action. If they are untimely in their judgments and actions, the tragic consequences, whether or not celebrated in the arts, will exact their retribution.

Inner experience is not the test of timeliness; only criticism can provide a test. Plainly, unhampered communication is indispensable to the search for and validation of legitimate standards, of art as well as of other cultural matters. Standards become legitimated when, through knowledge and understanding, a people come to agreement on fundamentals. The most generous tolerance of widely divergent opinions and their implications is no doubt a requisite for reaching agreement and for keeping the cultural processes alive. Serious art has traditionally been crucial in aiding the understanding by which men can come to agreement. Tragic poetry is the classic example by which the understanding has been raised to new heights. Being critical—and philosophical—it has provided men with images which criticism often found to be appropriate to their time. Yet, simply because poetry is high-minded and serious, it does not follow that it is either illuminating or appropriate. The task of criticism is necessary to distinguish the untimely from the timely. Some general categories of art, however far from traditional classifications, may help to make the analysis clearer. I wish briefly to consider serious art from the points of view of escapist art and apologetic art, and then somewhat more extendedly from the point of view of critical art.

Chapter 10

SOCIETY AND THE ARTS TODAY

IT IS COMMONPLACE TO REGARD ART AS AN ESCAPE from reality, from the dreariness of the world, or, it may even be, from its horrors. As Louis MacNeice one pointed out, all art is an escape, even though he is quick to add that not all art is escapist. In this, I think, lies a crucial distinction. Just because serious art is a transmutation of experience—a heightened and purified experience—which compresses its materials into an effective and intense expression, it necessarily escapes the tedium and redundancy of gross and relatively formless experience. Formlessness is, of course, antithetical to art, or, we may just say platitudinously, the aesthetic differs from the non-aesthetic. Escapist art, then, is a kind of art; it is aesthetic, but it lacks virility. And it lacks virility precisely because in its transmuted form it has lost contact with the world from which it took its rise. It comes to be constituted as an art of detachment, not an art of fulfilment. It seeks an inner experience, a kind of dream life, alien to and alienated from the world in which men live and move.

The escapist makes the awful separation between the spiritual and the material—awful because it alienates. This is a separation different from the metaphysical distinction, which, even though it interprets the world as ultimately spiritual, still acknowledges and attempts to absorb the irreducible facts of experience which common men denominate as material. Rather, the escapist point of view is Manichean—a world of good dramatically opposed to a world of evil, the life of the one being the death of the other. The drama can end only as melodrama, idyllic blessedness opposed to inhuman terror. The vision is a familiar one in the history of culture. The significant variations are the kinds of evil that the artist can dwell upon before he repudiates them. Blessedness is a vision more difficult to depict. Of the philosophical poets, Dante is most successful, but then this is because he could turn earthly shapes into visions of fulfilment and could find in love, not so much an escape, as a realization. Lesser poets fail to discern a continuity between the earthly and the spiritual.

The kind of separation which makes art escapist is the split personality—split between a compartment of love and a compartment of hate. No wonder, then, that the opposite of the dream world is not reality but the nightmare. In neither does the poet discern the realities which make life—and death—meaningful, for he is contending with phantasms which have no originals in the world of waking experience. Transcendental art, which breaks the continuities of experience into secular horrors and sectarian ecstasies, is the cardinal sinner. In its attempt to be universal art, it is parochial; in its attempt to be critical, it is crudely unobservant; and its would-be climaxes of pathos end up only as sentimentalism. In the face of the defects ingrained in transcendental art, literary skill, however enchanting, is not enough to save the art-form from breaking into its parts. The fissure is too deep to be held together by the beauty of metaphor.

The alternative to a serious art which would not be escapist is one which is created out of compassion for the world, not a loathing of it. I chance upon a recent essay in criticism that singles out, among others, T. S. Eliot whose poetry is said to have the "quality of withdrawal from the world" and which differs from Synge or Burns or Herrick in that their effect "springs out of an immediate love of existence."[1] Having already spoken of Eliot's withdrawal, I do not wish to press this criticism further. But there are others who in a variety of different ways also withdraw. Robert Frost in a more bucolic mood can also seek a blessedness in a withdrawal from the noisy world of bustling people. His "Me for the hills where I don't have to choose" is a variation on the theme of transcendentalism and would-be eternalism, however different in tradition from the more theologically minded poets. Not just literary criticism, but criticism in the plastic and also in the musical arts, I am certain, can support the thesis with innumerable examples.

One further comment, however, appears appropriate for correcting something of the starkness of this criticism and for arriving at a more balanced judgment. It is not difficult to find in the modern world—or in any epoch, for that matter—instances of horror, brutality, ugliness, mania, and infinite varieties of callousness from which the poet or any other sensitive soul feels an unsuppressable urge to withdraw. The world may well challenge us to the question, is life worth living? We may want to answer it as William James did by replying that it's worth living if you make it worth living, but the question hauntingly remains as a question. A Sodom and Gomorrah possibly deserve only extinction, but this is a judgment that calls for superhuman wisdom, not the wisdom that we can expect from the poet. Human agency cannot legitimately be dismissed as a force in the world, however realistically man needs to inform himself of the character and strength of the forces against which he may decide to pit himself. Withdrawal, except as strategic withdrawal, is no battle and contains the seeds of strangely listless meditating, not of a coping with or illumination of the problems of man.

If escapist art errs on the side of withdrawal, apologetic art errs on the side of identification and complacency. To be of one's time is not necessarily to be timely, but rather passively to resign oneself to it or actively to combat any threats to it. The attitudes of resignation and combat lead to different kinds of apologetics in art, namely, realism and reactionism, if I may be excused in employing these terms in their pejorative sense. Possibly there is no better statement of "realistic art" than that which conceives of it as sound and fury told by an idiot and signifying nothing. The contemporary world seems to be full of this kind of thing, bombastuous, raucous, cacaphonous art, insistent, deafening, and exhausting, without yielding any sense of gratification. The quality that makes it apologetic is its pretense of having serious intent. It is not just wild and bacchanalian and full of humor. It dwells on horrors and revulsion with an extravagance disproportionate to any enlightenment it contains. And for the most part it is totally unrelieved except for a sop to saccharine sentiment.

When one reads a "novel" that begins with a recital of preparations for Hate Week and is soon introduced to Winston's removing a blob of human hair from Mrs. Parson's sink, obtrusively displayed for the children to see, the reader can anticipate for himself big brother, torture rooms, rats, and mechanical spies, tempered only slightly by a synthetic love affair, more promiscuous than tender. The generous reader may try to read into this an analogy to high tragedy. To be sure, the latter can be revolting enough, what with such elements as, for example, Banquo's bloody ghost appearing at the dinner table, the ruthless, senseless slaughter of Lady MacDuff and her child, and finally a warrior carrying onto the stage Macbeth's ghastly head atop a long pole dripping with blood. (It does seem almost as if Shakespeare has gone too far in his venture.) But the analogy doesn't come off. In the modern version, there is no "vaulting ambition"; there is no awareness of human aspiration and its distortion; and there is no convincing image of the tyrant. Or in keeping with the demands of modern organization, there is not even any recognition of the dignity of any social pursuit, including work, or the possibility of co-operation on a level where men can with mutual respect for one another achieve anything significant. There is at best a vapid suggestion that memory is the essence of life and history its embodiment, together with the drill-hammered proposition that privacy is the supreme value of man and that this can be destroyed in man's body as well as in his mind. This is not the stuff of the tragic view of life. It is a reporter's version of his assignment to cover the "realities" of life.

Realism and reactionism, it becomes apparent, are not necessarily exclusive but may converge to reinforce each other. Propagandistic in intent, they seek the *status quo ante* and utilize the power of art to arouse fear in the form of the scare, which cannot be alleviated, for the turning back which they ask for can only involve more of the horrors, not in essence different from those which they depict as the present lot of man. Their own realism catches them up in a way which destroys their intent, and then reveals itself as sentimental instead of realistic. Their logic yields no clarification but only a strenuousness that fails to support the wisdom which was its purpose. Propaganda divorced from wisdom can only mar insight by a rigidity that has its outward expression in the brittle language of satire without humor, horror without purpose, and human beings without mentality. It places emphasis upon the sensational to the exclusion of the reflective.

Reactionism may, however, have its own brand of seriousness apart from realism, especially when the *status quo* is not considered to be threatened. In this case, the idealization of the world man lives in is embroidered in comforting colors of peace and success. Naked force is clothed with the garments of virtue, and the lawful is sanctimoniously bedecked with tinsel in order to draw the unwary from the temptations of lawlessness. Ambition is channelled in directions approved by customary morals, and happiness is said to be apportioned in accordance with righteousness. Such art cannot fail to be anaemic, for it is art by formula, thoughtless, sentimental, and stereotyped. Apologetic, it seizes upon what it takes to be the focus of a culture and makes it a guide to the perpetuation of a tradition, regardless of whether or not it meets the needs of society. Usually, it is reactionary in that it tilts windmills which in themselves are without function.

Critical art contrasts both with escapist and apologetic art in that the artist sees the world in a new way, a way which is timely, not eternal, and not just current. When it is not just carping, critical art has a profundity that jars man loose from his traditional attitudes toward the world and the way he thinks about it. It causes him to re-evaluate it, together with his destiny and his powers of life. Historically, the great poets and artists have given men a new version of themselves in their world. And it is to ends that they look, for art is concerned with finalities, however much the conception of them must change as the conditions of life change.

Critical art is an essential part of the cultural process. The artist as critic sees through the banalities and dogmas and inhumanities of a society and suggests, if only negatively, not solutions, but at least the obstacles to a more authentic kind of existence. As a negative critic, Aldous Huxley, for example, fired his shots with unerring accuracy at the foibles of a scientific society, free from pain and relying on the Pavlovian conditioning necessary for each Alpha, Beta, Delta, Gamma, or Epsilon to find his proper place in the world. The "feelies", the solidarity ceremonies, the blood surrogates—all are devised to reveal the shallowness of values derived from the intellect and separated from any feeling other than that which promotes maximizing pleasure and minimizing pain. It is true that Huxley incompletely criticized such a society in that he failed to take quite seriously the authentic basis of his criticism and concludes with an equally disastrous separation of feeling from intellect. This romanticism issues into a more than dubious idealization of the noble savage as opposed to the scientist. It makes love a catastrophic disturbance in society, not a principle of criticism with a power to create. The sciences that Huxley criticized were, it is true, the psychological and the biological sciences of the 1920's. Yet the point is well made that contemporary man confuses irrelevancies with the substance of life. In *Brave New World Revisited* he makes the point uncommonly clear:

> In regard to propaganda the early advocates of universal literacy and a free press envisaged only two possibilities: the propaganda might be true, or it might be false. They did not foresee what in fact has happened, above all in our Western capitalist democracies—the development of a vast mass communications industry, concerned in the main neither with the true nor the false, but with the unreal, the more or less totally irrelevant. In a word, they failed to take into account man's almost infinite appetite for distraction.[2]

The question Huxley forces upon our attention is one of man's relation to man and to nature. It is an old question, but it is in a new form, that is to say, in the impact of science and scientific technology on man.

The issue may profitably be cast in even broader terms—terms which include the kind of social relations possible if man is not to yield his scientific heritage and still preserve his identity as man. Huxley, in other words, doesn't go far enough in his criticism. The lively question is whether we can have science and man too. Otherwise man surely loses out, as the savage does in *Brave New World*—when in the end a pair of feet are seen to be dangling from a crown of an arch in a lighthouse. When science is looked at from the point of view of its authentic challenge, and not just from one of gadgetry or cookbook recipes, it can be as engaging, imaginative, and creative as anything in art. Those who denigrate it in order to adulate art do both an ill favor. Arcadia may, of course, be lost to art because of science. Yet the transformed world brought about by science constitutes but another opportunity to the arts to humanize and to make brave a new world without cynicism or rancor. This is the perennial task of critical art.

Few words should be wasted on what this art will be. It will be what the artists will make of it, nothing more and nothing less. Yet it is enticing and probably not wholly unwarranted to suggest some of the terms which such an art likely would have to take into account. If it is not to be escapist, dream-world art or apologetic, reactionary art, it would neither content itself with the heroics of an inner life nor the banalities of formal custom. Yet "somehow" it must combine the heroic and the formal by melting them into a new cultural amalgram. The "somehow" is the mystery which constitutes the challenge to the artist. Heroic his outlook must be, if man is not just to grovel in the world of morons, as much of our present-day literature insists upon. But not heroic in the sense of an inner world walled off from the world of practice and from the community. The greatness we look for may be that for which Whitman long ago so eloquently pled in *Democratic Vistas*—that democracy which "founds and luxuriantly grows its own forms of art, poems, schools, theology, displacing all that exists or that has been produced anywhere in the past, under opposite influences." His insistence is upon the need for

> . . . native authors, literatures, far different, far higher in grade, than any yet known, sacerdotal, modern, fit to cope with our occasions, lands, permeating the whole mass of American mentality . . . and . . . accomplishing . . . a religious and moral character beneath the political and productive and intellectual bases of the states.

Feudalism, the historical sense, tradition—none of these can meet the fresh requirements of today. Whitman's vistas, combining as they do his personalism and his sense of a community, is as relevant to post-World War II as it was to the post-Civil War period, excepting only that the native authors cannot but be required to regard their beloved States from an even further enlarged point of view.

The fissures in the States still need to be healed. The problems have since Whitman's time been exacerbated by the vast occurrences in science and technology and social organization. From any but the most provincial points of view, these problems are generally recognized. Mr. Allen Tate states it well in his criticism of the "illiberal specializations that the nineteenth century has proliferated into the modern world." He identifies them as specializations in which "means are divorced from ends, action from sensibility, matter from mind, society from the individual, religion from moral agency, love from lust, poetry from thought, communion from experience, and mankind in the community from men in the crowd."[3] His indictment of the fragmentation of the Western mind is a twentieth century charge that can be matched by Ruskin in the nineteenth century. The terms have, of course, changed in intensity and scope and call for solutions appropriate to the mid-twentieth century scene. Critical art, by its very nature, must be aware of the cultural issues which face us.

In its most abstract phase, the problem of the arts is the metaphysical problem—the relation of art to reality. In a sense, this has been the burden of the whole of this now extended discussion of the institutions of expression. Being ultimate, the issues cannot be conclusively decided by arguments. Indeed, there is a sense in which reality can never be satisfactorily coped with on the discursive level. One man's dream world is another man's reality; one man's deep concerns are another's trivialities. The question is whether we can really read the logic of events and discern the indispensable and controlling forces in human life. Philosophers have necessarily had to take this question as constituting their urgent, if not their supreme, one. And to the extent that the philosophical is relevant to art and society, to religion and practice, or to any other human enterprise, they too must take into account metaphysical notions, however much they must translate them into the concrete terms of their distinctive preoccupations.

If we do not give priority to the contemplative point of view —and there seems no necessity for this—we may seek for reality in what we have called the ambience of man. Space and time, we saw, are essential to any conception of ambience. But also, we saw, they are abstract and need to be made definite through interpretation. How can man move about in his world? Only as he has ideas which give him a sense of direction. Otherwise he can only stumble and clutch at any branch that provides but wavering support. If the world is to be definite and also to be one in which man can move about, he needs to reckon with the obstacles as well as with opportunities—and this means to reckon with the world of natural beings and with other men. But these are not original existences. They, man and nature, have already been transformed many times by cultural processes. The original may have been there in a state of nature, but the civil society has so altered the original as to make it irretrievable in its pristine state. The reality we have to contend with is the cultural reality, complex, illusive, tempting, sometimes satisfying, more often frustrating.

Art itself is a major force in the transforming process. It takes its material from a world already altered by man's being of it, and it further converts that world by the introduction of new kinds of artifacts which realign his being with it. If we wish, we may say, then, that man is thrice removed from the world of pristine nature, not because it is twice imitated, but because it is twice converted: once by virtue of the socializing of the world which comes about through man's interrelations with it in the processes of living and sustaining himself; and secondly, by virtue of the art-process, which takes the socialized world as its stuff to be further converted into forms of artistic expression. In the first conversion, the artist is born into the world of his social inheritance. In the second, he is the maker of an inheritance of an inheritance, through which in turn men come to see differently, to hear differently, and to feel differently. The mirroring of the world in art is distorted in the sense that its primary function is that of extending or completing it. The rainbow is a better image than that of the mirror to express the function of art. Taking its subject matter as continuities between light and water, it creates a new glory which proclaims the work of a new power. So art, taking its subject matter as the continuities already established between nature and man, produces new continuities between man and his artifacts, to the further enhancement of both nature and man.

The double process of conversion may be seen more clearly in the practical arts than in the fine arts. The sophistications of the latter often conceal the origins from which they have taken their rise. Arabesques, geometrical patterns, the "non-objective," which

269

is not limited to just painting, appear to have a life of their own. This independent existence of art is then regarded as constituting a sufficiency whose only end is the delight taken in the pure contemplation of the forms created by the artist. In the practical arts, however, the continuities are nearly always apparent. Tools, machines—in general, artifacts of use—are undeniably conversions of materials of nature and subject to the forces of nature. There is no doubt that the "material cause" belongs both to nature and to the thing made "for the matter is not only that out of which something is made but also that which persists in it." So, for anything of use. Beyond this, however, a thing may have an elegance of design which is not quite dictated by use. It follows function without being determined by utility. The first form of continuity requires no elaboration. The second requires at least some clarification.

The current reactions against the formula, "form follows function," happily serve to clarify some confusions that have plagued the interpretation of it. The principal confusion comes from those who would *identify* form with function. But this isn't what Sullivan said, and clearly it was not his intent, for he said that the one *follows* the other, where "follow" is used in a genetic sense, not in a logical one. The objections, then, especially in architecture, of those who are reacting against functionalism may not be well taken. However intimately related form is to function, it is not the same as function. It may in a perfectly legitimate sense then be said to be *non-functional*. The real quarrel, if in fact any there is, has its source in the ambiguity of the negation of function. It may mean anti-functional, involving a clutter of things, including decoration which is "stuck on" to artifacts as a kind of prettifying afterthought. Or again, it may mean the non-functional which, although differing from function, nevertheless completes it by virtue of giving to it aesthetic form which it would otherwise lack. Decoration of this sort is integral to the thing. It makes pleasing to the eye a form which evolves out of function and gives it a richness, a scope, a meaningful ambience, and especially a sense of completeness, which it would not have in the absence of the form.[4] Without aesthetic form, things are mean and niggardly. They are mere tools or crude shelters—

sheerly utilitarian things—but not works of art. If a thing is to have beauty as well as utility, it must have expended on it care and attention and it must give evidence of human sensibility, which is indispensable to a thing's becoming a work of art.

This analysis suggests now the difference between the practical and the fine arts as well as their affinity. In the practical arts come to aesthetic fulfilment, the object is at once the object of use and one of aesthetic form. In the fine arts, the object is never intended as one of use. But it reflects practical meaning inasmuch as its form is a further conversion of an already enculturated reality. Whereas in the practical arts there is one object which bears two kinds of values, in the fine arts there are implicitly two objects, each possessing a unique kind of value. This duality, of course, makes it possible to develop a theory of art which is cast in terms of a mirror (distorted) image. The image is much less convincing when applied to the practical arts, and even the Platonist has some doubts as to the correctness of seeking for an original laid up in the heavens of utilitarian things, especially should they be ugly. The alternative which appears more justifiable is one in which art is seen to be a conversion of fundamental realities of man's social existence. I should accordingly like to conclude this discussion by pointing up what appears to be the challenge to the arts today in a genuine culture.

Basically and bluntly posed, the challenge to the arts today is how to humanize a society committed to science and technology? This certainly appears to be the problem of the Western World as well as of Russia. When and as the rest of mankind become increasingly industrialized, it is fair to assume that they, too, will be confronted with much the same challenge. In posing the question, however, we have no right to presume that science and technology are illiberal in their outlook. They may be. But so may be the arts. The rise of science and technology, whether illiberal or liberal has, however, converted the focus of society from agricultural to manufacturing pursuits. A genuine culture today cannot but recognize the change in focus and take it into account as the formidable condition of achieving a rich and liberating kind of existence.[5]

In this as in all genuine cultures, the prime requisite is a community of outlook which adds to the integrity and effectiveness of the individual members and which liberates their vitalities instead of thwarting them. When, however, this community of outlook is specified as being scientific and technological, immediately two social conditions become apparent which constitute a serious break with the past. The first is the degree to which such a community is constituted as secular, and the second is the evolution of its growth into a mass society. From the beginnings of man's renewed interest in nature down to the Scopes trial, the struggle between the institutions of religion and those of science have been bitter, and the resolutions have been more by attrition and exhaustion than by reason and agreement. In rejecting revelation and authority and in insisting upon reason and evidence, science has turned men's serious attention to the laboratory and the field rather than to the Bible and inner experience. And by putting to use accumulated knowledge, technology has had the effect of shifting populations from country to town and of transforming town into city. Thus the massive organization required for modern production has produced mass society.

We have earlier had occasion to discuss the political forms which appear in the course of the rise of mass societies. It is not necessary to repeat that discussion. But it is necessary to re-emphasize two conditions that are essential to a genuine culture. They are, first, the emergence of a community which is based upon agreement, and, second, an agreement which is arrived at through critical intelligence. Otherwise, the community is only a society held together by force and terror in all their endless depravities. No sensibility of man is too puny to find expression in the open community, but no sensibility is worthy of becoming policy for a community unless it is capable of withstanding harsh criticism— harsh because of the need for recognizing the possible superiority of opposed sensibilities. Criticism, together with the sensibility it presupposes, is indispensable to the authentic community, a community which rests upon an acknowledgment by the vast majority of the fundamentals necessary to their common welfare.

When we look to the arts manifested in institutional form, we find potentialities of their critical function, however much they may fall short of them in practice. We have, in fact, discussed this function insofar as the *fine* arts are capable of serving it. The discussion pointed to the opportunity—in fact the urgency—of art to provide man with ever new images of himself. The new can be used to challenge the old images which are implicit in his attitudes and habits of action. We noted the need for the relevancy of these images to the actual ambiences which are open to men, and on this basis we distinguished them from art which is transcendental, escapist, or apologetic. It suffices for our purposes if we now relate this discussion to two other forms of art which are specially important for our day—the applied arts and the mass arts. Without attempting any detailed analysis of them, I wish nevertheless to show how they too may serve the critical function in relation to the demands of an authentic twentieth century culture.

The applied arts have one decisive advantage over the fine arts, and that is in the urgencies which make them take into account the realities of human existence. The pressures on men to economize both their strength and the use of natural resources are endless. And this is still more the case even when the applied arts that men are wedded to are largely obsolete, for under these circumstances the practical effect is to increase unnecessarily human suffering. No, the urgencies are a simple matter of economy —the use of limited resources, human and natural, to maximize well-being. Tools are necessary to convert things from one form to another; houses and clothing are necessary for protection against the elements; the gathering or production and preparation of foodstuffs is necessary for the preservation of life, and so on. Moreover, many of these demands are concurrent and require plans of actions which are capable of meeting them both simultaneously and serially. Modern industrial society bears a close resemblance to primitive societies in its applied arts, since in both, the need for conservation of resources is predominant. Luxury— that is, the luxury which is justifiable—is a matter of having a care for things in a way which satisfies the whole man, rather than being a matter of waste.

The pressures for economizing come primarily from man's relation to nature and secondarily from his relation to other men.

For this reason, the applied arts are inherently grounded in secular knowledge, whatever extra-secular sanctions may be superimposed upon them. Natural knowledge cannot consistently be defied without a toll on human welfare, however short this knowledge may be from satisfying deep-lying aspirations of men. Clearly, it is by reason of these aspirations that the applied arts can serve an aesthetic function as well as a practical one. The need for completeness drives man to seek beyond the practical to the aesthetic. Basically, he becomes aware of this further dimension by virtue of the fulfilments which inhere in perceptual experience. Perception is a delight, is a unity, is a fulfilment. Accordingly, things can be shaped to add this quality to what would otherwise be unpleasant, unharmonious, and not satisfying. The principle holds true in the least as well as in the most sophisticated of artifacts—from arrow heads to rockets.

Modern architecture reveals the principle in impressive and exciting ways. Frank Lloyd Wright insisted upon a new architecture primarily by his recognition of the human demand for a continuity between the inside and the outside of a house. The Aristotelian definition of a house as a shelter offering protection against wind, rain, and sun signifies enclosure, but so inadequately that the "essence" of a house gets manifested in a box-like structure, inhuman, degrading, and stifling. Wright brings sun and water, even wind and trees into a house, erasing the sharp separations between man and nature. His "essences" differ each from every other depending upon whether they become embodied in lake-shore structures, hill-side, or prairie-land—and even more, depending upon the unique contours of the land and seascapes. The motivating power of Wright was a romantic one—as far removed from the row-houses and square-blocks as possible. He looked once more for the individual and tried to remove him from the ambience of mass conformity to that of an eccentric independence.

Others, more willing to yield to the pressures of mass society, have rejected Broad Acres in favor of an urban architecture consistent with the needs of dense populations, rigid materials capable of indefinite repetition, and cubicled space more given to vertical than to horizontal expansion. Mies van der Rohe, for

274

example, is more concerned to cater to the exigencies of a society devoted to financial and business transaction than to the impulses to cultivate rose gardens. Nature becomes transformed into concrete, glass, and aluminum. Sunlight is converted into slant rays adjusted by slats or rays softened by passing them through a wall of drapes. The neo-technics which are applied to metropolitan architecture practically defy nature, including even gravity itself. Little wonder is it, then, that the conflict becomes transformed into one between urban and suburban life, with all the embarrassments it causes man in trying to bridge the two.

When we shift attention from architecture to that of machine-design, we are likely to find that modern technology provides much more happy solutions. The problems are, to be sure, less complicated inasmuch as the functions are simpler and the challenge to the human imagination less exacting. Machines, even those capable of multiple operations, are designed with a simplicity of purpose that permits a further elegance dictated only by the cravings of sight and touch. Elongations, rounded corners, polished surfaces—these may be enough to prove the care of the designer for human sensibilities. Modern methods of processing and packaging have an eye to color and shape, which often reflect both the biological virtues and beauty of natural products. The simplest, transparent packaging can employ natural light to cater to the kaleidoscopic joy that sophisticated man can still take in simple things. Thus the modern designer can create objects of beauty by capturing an integrity of movement from the mechanical to the biological to the social, enhancing the process at each step, even as the poet does in moving from verse to verse in a culminating creation.

The mortal sin against applied art consists in rupturing the art-process. When an insistent element is introduced which is false to the continuities, ugliness appears, not beauty. Whether it is rose medallions on machines that call for simplicity of line, or medallions of an extra wheel imprinted on the reverse side of an automobile trunk, the falsity trumpets the insincerity of the designer. The sports, whether appearing as pseudo-biological or pseudo-social *motifs,* are monstrosities and deserve to be treated as such. We have pretty well learned today that we should not mar physical beauties by plastering on them biological design. We are a long way from having learned to distinguish social continuities from disruptive elements—especially in regard to those things designed for retail consumption. Designing for flashy competitive obsolescence, we often exaggerate surface features out of all proportion to functional continuities. As in dress design, we are asked to substitute fad for beauty. The perversion is obvious when style, which in the arts is the essence of integrity, becomes converted into the fashion of the day, always distinguishing but seldom distinguished.

Although the need for social continuities is detectable in the applied arts, it is positively insistent in the mass arts. Allied as the latter are with technical processes of photography and sound-recording, they live in an appeal to a mass audience. The techniques required for the production of a radio program, not to speak of TV, rest on a phenomenally complicated knowledge, however many there are who possess it. There can be no doubt of the propriety of applying the phrase, "the institutions of expression," to the mass arts. The organization of technical skills, the bringing together of creative talent, the means of assembling a mass audience—these are but a bare indication of the scope required to make the mass arts into a reality. But even more to the point, the convergence of the institutions of power and the institutions of expression is crucial to the maintenance of each. The issues arising out of this convergence turn upon some of the most complicated and controversial questions of the day. Among these is one which is most relevant to our discussion: can the mass media serve in the creation of an authentic culture, as well as provide the kind of expression which is essential to it?

The question admits of no easy answer, and I do not propose to supply one. Instead, I wish merely to designate some of the major conditions necessary to anything like the emergence of mass arts which can excite and engage the creative instincts. The indications are that we have a plethora of distinguished creative writers for the mass arts.[6] It even seems likely that those writers are willing to make necessary concessions to the co-operative requirements of these arts, as have playwrights from time immemorial and, more recently, movie script writers. Inherently, the medium is one which calls for a multitude of co-operating talents, some with technical skills, some with productive sensibilities as well. Mechanical features, including time allotment, must be respected if there is to be anything at all like an adequate production. One may, however, regard these as the requirements of the medium which, although different from the fine and the applied arts, are nevertheless comparable. The crucial difference between this art and the fine arts (less so, but still appreciable in regard to the applied arts) is the kind of patronage it involves. This patronage is so thoroughly organized that it can bring more than economic sanctions to bear upon artists: it can often control public sentiment itself and therefore the censure which the whole population may visit upon its aberrant artists. This often strains the very conception of culture, and therefore of cultural focus. Inquisitorial, it can terrorize and beat into submission, sometimes through blandishment, sometimes through naked force, whole vast populations, without there being any effective restraints upon that power.

That power which has manifested itself today shows up in one of two ways, or a combination of both. Either it is the power of private organizations which substantially control public policy or of state organizations which through their directors impose policy on the masses. The curious combination of the two shows up as fascism, in which arbitrary power is in essence an extreme extension of private enterprise.[7] In either case, propaganda is the technique which is used to distort the social process. And whatever other refinements may be employed depend upon the ingenuity of those in power to bring about the results they desire. I am not suggesting that propaganda is intrinsically false in art. It may or may not be. It is false when it disrupts the continuity of the art-process; it is not, so long as it effectively advances it.

Our question as to whether the mass arts can effectively and legitimately employ talent in the service of a genuine culture reduces to the question whether there can be a shift from private to public or quasi-public sanctions that can evoke talent instead of destroying it. Private sanctions will not do in the mass arts for one and only one reason—they are irresponsible. Whether it is a cigarette sponsor who insists that a script writer must substitute the term "fortunate" for "lucky" in his writing, or whether it is a religious sect that insists its particular brand of morality must prevail in the mass arts, or whether it is a patriotic organization that imposes black lists upon producers and therefore makes an orthodoxy of the kind of content which the mass arts may explore —all are sinners against the spirit of a genuine culture. Substituting privacy, prejudice, and orthodoxy for what should be public, critical, and tolerant, they reduce the mass arts to an adolescent level, which can at best amuse, but probably just distracts minds from advancing into the spontaneities which are the birthright of creative genius. To suggest that these private organizations be silenced is, of course, no help. It merely converts one kind of tyranny into another. And although the immediate merits of the case may seem to warrant it, tyranny by being publicly sanctioned can lead only to even blacker lists.

The political question, it seems, is an intrinsic part of any intelligent treatment of the mass arts. It cannot be evaded. We are squarely confronted, then, with the issue of whether there can be a genuine culture in a mass society—whether the political virtues of intelligence, tolerance, sensitivity, power, and creative advance can all be combined in a community intent upon the fulfilment of its human vitalities. Those who take the dim view may pride themselves on their realistic appraisal of human beings *en masse,* concluding that the vast majority are incapable of exercising the necessary virtues, and that even if they did possess them, the mere mechanics of mass society makes it impossible for them effectively to put them to use. The formulation of policy, the making of decisions, and their effective implementation in social action must be engineered by the few and can never be undertaken by the masses. However strong the case may be, I have already tried to show its inherent weaknesses. Whether in the more romantic form, such as Nietzsche proposed, or in the more brutal form of the garrison state, one may examine them to ascertain whether they can possibly satisfy the demands of a genuine culture. Surely their very essence prohibits a culture in which the vast majority can be full participants, stimulated to the utmost to use their talents, to enjoy the rewards of both the institutions of power and the institutions of expression, and to achieve a life of the community in which common ends prevail by agreement, not by ignorance, fiat, or terror. The alternatives appear to be an industrial system in which the mass arts contribute to the establishment of a genuine mass culture or else one in which greed and brutality serve to stupify the masses through distractions and inanities to prevent them from rising much above the level of simple-mindedness. The alternatives exist partly in the mass arts themselves, but mostly in the political mentality which has the power of strangulating or of liberating them.

It becomes apparent that no automatic system, whether placed in the hands of private organizations or in public ones, can guarantee the liberation of the mass arts. Here as in all public virtues there is no substitute for intelligence, education, sensitivity, generosity, and a fearless sense of public well-being. When these virtues are supported by the institutions of power, the genius that comes from the arts, fine, applied, and mass, in wrestling with the problems of men and expressed in the media in which the artist has expertise—that genius inevitably comes to fruition. Our discussion has intended to show, however, that the arts cannot flourish without institutions of power, which can either promote or defeat the arts. The conclusion is clear: those who would ignore the part that institutions can and do play simply blind themselves to an effective condition of the life of the arts. Transcendentalist and escapist in their outlook, they remove themselves from effective participation in shaping a virile art for a virile people intent upon recognizing ever new continuities of life. They defeat the social processes; they do not enhance them. Although it is obviously true that it takes an artist to make a work of art, it is also true that it takes a society to make an artist. And the kind of artist is never quite independent of the kind of society. Some concluding words are appropriate, therefore, concerning the potentialities of a concurrent development of each towards the establishment of a more genuine culture.

Our earlier discussion led us to conclude that two opposite elements figure in the development of a more satisfactory culture. Paradoxically, they are the developments into both a smaller and a wider community of interests. The one is a cultivation of regions in the world where proximity, terrain, and economic self-interest cry out for a rational politics which can give expression to social need. The other is an equally insistent demand for a realignment of national institutions into political forms which are bent upon ends of mutual well-being instead of those of destruction. The arts, too, as they pursue the needs of modern man cannot but reflect them in their creations. The new political virtues called for may be expected to be a boon to the arts as well as to politics. Whether these virtues will be practiced and whether they will issue into revitalized arts are guesses that we fortunately need not try here to make, ominous as the negative alternatives clearly are.

Although the modern region is not self-contained or self-supporting, it can nevertheless measurably exploit its own self, economically, socially, and artistically. It can develop its own resources, while still recognizing that its people are part of the human race. Its local color need not be just quaint; it can be genuine to the extent that its ambience is native to its own terrain and its customs are expressions of its sensibilities. Even mawkish neon lights and Coca-Cola cannot destroy a cultural tradition rooted in a geography, an occupation, an architecture, and a language which are embedded in the minds and loves of a people. A kind of political decentralization which has a concern for these minds and their loves can be a movement towards an autonomy of a people which needs not be contrary to the universal rights of persons. Their problem will unquestionably be one of absorbing experiences from the outside without being absorbed by them. The artist, who has an unusual sense of independence, can in his own way be a most important critic of what can and what cannot be absorbed without destroying the authentic elements in the life of a region. Irony, satire, and wit are as important to the process of criticism as love, sympathy, and reverence. How these can be fitted to the exigencies of an industrial world is a challenge for the poet and the statesman as well as for the industrialist and the financier.

The opposite face of the region is the universe of man with his common hopes and fears—in short, his common humanity. This, too, has a way of changing with knowledge and institutions that can be shared by at least most of the populations of the world. Industry and trade have placed their imprint upon every continent; and increasingly a world is sharing in and contributing to that source from which they came—namely, science. Poets often lament the rise of science, believing that it has destroyed the taste of cherries, that is, the natural and unadulterated realm of sense experience. But they are mistaken. Science has altered our world. It is up to the poet to find new beauties in it, and to the painter to discover new symmetries, and to the composer to disclose new harmonies. When the artist learns better the lesson that science, too, is creative, he can come to recognize that art can interpret a whole new range of experience and make it more germane to the life of man. He can find that in aiming to make experience consummatory he can probe more deeply than sheer aesthetic surfaces and that he can reveal to modern man hitherto undetected connections between the intimate world of emotion and the outer world of thought and perception. Then it will be that the scientist and the artist can recognize themselves as kinsmen.

Having said this, we are still left with an imponderable. How are we to relate the world and the region in an art which can do justice to both? Perhaps all we should say is that this art can be nothing less than the philosophical art of the future. Lucretius, Dante, and Goethe did it for their ages. Perhaps some philosophical poet will do it for ours. We know some of the conditions that are necessary for this kind of philosophico-poetic synthesis. We have not yet produced the talent that can make it a reality. When we do, we will come to understand better the reciprocal relations between the institutions of power and the institutions of expression.

NOTES

PART I

CHAPTER 1

1. Ruth Benedict, *Patterns of Culture* (Boston: Houghton Mifflin, 1934).

2. D. F. Aberle et. al., "The Functional Prerequisites of a Society," *Ethics*, LX 2 (Jan. 1950), 100-111.

3. Cf., however, Stephen Pepper's interesting statement of the function of religion as providing social solidarity. But note that solidarity can be attained by religions other than religious—e.g. political, economic, military, or even aesthetic. *The Sources of Value* (Berkeley and Los Angeles: University of California Press, 1958), pp. 584 ff.

4. B. Malinowski, "Culture," *Encyclopedia of the Social Sciences*. Vol. 4: "The savage is not more rational than modern man nor is he more superstitutious. He is more limited, less liable to free imaginings and to the confidence trick of new inventions. . . There are domains on which magic never encroaches. The making of fire, basketry, the actual production of stone implements, the making of strings of mats, cooking and all minor domestic activities although extremely important are never associated with magic. Some of them become the center of religious practices and of mythology, as, for example, fire or cooking or stone implements; but magic is never connected with their production. The reason is that ordinary skill guided by sound knowledge is sufficient to set man on the right path and to give him certainty of correct and complete control of these activities." p. 636.

Also: "But magic is never used to replace work. In gardening the digging or the clearing of the ground or the strength of the fences or quality of the supports is never scamped because stronger magic has been used over them. The native knows well that mechanical construction must be produced by human labor according to strict rules of craft. He knows that all the processes which have been in the soil can be controlled by human effort to a certain extent but not beyond, and it is only this beyond which he tries to influence by magic. For his experience and his reason tell him that in certain matters his efforts and his intelligence are of no avail whatever. On the other hand, magic has been known to help; so at least his tradition tells him." p. 637. Copyright 1931, The Macmillan Company. Quoted by permission.

5. A. L. Kroeber and Clyde Kluckhohn, *Culture: A Critical Review of Concepts and Definitions* (Papers of the Peaboby Museum of American Archaeology and Ethnology, Harvard University. Vol. XLVII, no. 1. Cambridge, 1952).

6. *Op. cit.*, p. 46. Cf. also Franz Boas, *Mind of Primitive Man* (New York: Macmillan, Rev. Ed. 1938), p. 159.

7. Cf. Malinowski when he writes: " . . . the institution is the real isolate of culture." And, "The study of any culture must . . . be carried out in terms of institutions." And further, "We have found that everywhere the business of life is carried on by a number of institutions." *Freedom and Civilization* (New York: Roy Publishers, 1944), pp. 154, 167. Also cf. Ogburn and Nimkoff, *Sociology* (Boston: Houghton Mifflin, 1940), pp. 46-7, and pt. VI.

8. Cf. Ralph Linton on what he calls "Alternatives" in *The Study of Man* (New York: Appleton-Century, 1936), pp. 273 ff. Professor Schattschneider has collected an amusing list of organizations which represent a wide variety of interests. Cf. *Party Government* (New York: Rinehart, 1942), pp. 25-6, and his discussion, Ch. 2.

9. For an extended, detailed, and discriminating study of this, cf. Stephen Pepper, *op, cit.,* especially Chs. 18, 19. Also for a critical discussion of it see my review in the *Journal of Philosophy,* vol. LVI, no. 8 (Apr. 9, 1959), pp. 358-68.

10. A. L. Kroeber, ed., *Anthropology Today,* "Universal Categories of Culture" (University of Chicago Press, 1953), p. 521.

11. *Encyclopaedia of the Social Sciences,* "Culture," p. 645.

12. Ruth Benedict attempts to deny this when she insists, "The significant sociological unit from this point of view [i.e. the using of any occasion "to channel purposes generically unrelated"], therefore, is not the institution, but the cultural configuration." *Op. cit.,* p. 244. Her denial, however, is not very convincing, since her insistence amounts merely to an allegation of culture as being the only self-sustaining social unit. We may allow the conclusion and still hold that culture, being complex, is capable of analysis into components, even though culture itself is regarded as a "pattern" or "configuration." Otherwise, we are reduced to the position that culture is not analyzable, a conclusion which, for a social scientist, is surely sorry and misleading, as well as one which belies the rendering of any intelligible account of social life. Besides, the statement above quoted hardly squares with what she writes earlier when she declares, "The first essential, so it seems today, is to study the living culture, *to know its habits of thought and the functions of its institutions. . . .*" p. 49. Quoted by permission. (Italics mine.)

13. *Selected Writings of Edward Sapir in Language, Culture, and Personality,* ed. by David Mandelbaum (Berkeley and Los Angeles: University of California Press, 1951), p. 311.

14. Cf. *Ibid.,* pp. 308-311.

15. Cf. Pepper, *Op. cit.,* "Priorities among the Norms within a Cultural Pattern," pp. 597 ff.; J. K. Feibleman, *The Institutions of Society,* Ch. XVI, "The Leading Institution" (London: Allen and Unwin, 1956); and especially, M. J. Herskovits, *Man and His Works,* "Cultural Focus" (New York: Knopf, 1948), pp. 542 ff.

16. *Ibid.,* p. 542. Cf. also the following statement: "We characterize Egypt by saying that here economics and politico-religious concerns predominated. Athens of the classical period is described as a democratic society wherein the quest for truth and the search for a balanced view of the universe prevailed. In Rome, the principle of organization, particularly as manifested in political organization, but pervading other aspects of the culture as well, was outstanding. During the

Middle Ages, the emphasis shifted to regard for the other world, with a hierarchical concept of the universe shaping modes of life as well as belief. The Renaissance again marked a gain in stress, with emphasis on secular matters, learning, and the arts. The Industrial Revolution initiated a period that, in the twentieth century, has produced a society that patently centered about the technical and economic facets of life." p. 542. Quoted by permission.

17. *Ibid.,* p. 543.

18. Cf. Herskovits on "Universals," *Ibid.,* p. 77.

19. G. H. Mead, *Mind, Self and Society* (Chicago: University of Chicago Press, 1934), pp. 285-6. Copyright 1934 by the University of Chicago. Quoted by permission.

20. Cf. Werner Jaeger, who writes: "Other nations made gods, kings, spirits: the Greeks alone made men." *Paideia* (Oxford: Blackwell, 1939), vol. 1, p. xxiii.

21. Introduction to Ruth Benedict, *Patterns of Culture,* Mentor edition (New York, 1946.)

22. *Selected Writings, op. cit.,* pp. 314-5. Cf. also: "It [i.e. the genuine culture] is not a spiritual hybrid of contradictory patches, of water-tight compartments of consciousness that avoid participation in a harmonious system." p. 315. Quoted by permission.

23. *Ibid.,* p. 315.

24. *Ibid.,* p. 316.

CHAPTER 2

1. Those who believe in an elite culture do, of course, gainsay this. But they encounter the difficulty, as I shall later argue in detail, of justifying their dogmas, just because they cannot appeal to those they have excluded from the elite. T. S. Eliot makes it doubly difficult for himself, since on the one hand he excludes the vast majority and then is self-contradictorily led to appeal to them. Cf. his *Notes Towards the Definition of Culture* (London: Faber and Faber), 1948.

2. The same criticism applies, *mutatis mutandis,* to Whitehead's theory of "eternal objects" and the theory of "ingressions." Cf. my essay, "The Art-Process and the Aesthetic Fact in Whitehead's Philosophy, *"Library of Living Philosophers, Volume III: The Philosophy of Alfred North Whitehead,* ed. by Paul Arthur Schilpp (Evanston and Chicago: Northwestern University), 1941.

3. Cf. J. K. Galbraith, *The Affluent Society* (Boston: Houghton Mifflin: 1958), ch. XVIII.

4. Cf. Lon Fuller on "Legal Fictions," *Illinois Law Review,* vol. 25 (1930-31).

5. I am, of course, drawing freely upon Lewis Mumford's *Technics and Civilization* (New York: Harcourt, Brace, 1934). This volume is a landmark in disclosing the connections between the materials of a culture and superimpositions they will bear.

6. Professor Melville J. Herskovits, following Boas, has covered the development of the concept. Cf. his *Man and His Works, op. cit.,* ch. 31; also his *Acculturation* (Gloucester, Mass.: P. Smith, 1958).

7. Cf. Richard Brandt's criticism of acculturation in Hopis in his *Hopi Ethics* (Chicago: Chicago University Press, 1954), ch. XIX.

8. Cf., for example, A. MacBeath, *Experiments in Living,* Gifford Lectures for 1948-9 (London: Macmillan, 1952).

9. This does not signify, however, that only goodness is good; for goodness is no more good than redness is red. If, for example, the office of a principle is to guide us to something, clearly it may do so without itself being that to which it guides us. The form of a thing may be what leads us to something without itself possessing the quality to which it leads, just as the nature of a thing, such as "the nature of being" which does not itself have "being," is different from the thing itself. Kant, of course, pointed out this error in his criticism of the ontological argument. If I have understood G. E. Moore correctly, he committed the same error in speaking of good as a quality like "yellow." Amended, good should be a quality like "yellowness," which, of course, is not yellow.

10. This is not so if one adopts F. J. E. Woodbridge's reading of the *Republic* in his *Son of Apollo* (Boston. Houghton Mifflin, 1929).

11. The anthropologist's favorite, and not always happy, term for this is "ethnocentrism."

12. One should not belittle the role religion, especially in the form of the churches. But it was, as Max Weber and R. H. Tawney have so persuasively shown, a new role appropriately related to the new secularism, or, following them, one may say, the new *monasticism.* Cf. Weber's *The Protestant Ethic and the Spirit of Capitalism,* and Tawney's *Religion and the Rise of Capitalism.*

13. *Freedom and Culture* (New York: Putnams, 1939), p. 154.

14. My colleague, Professor David Hawkins, terms this the mechanistic view of science, as opposed to the idealistic view, which is one in which the scientist interacts with nature and thus alters both nature and himself in the very processes of knowing it.

15. Cf. Professor Ayres' very interesting and incisive essay on this topic, "The Conflict of Values" in *The Colorado Quarterly,* Autumn, 1957. In this essay, Professor Ayres provides an impressively forthright argument that only as man is capable of substituting the "scientific-technological" system of values for the "legendary-ceremonial" is there any hope for his authentic fulfilments. The essay should be read in the light of his more inclusive statement to be found in this *Theory of Economic Progress* (Chapel Hill: University of North Carolina Press, 1944).

16. George Mead makes this pivotal distinction very effectively. In a different, but comparable language Collingwood does the same. Cf. Mead's *Mind, Self and Society, op. cit.,* pt. III; and R. G. Collingwood, *The New Leviathan* (Oxford: Oxford University Press), Ch. XIX. Also Cf. Professor Arthur Murphy's Presidential Address, "The Common Good" in *Proceedings and Addresses of the American Philosophical Association,* 1950-1951.

17. Professor Richard Brandt so conceives of cultural relativism, or better, what he calls "ethical relativism" that two opposite judgments such as X asserts "A is wrong" and Y asserts "A is not wrong" can both be correct, or at least neither is incorrect. This is entirely different from what I take cultural relativism to be, for I assume the essence of it to be that cultures (genuine) are equally good. Particular customs, however, may be regarded as either good or bad, but, as he

suggests, an indicator word such as "this" or "now" would be required in order that a custom could be referred to one culture or another, in the context of which it would properly be regarded as good or bad. Good and bad in this sense do not then signify, "I approve" or "He disapproves," but such and such is "approvable." The relativism is thus of custom to culture, and of neither of them to judgments of approval. See Professor Brandt's very interesting treatment of these questions in his *Hopi Ethics, op. cit.,* chs. VI, XVI.

18. MacBeath makes what I regard as an effective case for refusing to separate moral actions from the cultural context, the summary of which can be expressed in his own words as follows: "What concerns us, however, is whether such atomic absolutes, which contain the grounds of their rightness or goodness within themselves, can in fact be found. The unanimous and oft-repeated view of recent and contemporary social anthropologists is that, among primitives at least, they cannot. They hold, in effect, that the results of any attempt to apply the method of isolation to the moral judgments of primitives are not only valueless but misleading. Indeed, as we have seen, their main criticism of the earlier anthropologists is just that they used the method of isolation, and tried to understand primitive actions and customs and value-judgments without taking account of the cultural context which alone renders them intelligible. According to their view, what we find among primitives is not rules who obligatoriness is self-evident when they are considered in isolation, but rules which are the conditions of the working of certain interrelated institutions; not acts which have intrinsic goods as consequences, but acts which are good in their context; not a scale of values whose relative order can be decided in abstraction, but a system of values embodied in a way of life which determines their order of preference at any given moment." *Op. cit.,* p. 355. Quoted by permission.

19. T. S. Eliot, *Murder in the Cathedral.*

PART II

CHAPTER 3

1. Hobbes' interesting formulation of this, from which I have drawn freely is: "Felicity is a continual progress of the desire, from one object to another; the attaining of the former, being still but a way to the latter." By way of explanation, he continues, "The cause whereof is, that the object of man's desire, is not to enjoy once only, and for one instant of time; but to assure forever, the way of his future desire."

2. Cf. Louis Sullivan, *The Autobiography of an Idea* (New York: Dover Publications, 1956).

3. Sometimes Hobbes couched the reason in terms of natural law, sometimes in terms of "peace and security," and sometimes, and I think most importantly, as I emphasize in the text, in the inherent character of the civil state.

4. *Leviathan,* pt. 1, ch. 13.

5. Mill's modifications of Bentham's hedonism emphasize the need for quality or excellence. Harold Laski rightly found in Bentham a conception of "the

positive state." See his *Decline of Liberalism,* Hobhouse Lecture no. 10 (London: Oxford University Press, 1940).

6. *Mutatis mutandis,* the same is true, of course, of W. D. Ross in connection with his doctrine of "right."

7. Three comments seem to be appropriate in the absence of extended analysis which would carry us far afield from the topics in moral theory. (1) The use of a common name "good" is grossly insufficient as evidence for the theory that all values have something in common and are therefore of the same order. (2) The non-naturalist seems to be confronted with insuperable difficulties in the interpretation of negative values. Can "bad" too be properly regarded as a simple, unanalyzable quality? If so, what does it have in common with "good"? If nothing, why call it, according to non-naturalistic logic, a value? If something, then it is not simple, but complex and therefore analyzable. (3) Plato, who may be regarded as the father of "non-naturalistic" ethics, felt compelled in the *Philebus* to forsake the theory that there is one Good, and at least for human life to include pleasure (at least the innocent ones) as one of the mixed goods of the good life.

8. Cf., for example, Charner Perry, "The Arbitrary as Basis for Rational Morality," *The International Journal of Ethics,* vol. XLIII, no 2 (Jan. 1933), pp. 127 ff.

9. Cf. *Ibid.,* p. 141.

10. Cf. Sir Ernest Barker's Introduction to *Social Contract* (Galaxy Edition, New York: Oxford University Press, 1948), pp. xiv and *seq.*

11. *The Social Contract,* trans. by G. D. H. Cole (New York: E. P. Dutton), bk. I, ch. 8.

12. In his definition of the "public," Dewey discusses this in a way to which we may well subscribe. Cf. *The Public and Its Problems* (Denver: Alan Swallow, 1954), ch. I. Although the public is usually regarded as the special province of politics, it need not be so, unless of course the formal definition makes it so necessarily. Cf. on this point, Pepper, *The Sources of Value, op. cit.,* p. 603.

13. Cf. Professor Schneider's very careful and illuminating statement of this in his definition of a public utility as "an equitable sharing in providing for possible needs, the costs of which if and when they become actual are difficult to bear personally." Herbert Schneider, *Three Dimensions of Public Morality* (Bloomington: Indiana University Press, 1956), p. 111.

14. Cf. also in this regard the classical definition of a public service by Leon Duguit as follows: "Any activity that has to be governmentally regulated and controlled because it is indispensable to the realization and development of social solidarity is a public service so long as it cannot be assured save by governmental intervention." *Law in the Modern State,* trans. by Frida and Harold Laski (New York: Huebsch, 1919), p. 48.

15. In *The Political Works of James I,* ed. by C. H. McIlwain (Cambridge: Harvard University Press, 1918), p. 55.

16. Adolph Hitler, *From Speeches* 1933-1938 (Berlin: Terramare Publications, 1938), pp. 61-2. Cf. the title-page quotation from Hitler as follows: *"Ein Ziel habe ich, ein einziges politisches Glaugensbekenntnis kenne Ich, einene einzigen*

Lebenszweck habe ich mir aufgestellt, der heiszt ganz einfach: Deutschland, mein Volk und mein Vaterland!"

17. Hans Kelsen, "Foundations of Democracy," *Ethics,* vol. LXVI, no. 1, Pt. II (Oct., 1955), p. 6.

18. In this respect Professor Ayres is quite right in rejecting the "ceremonial-legendary system of values." Cf. "The Conflict of Values," *The Colorado Quarterly, loc. cit.*

19. Even von Hayek allows for the provision of services pertaining to food, warmth, care of aged, and the like. Cf. his *Road to Serfdom* (Chicago: Chicago University Press, 1944), pp. 120 ff.

20. A. L. Kroeber and Clyde Kluckhohn, *Culture: A Critical Review of Concepts and Definitions, op. cit.* These "universals," incidentally, do not confute cultural relativism, first, because they are negative and, secondly, because they are principles rather than institutions.

21. Professor Clarence Morris examines this subject carefully in his able discussion of problems in torts. Cf. *Morris on Torts* (Brooklyn Foundation Press, 1953), pp. 85ff.

CHAPTER 4

1. Cf. not just the contract theorists, but also Hegel who writes as follows of the well-constituted state: " . . . a State is then well constituted and internally powerful, when the private interest of its citizen is one with the common interest of the State; when the one finds its gratification and realization in the other." *Philosophy of History,* trans. by J. Loewenberg (New York: Scribner's Modern Students Library, 1929), p. 369.

2. In addition to these exceptions, already footnoted, see von Hayek's distinction between the "rule of law" and "substantive rules" in his *Road to Serfdom, op. cit.,* ch. VI.

3. Cf. Hannah Arendt, *The Origins of Totalitarianism* (New York: Harcourt Brace, 1951). The question is also raised whether there are any limits to power, since it proceeds from a capricious will which, as long as it exists and determines effects, is uncontrollable. Plato, of course, makes out the classical case in his discussion of tyranny.

4. In discussing various forms of social determinism, critics have endlessly revelled in pointing up the paradoxes which result from, on the one hand, asserting that there is a single, inexorable, controlling determinant of social life, and on the other, asserting that human agency *should* intervene in making more effective this determinant. Formally, the paradox is awkward even if it does not contain an outright contradiction.

5. *Utilitarianism,* ch. 3.

6. Professor Stephen Pepper underscores this in his *The Sources of Value* when he asserts that conscience is a social sanction because it is "the incorporation into the personality of the demands of the environing culture." *Op. cit.,* p. 568.

7. Although the theory of continuity and means-end relation is ubiquitous in Dewey's philosophy, the following are typical discussions: *Human Nature and*

Conduct (Mod. Library Edition, New York: Random House), pp. 24ff., 34ff., 270 ff.; *Ethics*, Rev. Ed., 195ff.; *Experience and Nature* (New York: Norton, 1929), ch. 3; "Theory of Valuation," *International Encyclopedia of Unified Science* (Chicago: Chicago University Press), vol. 2, no. 4, pp. 33ff.

8. Cf. Fritz Kaufmann's fine aperçus on the subject in his *Thomas Mann: The World as Will and Representation* (Boston: Beacon Press, 1957), especially Part I.

9. Dostoyevsky may play on the theme of idiots as being possessed of supernatural powers, but we must regard this as a literary *tour*. Societies sometimes take such attitudes, as when the Greeks regarded epilepsy as being a divine visitation. Whether "lunacy" is generally believed to be the mark of a viable supernatural possession is surely open to question.

10. Although any scholar of Marxism can cite passages in which Marx and Engels confute this narrow interpretation of dialectical materialism, to take seriously these confutations requires a more thoroughgoing revision of Marxist doctrine than they appear willing to make.

11. Cf. my "The Dignity of Man," *Ethics*, vol. LVII, no. 1 (Oct. 1946).

12. I have dealt with this in some detail in "Ruskin on the Pathetic Fallacy, or How a Moral Theory May Fail," *Journal of Aesthetics and Art Criticism*, vol. XIV, no. 2 (Dec. 1955), pp. 248-266.

13. Professor George Gamow of the University of Colorado has at least informally suggested this position.

14. Cf. Galbraith's discussion of "The New Position of Poverty" in *The Affluent Society, op. cit.*, ch. XXIII.

15. This assumes that there is no concentrated and widespread effort to relieve at least some of the major hardships suffered by non-industrial peoples.

16. *Experience and Nature* (New York: W. W. Norton, 1939), p. 161.

17. Cf. Baker Brownell's thoughtful criticism in *Art is Action* (New York: Harper, 1939).

18. On the contrary, the fashion is to trace vividly the bestialities of the industrial society, often without any very clear realization of what the alternatives are. Although Huxley was capable of magnificent satire in *Brave New World*, his alternative to it was cast in the form of the sentimental primitive. Orwell's *Animal Farm* was an aborted attempt at satire; his *1984* a bitter bit of journalese.

19. This might be regarded as a rough paraphrase of part of an argument by Charner Perry quoted earlier. Cf. again his "The Arbitrary Basis for Rational Morality," *The International Journal of Ethics*, Jan. 1933. The criticism can also be traced to those who atomize society into its individual components.

20. I earlier suggested a distinction between the personal and the private. Since, however, the latter is characterized by its complete subjectivity, it does not pertain to action and consequently cannot intelligibly be thought of as having any relevance to choice and the making of decisions.

21. For reasons stated above, there is still the realm of the private to which not even moral sanctions apply—that is, in the realm of the purely hedonic.

Part III

CHAPTER 5

1. Jean-Paul Sartre, *Being and Nothingness,* trans. by Hazel Barnes (New York: Philosophical Library), especially Part Four. Cf. also Professor Barnes' helpful glossary of terms in the Appendix.

2. *Ibid.,* pp. 436, 439. Karl Jaspers speaks of this as "to take a leap." *Man in the Modern Age* (New York: Doubleday Anchor Books, 1957), p. 185.

3. *Op. cit.,* p. 439. Cf. Jaspers' statement, " . . . man cannot surrender himself." *Op. cit.,* p. 181.

4. Cf. Marjorie Grene, *Dreadful Freedom* (Chicago: University of Chicago Press, 1948). Mrs. Grene, following Sartre, has made popular the expression, "dreadful freedom." Cf. also *The Transcendence of the Ego,* trans. by Forrest Williams and Robert Kirkpatrick (New York: Noonday Press), p. 102.

5. Cf. "The anonymous, the nameless, is not only the true being of man, which tends to vanish in dispersion, but also the true not-being, which seems, however, to claim the whole realm of life. The problem of the nameless powers is a problem of human existence itself." *Op. cit.,* p. 179.

6. Sartre, *op. cit.,* p. 410.

7. *Ibid.,* pp. 424, 429.

8. Jaspers, *op. cit.,* p. 196.

9. Quoted by Benjamin Farrington, *Greek Science,* British Penguin, p. 73.

10. Cf., for example, Hobbes' definition of freedom as follows: "Liberty, or Freedom, signifieth (properly) the absence of Opposition; (by Opposition I mean external Impediments of motion;) and may be applied no lesse to Irationall, and Inanimate creatures, than to Rationall." *The Leviathan,* Part 2, ch. 21.

11. R. H. Tawney, *Equality* (London: Allen and Unwin, rev. ed., 1952), p. 258.

12. For a recent, sensitive version of this liberal point of view, see Professor Wilson O. Clough's engaging "Some Uses of Cant" in *Southwest Review,* vol. XLI, no. 4 (Autumn, 1956).

13. Cf. A. A. Berle, Jr., *Twentieth Century Capitalist Revolution* (New York: Harcourt Brace, 1954), p. 25.

14. Cf. Carl Stephenson, who writes: "First of all, the bourgeois enjoyed free status. No matter what his origin, the man who lived in a town unchallenged for a year and a day secured complete liberty. The town air, it was said, made him free." *Medieval History* (New York: Harper, 1935), p. 357.

15. Speaking of the origins of Greek art, Jane Harrison observes, "Moral and social are, in their final analysis, the same. That human, collective emotion, out of which we have seen the choral dance arise, is in its essence moral; that is, it unites." *Ancient Art and Ritual* (New York: Henry Holt, 1913), p. 218.

16. This is the thesis of the argument vigorously and interestingly presented by Mr. Berle, *op. cit.*

17. Professor Galbraith concludes that the power of advertising is effective because important needs are satisfied and people willingly allow themselves to be swayed in regard to other things which are of little consequence to them anyway. Cf. *op. cit., The Affluent Society,* especially chs. X, XI.

18. Cf., for example, Professor Clair Wilcox's classic TNEC report, *Investigation of Concentration of Economic Power,* Monograph No. 21, "Competition and Monopoly in American Industry" (Washington: U.S. Government Printing Office, 1940), ch. IV, pp. 176ff. and the especially interesting discussion of market sharing in the meat industry, pp. 182ff.

19. I am indebted to my colleague, Professor Reuben Zubrow of the University of Colorado, for this suggestion.

CHAPTER 6

1. One interesting attempt of this kind is the *National Resources Development Report* for 1943 (U.S. Government Printing Office, Jan. 1943). In this report attention is given not merely to "The Four Freedoms" but also to "A New Bill of Rights" as a supplement to the traditional Bill of Rights. In an entirely different kind of context the International Bill of Rights is an attempt to recognize the political question as a legitimate world-wide question.

2. See on this subject a classic work by Benjamin Cardozo, *The Nature of the Judicial Process,* especially Lecture III, entitled "The Method of Sociology. The Judge as a Legislator" (New Haven: Yale University Press, 1921).

3. I borrow freely, of course, from Francis Bacon's *Novum Organum,* Bk. I, sec. 104.

4. Cf. his classic, *The Engineers and the Price System.*

5. Mr. Lippmann has consistently and vigorously argued the case from at least the time of his *Public Opinion,* 1922, and *The Phantom Public,* 1925, to his recent *The Public Philosophy,* 1956.

6. Cf. *The Public Philosophy* (Mentor Book, 1956), p. 29, and especially pp. 30ff.

7. Cf. *Ibid.,* p. 40.

8. On this important topic, cf., for example, Professor Dorwin Cartwright, "Public Opinion Polls and Democratic Leadership," *Journal of Social Issues,* vol. 2, no. 2 (May, 1946), pp. 23-32. Also Professor Angus Campbell's summary, pp. 58-66. Professor Cartwright has serious reservations about the extension of public education as a simple answer to public ignorance. And both he and Professor Campbell insist, as the latter puts it, "Leadership and social inventiveness must necessarily come not from the public *en masse* but from more gifted individual members." p. 65. With respect to the soundness of public policies, Professor Cartwright asserts, "Sample surveys can be very useful in determining whether a program that is sound from an economic point of view will be at all satisfactory when the 'human element' is considered." p. 32. Although he narrows the kinds of issues in which 'the human element' is relevant, he recognizes some issues on which there can, through "public discussion and issues clearly drawn" be a mandate from the people. p. 29.

9. Henry A. Kissinger indicts this ebbing condition of politics in an incisive essay in *The Reporter,* entitled, "The Policymaker and the Intellectual," vol. 29, no. 5 (Mar. 5, 1959).

CHAPTER 7

1. Sweezy v. New Hampshire, 354 U.S. 235 (1957).

2. In Pericles' Funeral Oration, bk. II, ch. 6 of *The Peloponnesian War*.

3. George J. Stigler, *Five Lectures on Economic Problems* (New York: Macmillan, 1950), p. 10. Cf. also: "Rule of thumb guides such as greater equality and maximum output are insufficient to distinguish policies that lead to a very different type of society, and therefore insufficient to distinguish good from bad policies," p. 8.

4. Henry Alonzo Myers observes the necessity of man's wholeness, his "infinite worth," as desperately requiring a sharing of "his values with others and with the universe" in order to avoid "the spiritual sickness which overcomes him when he no longer feels united with his world." He regards this sharing, however, in terms of a universality which disregards what appear to be the realities of cultural life. Cf., however, the strong case he makes in his *Are Men Equal?* (New York: Putnams, 1945), pp. 30 and *passim*.

5. Only by virtue of the all-important fact of tradition and custom can "utilities" be asserted in an economic scheme whether capitalistic (including their monopolistic or oligopolistic phases) or socialistic. Planning is possible in both schemes only because the range of variation takes its point of departure from customs already at work in the market and does not attempt to formulate a schedule of utilities apart from the direction which custom provides.

6. R. H. Tawney, *op. cit., Equality*, p. 49. Cf. also pp. 35, 40.

7. As significant approaches to this problem, cf. John Dewey's *The Public and Its Problems* (Denver: Alan Swallow, 1954), especially pp. 149ff. Professor Herbert Schneider has admirably spelled out the consequences of this point of view in his *Three Dimensions of Public Morality* (Bloomington: Indiana University Press, 1956). And in a somewhat specialized context, cf. Professor Gregory Vlastos, "The Religious Foundations of Democracy," *Journal of Religion*, vol. 22 (Jan. 1942, Apr. 1942).

8. Cf., for example, Borsodi, *Flight from the City* (New York: Harper, 1933), Baker Brownell, *The Human Community* (New York: Harper, 1950), and Lewis Mumford, *Culture of Cities* (New York: Harcourt, Brace, 1934).

9. For a devastating and well-worked out criticism which, although it is much too urbane to countenance the suggestion of a "tribal morality," nevertheless insists upon morality as the ground of criticism of both business and subjective feelings, cf. E. Jordan, *Business Be Damned* (New York: Henry Schuman, 1953).

10. *TVA: Democracy on the March* (New York: Pocket Book, 1952), p. 57.

11. Professor Robert MacIver must be credited with having clearly enunciated this point. Cf. his *Web of Government* (New York: Macmillan, 1947), ch. XII and especially p. 370.

12. On the more specific subject of philosophy's concern with literature, Professor Joseph W. Cohen has significantly elucidated this in his "Aspects of the Relations between Philosophy and Literature," *University of Colorado Studies*, vol. I, no. 2 (Boulder, June 1940).

PART IV

CHAPTER 8

1. J. Middleton Murry illustrates this nicely in his *Studies in Keats* by showing how Keats needed to pass from nature to "the agonies, the strife of human hearts" before he could finally disclose the spirit of poetry. Cf. ch. 2, "On First Looking into Chapman's Homer" (New York: Oxford University Press, second ed., 1939).

2. *Ibid.,* p. 32.

3. Professor Birkhoff does provide an interesting discussion of a mathematical approach to form, far more sophisticated than Plato's. Cf. his *Aesthetic Measure* (Cambridge: Harvard University Press, 1933).

4. *Vision and Design* (Pelican Ed., 1937), p. 39.

5. *Art Now* (London: Faber and Faber, 1933), p. 74.

6. Cf. Herbert Read's comments on this, *ibid.,* pp. 67ff.

7. Louis MacNeice, from "Snow," *Poems by MacNeice* (New York: Random House, 1937).

8. For an extended discussion of this see the writer's "Ruskin on the Pathetic Fallacy, Or on How a Moral Theory of Art May Fail," *Journal of Aesthetics and Art Criticism,* vol. XIV, no. 2 (Dec. 1955), pp. 248-266.

9. This is quoted by Katharine Gilbert, "Ruskin's Relation to Aristotle," *Philosophical Review,* XLIX (1940), p. 58.

10. Various forms of transcendentalism do, of course, deny this, but in doing so, they are compelled to forsake the natural and social environment of man. Asceticism in its various forms of mysticism do just this. Also existentialism, to the extent to which it is ascetic, does this.

11. The Gauguins may seem to be exceptions to the principle. It is interesting to observe, however, that Gauguin rejected, as far as possible, his own culture in order to create his sophisticated primitivism.

12. I realize this is a difficult proposition to support empirically. A sampling of the lives and letters of the classical artists does, I believe, bear out the proposition, but this is surely not adequate to eliminate some dogmatism.

CHAPTER 9

1. I am elaborating an argument here earlier sketched in an article, "Philosophy of Criticism," *Philosophical Review,* Nov. 1946.

2. Little wonder that Plato gives such different accounts of art such as in Bk. X of the *Republic* as contrasted, say, with his account in the *Ion.*

3. Cf. on this topic his *Notes Toward the Definition of Culture* (London: Faber and Faber, 1948).

4. *Society and Solitude,* "Art."

5. *The Sacred Wood,* 4th ed. (London: Methuen, 1934), p. 58.

6. *The Confidential Clerk* is in some ways the more interesting work to illustrate Eliot's opposition of two worlds. Sir Claude early says of Lady Elizabeth that "She has always lived in a world of make believe, / And the best one can do is to guide her delusions / In the right direction." (p. 43) And a little later he finds a more positive value in the world of escape, when he says:

> To be among such things [i. e. those made by the potter]
> If it is an escape, it is escape into living,
> Escape from a sordid world to a pure one.
>
> . . . .
>
> I want a world where the form is the reality,
> Of which the substantial is only a shadow. (p. 46-47)

Again, he asserts of the make-believe world that "the make-believing makes it real." (p. 47) Other allusions are liberally sprinkled throughout the play, although they are sometimes to the "secret garden." (p. 63) From *The Confidential Clerk*, copyright 1954, by T. S. Eliot. Used by permission of Harcourt, Brace and Company, Inc.

7. Cf. J. Middleton Murry, *Aspects of Literature* (New York: Alfred Knopf, 1920), p. 180. Cf. also "The Function of Criticism," pp. 1ff and "Poetry and Criticism," pp. 176ff. His classicism is apparent when he writes: "This [i.e. the identity of the good and the beautiful] is why we have to go back to the Greeks for the principles of art and criticism, and why only those critics who have returned to bathe themselves in the life-giving source have made enduring contributions to literature. They alone are—let us not say philosophic critics but—critics indeed." p. 9.

8. Cf. Lionel Trilling, *The Liberal Imagination* (Garden City: Anchor Books, 1954), p. 160.

9. Professor Cambell Crockett, for example, confesses a hospitality to Ernest Jones's psychoanalytic interpretation of Hamlet, when of his *Hamlet and Oedipus*, he writes, "I personally find this interpretation persuasive." In his discussion of "Psychoanalysis in Art Criticism" Professor Crockett makes some telling points in reference to the clarification of the kinds of questions that need to be raised in connection with psychoanalytic theory. Cf., *Journal of Aesthetics and Art Criticism*, vol. XVII, no. 1 (Sept. 1958), pp. 34-44.

10. *Collected Papers* (Hogarth Press and the Institute of Psycho-analysis, 1925), IV, 19.

11. Cf. Ludwig Marcuse, "Freud's Aesthetics," *Journal of Aesthetics and Art Criticism*, vol. XVII, no. 1 (Sept. 1958), especially pp. 5ff.

12. *Hamlet and Oedipus* (London: Victor Gollancz, 1949), p. 75.

13. *The Forlorn Demon* (Chicago: Regnery, 1953), p. 3. Perhaps in fairness to Mr. Tate, his question and at least a whole sentence answer should be reproduced. At the outset he says, "To the question, What should the man of letters be in our time, we should have to find an answer in what we need him to do. He must do first what he has always done: he must recreate for his age the image of man, and he must propagate standards by which other men may test that image, and distinguish the false from the true." Incidentally, this is an interesting point of view, coming as it does from one of the "new critics." Professor Irving J. Howe makes some pointed comments on the new critics, especially

in distinguishing their conception of life from their techniques of analytic, textual criticism. Cf. *The Nation,* Nov. 22, 1958. I have not included the new critics in a special category of theorists of criticism because they emphasize primarily textual criticism rather than range afield as Mr. Tate suggests in the above quotation. The new critics do, of course, raise embarrassing questions pertaining to the relation of a poem to understanding and criticism. Cf., for example, Mr. Tate, *Ibid.,* pp. 101-2.

CHAPTER 10

1. Colin Wilson in an essay entitled, "Existential Criticism" in *Chicago Review,* Summer 1959.

2. *Op. cit.* (New York: Harper & Bros., 1958), p. 44.

3. *The Forlorn Demon,* p. 14.

4. Ruskin develops a significant theory of decoration in architecture in his insistence that it be sculptural and therefore integral to the architectural line. Cf. the author's "Ruskin on the Moral Imagination in Architecture," *University of Colorado Studies, Series in Language and Literature,* no. 6 (Jan. 1957).

5. Without in the least minimizing the importance of either Russia or the non-industrialized countries, I shall, except for obvious and inescapable allusions, concentrate attention here upon the challenge to the Western democratic world, and especially to America. My belief is that the challenge in the broad is much the same for any culture which is constantly growing more industrial and more secular.

6. Cf. Marya Mannes, "The Captive Writer," *The Reporter,* Aug. 20, 1959, pp. 31-4. Also, Gilbert Seldes, *The Public Arts* (New York: Simon and Schuster, 1956).

INDEX